ADVENTURE TRAILS

in

MONTANA

by John Willard

Published by John Willard
Sponsored by Montana Historical Society

Illustrations, Courtesy of Montana Historical Society,
by these famous western artists.

Karl Bodmer	Frederic Remington
Fanny Y. Cory	Charles M. Russell
Bob Hall	O. C. Seltzer
Alfred Jacob Miller	Irvin Shope
Thomas Moran	Gustav Sohon
Edgar S. Paxson	William Standing
J. K. Ralston	Von Schmidt

Cover—"Nature's Soldiers," a water color by C. M. Russell.

———

The material in this book is reproduced by courtesy of the
MONTANA AUTOMOBILE ASSOCIATION

The chapters appeared in original form in the "Montana Motorist".

———

Copyright 1964
by **JOHN WILLARD**

———

Printed by
STATE PUBLISHING COMPANY
Helena, Montana

Foreword

No one has roamed the Big Sky Country more gregariously, with greater observation and appreciation than has John Willard. One of Montana's dedicated sportsmen; yet a true conservationist, John has undoubtedly visited more pristine high mountain sheep, goat and grizzly meadows, dropped a trout fly in more lakes and streams, and reported such outdoor pleasures and observations journalistically with more gusto, than anyone since Sir St. George Gore in 1855. There the similarity ends. In my book the so-called "Irish Sportsman" should have been called the "Slaughterer of Sligo". (He boasted of killing 3705 buffalo, elk, bear and deer). Sir George travelled in pomp and ceremony with one of the most elaborately equipped expeditions ever—which is more than can be said of "Sir" John, who travels lightly on foot, in well-worn boots and brush-tattered garments, more with camera and note pad than with rod or gun. Perhaps, rather, the more apt comparison would be with the Irish Baronet's Montana guide, able Mountain Man Jim Bridger who carried the map of the West in his head, observed every living thing, and like John, spun fascinating yarns of the wild places he had been and the unbelievable things he had seen.

At any rate, John Willard is my ideal combination of a latter-day Baedeker, George Bird Grinnell, Prince Maximilian, Audubon, Catlin and John Muir—with a little bit of contemporary John Gunther thrown in for full measure. He has really gotten around our scenic wilderness since his boyhood days out of Augusta. But along the way he has visited more historic sites and mountain passes, swapped more stories in out-of-the-way hamlets with stockmen, miners, roust-abouts, sheepmen, hayhands and trappers; and covered more miles of Montana highways, trails, rails and down-timber draws, than anyone else.

Therefore, this book is one of the most spritely, intimate and companionable pleasures in our literature. If you want to live vicariously; with the pungent smell of sagebrush and juniper in your nostrils, with the sound of elk crashing in aspen or the quiet play of grayling in a limpid pool—all permeated with the deep heritage of pioneers and distant gunsmoke and long-gone warriors—this is it!

Whether you be dude, casual visitor, or fourth generation Montana native, here is the most entertaining guide to Montana, "as it was, and as it is" in print. The Big Sky Country is huge, complex and deep-fasceted. But herein John Willard saves us millions of steps and many storied miles—transmitting his enthusiasm, love, understanding and intimacy with his native land into unforgettable, legend, lore, history and fact.

Most of this material has delighted segments of Montana and Western readers for many years. Now it's all here together as it should be, a delightful centennial addition to our proud place on the last frontier, yesterday and today.

MICHAEL KENNEDY, Director

Montana Historical Society
Helena, Montana, March, 1964

Contents

Foreword	Michael Kennedy	III
Introduction	Harold McCracken	VI
Montana—The Living Past		1
Southwest		5

    Bloody Junction 13
    The Nervous Tree 16
    The First Hooves 18
    Jim's Wagon Trail 21
    Wealth Under the Alders 23
    Day of Decision 27
    Sterling in the Rough 30
    Death House on the Ruby 32
    Grasshopper Diggins' 36
    The Gold Gulches 39
    Colors in the Sage 43
    Peaceful Fort 45
    Valley of Flowers 47

Northwest 51

    The Name-Lore of Glacier Park 63
    Sign of the Cross 73
    Stone Writing 76
    Trail to the Buffalo 78
    Disaster Falls 81
    Council of Peace 83
    Ice-Locked Waters 85
    Slim's Lake 87
    When Men Feared Gold 89
    Finan's Winter Tents 91
    Medicine Tree 93
    Flat-Tailed Monarch 95
    Tommy's Nuggets 97
    To Map an Empire 99
    Deer House Plains 102
    Buffalo—At Home on the Range 104
    Chapel of the Snows 107
    Evergreen Pulpit 109
    Justice by Rope 111
    Cruel Christmas—1813 113
    Travelers' Rest 115
    Ranger Station No. 1 117
    Silver Dollar Summit 119

Contents—(Cont.)

Northeast 123

- The Agony at Bird Tail Rock 135
- The "Kid's" Wolf Pack 139
- Castle of the Silver Kings 144
- Rising Wolf's Meadow 147
- The Mill on the Mountain 150
- Last of the Buffalo 153
- The Captain's Wagons 155
- Carroll's Cutoff 158
- Clagett's Landing 160
- The Snow-Shrinker 162
- Death at the Bluff 164
- Blood on the Grass 166
- Nepee's Secret Gold 168
- Sleeping Buffalo 170
- To Know the Faith 173
- Fort on the Medicine Road 175
- Mail in the Saddle Bag 177
- Love's High Price 179
- The Lasting Wound 181
- Paddle-Wheel Port 183
- Sublimely Grand Waters 187
- Fort of the Daring 189
- Father of the People 191
- Ghost of the Judith 193
- Stockade at the Forks 197
- Fight No More 201

Southeast 205

- The New Land 215
- The Battle Custer Won 217
- Little Big Horn—Bloody Mystery 220
- Little Pomp's Tower 224
- Red Farmers 226
- The Waters of Little Moon 228
- John Colter—Salesman 230
- Wilderness White House 232
- Trail Above the Eagles 234
- Hayfield Victory 236
- Ice Age Trophy 238
- Bear Coat's Fort 240
- Torch to the Wagon 242

Index 244

Introduction

Where in all the exciting and glamorous West are there so many interesting *Adventure Trails*, so well worth following, as in Montana? And a most capable guide is John Willard—to lead one along the time covered trails into the historical byways of the past, as well as the present day trails to adventures to suit most any degree of desire. The writer of this brief INTRODUCTION has known the AUTHOR of this book for a good many years, and along with many others has come to highly respect him as a scholarly journalist (a rare bird in any area) always devotedly delving into the fascinating facts which have given Montana the well deserved nicknames *Treasure State*, *Charlie Russell Country*, and *Big Sky Country*. All these factors are ideal ingredients for a fine book—and here you have it.

For the arm-chair adventurer, to the most serious historical researcher, there is an almost endless wealth of material ranging from the days before Lewis and Clark to the end of the Old West as an era. To cover it all, even superficially, one would have to start as a teenager and live to a ripe old age. For those who want to see and do for themselves, there's aplenty ranging from catching a big rainbow trout on a worm-baited hook, to getting a pugnacious grizzly bear, or just taking the family to sit by a highway and gaze at some of the finest sunsets and scenery in all the country—they can find it all in Montana. But they'll have a hard time finding a better condensed guide book than *"Adventure Trails in Montana."*

HAROLD McCRACKEN.

Montana –
The Living Past

Montana is a respectable lady who has had some moments in the past that she doesn't mind talking over at times, even with strangers.

This rough and generous state was spawned on the battlefields of the Indian campaigns and the Civil War. Its father was a fur trader with the morals of a tomcat, and its mother was an Indian maiden with a big love for trade jewelry or foo-feraw. Its childhood was not too tenderly cared for by an odd assortment of cowpunchers from the Rio Grande, soldiers from Fort Laramie, gold miners who lived through the blood of Gettysburg or Shiloh and dance-hall girls whose tarnished favors were bought with purest gold.

There still are enough of Montana's childhood memories around to delight the curious and the history buffs. Those who like sagging saloon floors, greying mine timbers and grizzled stage stations which served sour bread and sagebrush tea to wayfarers will embrace Montana's still living past.

For those whose nerves are gentled by an early morning moose grazing in an emerald meadow just below timberline, there is plenty of that, too. There are mountains that rear as defiantly as a snorting cayuse, wrapping their snow blankets around them even in midsummer. There are mountains blue as a Montana sapphire, covered with virgin forests that were young when Norsemen visited New England. There are lakes which wet the feet of monstrous tamaracks and cover their beaches with "larch balls," those strange products of wind, wave and tamarack needles shed at the urging of the first fall frosts.

There are lakes whose waters never lose the feel of ice and whose stunted trout barely survive from one brief summer to the next in the granite grip of an alpine basin. There are lakes with miles of blue water held in by badland bluffs or timbered mountains. There are lakes that you come upon surprisingly in the deep timber, mere cups covered with lily pads and smartweed and hiding brook trout under their submerged snags—lakes for any taste and of any size.

Creeks and rivers carry Montana waters to three oceans—Pacific, Atlantic and Arctic. From the shoulders of one mountain in Glacier National Park the melting snows flow to all three. The Missouri unites the waters from southwestern Montana's mountains, collects the drainage of northern and central Montana's grain and range lands, hurries it into Fort Peck Reservoir and out into Dakota. The Yellowstone rises within miles of the Missouri headwaters, and both it and the Missouri wash the "breaks" and badlands of eastern Montana before they flow together at the Dakota border. The Clark's Fork of the Columbia picks up the sparkling, twisting rivers and creeks of the western slope and pours them through a dark-cliffed canyon into Idaho's lakes. The Kootenai swings its blue-green loop of glacial waters into northwestern Montana from British Columbia and then forsakes Montana for Idaho in a canyon bottom that marks the state's lowest altitude at under 2,000 feet, more than 10,000 feet below its highest point.

Only the St. Mary, spawned in the glacial, east-side cirques of Glacier Park, and the Belly-Waterton, with a similar birth, plunge their ways northward to join Canada's massive drainage into Hudson's Bay.

It is the mountain snows that feed all Montana waters. These reservoirs of liquid plenty may lie against the northern slope of Granite Peak, Montana's loftiest at 12,799 feet, hard against the Wyoming border, in the shade of a solemn spruce in the Missions or against a boulder in the Little Rockies, far out on the eastern plains.

In western Montana's mountains a grassy prairie or level meadow is a welcome surprise in the grandeur of rock and timber. In central Montana blue ranges of mountains alternate nicely with rolling hills and wide valleys covered with haystacks. Eastern Montana's endless strip-cropped wheat fields, wide stretches of open range and flat-topped buttes rise slowly from the horizon, like a blue mirage, hardening slowly into reality.

The Continental Divide, snaking southward across the state from Glacier Park, cuts off the western third of Montana, yet allows free passage for travelers through its fir-laned passes, old in history and older yet in geology.

From the plains of the east, this divide gives warning in the Crazies that glisten to the north of the Yellowstone and in the peaks of the Little Rockies that warned Lewis and Clark that a greater mountain barrier lay ahead.

These same landmarks that separated the Indian tribes, and pointed the way for the wagon trains and the beef drives from Texas will give you a friendly sentinel as you pioneer your own way into Montana. Each mountain range is a goal, for in its folds of rock and trees and grassy "parks" is both history and lifeblood. Here are the aging mining towns, the fishing streams and lakes, the timbered slopes with their inviting spots to camp and eat lunch.

People making a living are part of this picture, too. Shovels digging copper out of a wound in the side of a mountain, cowpunchers working cattle against a brown hill, a sheepherder's wagon and his band white-dotted against the range, a sweating crew sinking an oil well, a wheat farmer mechanically turning waving gold into a staple of the breakfast table and a pungently-smoking mill converting amber logs into raw materials for homes.

Montana's first citizens, for they were here before any other, will welcome you. Antelope, camouflaged brown and white against the range grass and wheatfield, challenge the eye in eastern Montana. At dusk or in early morning the numerous mule and white-tailed deer are roadside scenery, especially in spring when the alfalfa is new and tempting. Mallards with heads of emerald satin are common in the borrow pit sloughs, as common as the pheasant, the "fancy-Dan" of the grain fields and irrigated valleys. Jack rabbits lope across the blacktop, and sharp-tailed grouse rise thunderously from the stubble.

These things, then, are Montana. Its history and its life are woven around them. Sharing them with others is a big part of the fun of owning them.

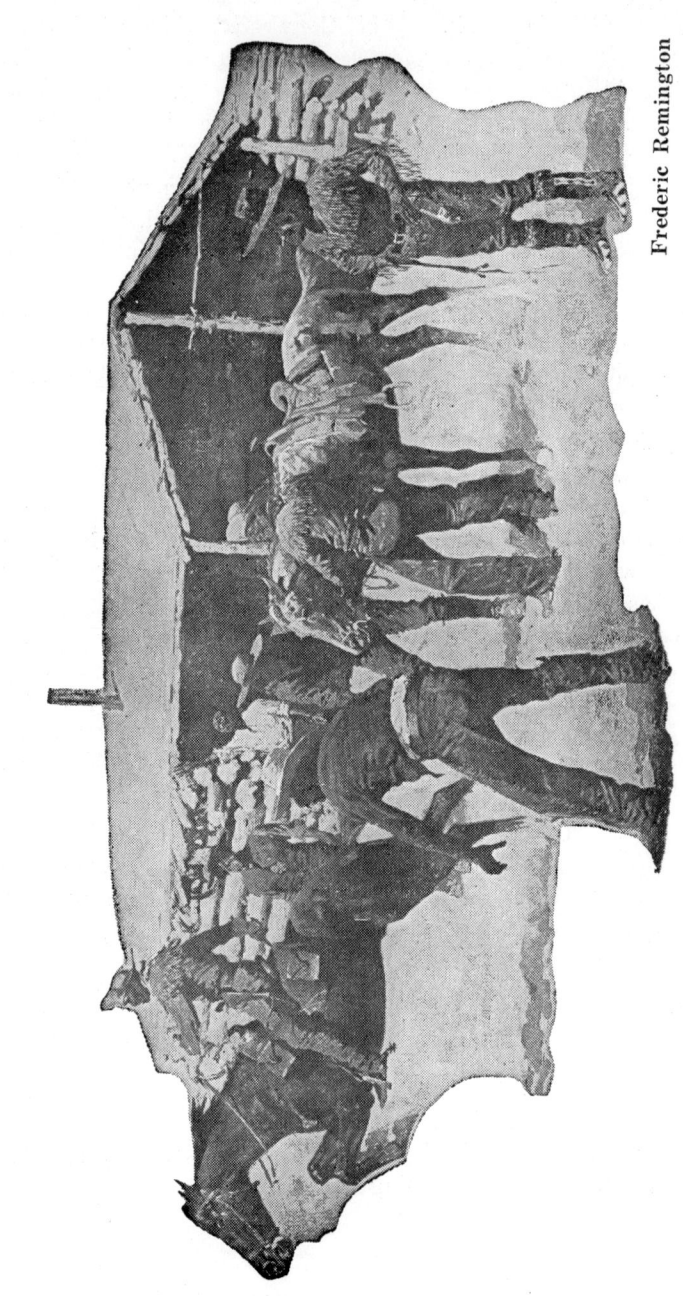

Frederic Remington

Southwest — The Headwaters Country

Montana as we know it was born here. Above the Three Forks of the Missouri the waters spread out like fingers into the mountains, and there is a story at every finger tip. The palm of this hand of history can be read, too, by those who look for the signs left by the fur traders, the miners and old cowmen who raised beef for the men who worked the placers.

It was here that Lewis and Clark found the source of the Missouri, which they had been told by President Jefferson to do. Here, likewise, they found a way across the Continental Divide and learned of the route to the Pacific through the mountains.

Montana's first and second territorial capitals, Bannack and Virginia City, grew from tent-and-shack towns to respectable seats of government, then withered away. Helena was born, too, in the placers of a tiny creek, became capital of the young state and stayed that way. In her youth Helena was the financial and administrative head of the livestock and mining businesses that were growing up all around her.

Wherever you go in the southwestern valleys there are traces of a state a-borning. Montana's first railroad came across the divide from Idaho in 1881, and its first cattle came in from the south to start an industry that still is a giant in Montana.

It's a country of strange and wonderful contrast. Pungent sage grows in the valleys, and antelope roam across its wide benches. There are more moose here than anywhere in the continental United States south of Alaska. Elk and deer are plentiful in the foothills. Its rivers without doubt are the most productive of game fish of any in the nation. This is the home of the grayling, that delicately colored, high-finned beauty of the mountain lakes and headwaters.

It was across this country that Chief Joseph brought his Nez Perce in 1877, fighting the army at the Big Hole battlefield on a crisp summer morning. Joseph, in leaving, crossed Yellowstone National Park, and so do most of his modern followers in their fancy automobiles and trailers.

Yellowstone really is a part of this southwest, although part of it drains off into Wyoming and the rest divides itself between the Yellowstone valley and the Madison.

The overtones of the old southwestern valleys all were golden. Today they have changed to other colors of metal and minerals, but the headframes of the mines still are here. So are the ranches whose first customers mined the same hills that grew grass that grew beef. Many of these ranches bear the names of grandsons or the husbands of granddaughters of those pioneer cowmen. There's a family flavor to the history and the economy.

How They Got Their Names — Lakes and Streams

Jefferson River—From Three Forks of the Missouri to Twin Bridges, where it is formed by the Big Hole and Beaverhead rivers. Named by Lewis and Clark for President Jefferson, because it was the westernmost fork of the Missouri and the one the party followed to reach the Continental Divide.

Beaverhead River—From Twin Bridges to its headwaters in the Beaverhead Mountains and ranges between the Beaverhead valley and the Ruby. Named from Beaver's Head rock, so called by the Shoshone Indians, which rises about 150 feet directly from the river on its west bank about 12 miles south of Twin Bridges. Lewis and Clark named the river from this rock, now called Point of Rocks, which Sacajawea recognized and pointed out to the explorers that they were near the summer retreat of her people, the Shoshone. South of Dillon is another Beaverhead rock, not as high as the one which named the river. The southerly one was called Rattlesnake Cliff by Lewis and Clark. In their journal, the explorers referred to the Beaverhead as the Jefferson River as far upstream as Horse Prairie Creek.

Big Hole River—From Twin Bridges to its headwaters in the Bitter Root and Pioneer mountains. Drains one of Montana's largest and highest mountain valleys and flows in a huge loop to join the Beaverhead and form the Jefferson. Lewis and Clark named the river "Wisdom River" as a tribute to Jefferson's wisdom, August 6, 1805, and called it a "bold, rapid and clear stream." Later pioneers, less impressed with

Jefferson, changed the name. Mountain valleys were called "holes" by early mountain men, and since this river flowed from the biggest "hole" in the area, they called it the Big Hole River. Clark called the Big Hole valley "hot spring valley" after the warm springs there.

Ruby River—This river, which flows into the Beaverhead River just above Twin Bridges, originally was called Philanthropy River by Lewis and Clark when they reached this area on August 6, 1805. They named this river and the Wisdom, later the Big Hole River, at the same time "in commemoration of two of (President Jefferson's) cardinal virtues, which have so eminently marked that deservedly selibrated (sic) character through life." Pioneers downgraded the name considerably to Stinking Water because of rotting buffalo carcasses found in it one spring, but fussier descendants called it Ruby after the garnets found in its placer gravels. You can still find them if you look.

Blacktail Creek—Flows into the Beaverhead just above or south of Dillon from the east side. Named for many mule deer in the area, mistakenly called "blacktail" deer by pioneers.

Grasshopper Creek—Flows into the Beaverhead from the west upriver from Dillon and from the west side. First named Willard Creek by Lewis and Clark after Alexander Willard, an expedition member. Early prospectors changed the name because of the numerous grasshoppers found along its banks. On this creek is old Bannack, Montana's first capital.

Horse Prairie Creek—Near the mouth of this creek in the late summer of 1805, Lewis and Clark met the Shoshone Indians and were taken to the summit of Lemhi Pass, at Horse Prairie's head, where the explorers first crossed the Continental Divide. Open meadows on this creek were grazing grounds for Indian horses. Lewis and Clark left their caches of provisions and their boats at the mouth of this creek when they ascended the Rockies on their way west.

Red Rock Creek—Joins Horse Prairie Creek at Armstead to form the Beaverhead. Named for the red rocks in its bed. Drains Red Rock Lakes, where the largest flock of trumpeter swans in North America nests and lives.

Wise River—Flows northward out of the Pioneer mountains to join the Big Hole River at the town of Wise River. This is all that's left of Lewis and Clerk's good intentions to honor the wisdom of their president.

Madison River—Lewis and Clark didn't dream there was such great trout fishing in this stream when they named it after Secretary of State James Madison. The middle fork of the Missouri, the Madison rises in Yellowstone Park and flows north to Three Forks. Near its head a 1959 earthquake tossed a mountain into the river, creating Quake Lake and taking a terrible toll of lives of campers in the Madison Canyon.

Firehole River—Unites with the Gibbon River at Madison junction in Yellowstone Park to form the Madison. Named for the hot waters entering it from geyser and hot spring overflow in the park. This mineral fertility is largely responsible for the Madison's excellent fishing.

Gibbon River—Named for General Gibbon, who led his troops through Yellowstone Park in pursuit of Nez Perce Chief Joseph in the summer of 1877. Rope marks on trees in the park where the troops lowered their wagons during the pursuit still are visible.

Gallatin River—The eastern fork of the Missouri, this river flows north from the northwest corner of Yellowstone Park through a forested canyon. Lewis and Clark named this branch for Albert Gallatin, Secretary of the Treasury in Jefferson's cabinet.

Boulder River—Flows south and east out of the Elkhorn and Bull mountain area to join the Jefferson River at Cardwell. Named for the big boulders in its bed.

How They Got Their Names — Mountain Ranges

Beaverhead Range—Sometimes called an extension of the Bitter Root Range, it snakes between Montana and Idaho southward from Gibbon's Pass to Monida Pass on Highway 15. Historic passes in this range, named after the Beaverhead River, are Lemhi, west of Armstead, where Lewis and Clark first crossed the Continental Divide in late summer, 1805, and Bannock, south of Brenner, used by the Bannock Indians on their trips from Idaho to Montana. Highest peak, Ajax Mountain, west of Jackson, 10,900 feet.

Big Belt Mountains—From southwest of Great Falls to Sixteen-Mile Creek, along the east bank of the Missouri River. Named for Belt Butte near Belt town. Their western slope is mostly historic gold country.

Bull Mountain—South of Boulder. Named for the big bull elk for which this range is noted.

Elkhorn Range—West of the Missouri River between Three Forks and Helena. Named for old Elkhorn, once a rip-roaring mining town and now "ghosted," which lies on its southwestern slope. Lewis and Clark Cavern State Park is on the south end of this range.

Gallatin Range—Between the Gallatin and Yellowstone rivers. Named by Lewis and Clark after Gallatin River, namesake of Albert Gallatin, Secretary of the Treasury. Highest peak, Mount Blackmore, 10,900 feet, west of Emigrant. Spanish Peaks, at the north end, named for Spaniards who prospected along Spanish Creek.

Gravelly Range—South of Virginia City. This one was easy to name after its gravelly soil. A lake in this range contains the only Oxalatl, or amphibious lizards, north of Mexico.

Highlands—South of Butte. Named to distinguish them from the "lowlands" or nearby lower mountains at the head of the Silver Bow valley.

Bridger Range—Northeast of Bozeman. Named for Jim Bridger, famed army scout and expedition leader, whose Bridger trail from the Yellowstone to Virginia City led across these mountains.

Madison Range—Between the Madison and Gallatin rivers. Named by Lewis and Clark after James Madison. At the south end of this range is Targhee Pass between Yellowstone Park and Idaho, named after the famous Bannock Indian chief. Highest peak is Gallatin Peak, east of Jeffers, at 11,015 feet.

Pioneer Mountains—In the loop of the Big Hole River east of Wisdom and west of Melrose. Name honors the pioneers who first settled Montana at Bannack on Grasshopper Creek, which drains the southern end of this range.

Ruby Range—Between Beaverhead and Ruby rivers. Garnets are easy to find in the Ruby valley placers, and early prospectors mistakenly called them "rubies."

Snowcrest Range—Between Lima and Ruby reservoirs. Their snowy peaks are a landmark in this high country, at the head of Blacktail Creek.

Tendoy Mountains—West side of Red Rock Creek between Dell and Armstead. An isolated range named after Chief Tendoy of the Bannock Indians of Idaho and southwestern Montana.

Tobacco Root Mountains—Indians and early trappers found a root in these mountains that, when dried and mixed with larb, made a suitable substitute for real tobacco. The root was a species of mullein. Between the Ruby-Jefferson and Madison valleys. Hollow-Top Mountain, its highest, is 10,513 feet.

Horse Shoe Hills—Rough hills north of Manhattan and Logan. Named for their horseshoe shape.

How They Got Their Names — Towns and Cities

Alder—Alder Creek, which washed the lodes of Virginia City and was named for the alders on its banks, flowed through town.

Amsterdam—Center of the so-called Holland settlement, a fertile country farmed by thrifty Dutch and their descendants.

Basin—Basin Creek, which flows through town, drains an old-time mining area, and some of the evidences still are obvious.

Belgrade—A Serbian nobleman and investor in Northern Pacific railway named this town after the capital of his homeland. The Serbian was on a special train carrying the Northern Pacific party of capitalists and officials westward to drive the Golden Spike in the road at Garrison in 1883.

Boulder—Through town flows the rocky-bottomed Boulder River, one of two in the state.

Bozeman—John M. Bozeman, who left a city, a pioneer trail and a mountain pass named for him, led the first settlers into the Gallatin valley in 1864 and in 1867 was killed by Indians east of Livingston.

Canyon Ferry—Beneath the waters of Canyon Ferry Lake lies a canyon that pinched the Missouri River. A pioneer ferry across this point carried the stage and freight wagons that connected Helena with the Carroll road and the gold mines of the Belt Mountains across the river. Crossing it regularly in the late 60s was the St. Paul, Minnesota-Helena Pony Express mail, delivered at this point to a stage.

Dillon—The Utah Northern Railroad, first into Montana, reached this point on the Beaverhead River September 16, 1879, and it was only natural the town be named for the railroad's president, Sidney Dillon.

Gallatin Gateway—The town is a genuine gateway to the Gallatin Canyon, beautiful route to Yellowstone Park.

Helena—Capital of Montana since 1875. Originally called "Crab Town," after John Crab, one of the "Four Georgians," who discovered gold in Last Chance Gulch July 14, 1864. Helena's principal street runs down Last Chance. There are two versions for the name "Helena." One is that a public meeting named it for Helen of Troy and the other that it was named for Helena, Minnesota, by John Somerville, a former resident of that place.

Jackson—Probably after David Jackson of the Rocky Mountain Fur Company, who spent much time in southwestern Montana.

Jefferson City—President Thomas Jefferson left his name several places in Montana, thanks to his loyal disciples, Lewis and Clark.

Logan—Probably after Captain William Logan, killed in the battle of the Big Hole by Nez Perce Indians in 1877.

Manhattan—A group from New York, known as the Manhattan Company, operated big farm and ranch holdings near here.

Monida—Straddling the Continental Divide and the Montana-Idaho boundary, the town took half its name from each state.

Ringling—After John Ringling of circus fame and former president of the White Sulphur Springs and Yellowstone Park Railway.

Sheridan—After General Philip S. Sheridan of Civil War fame. After the war he was commander of the military department which included Montana.

Silver Bow—Took its name from nearby Silver Bow Creek, named for its likeness to a silver bow.

Townsend—Named for a Northern Pacific Railway official.

Three Forks—Just north of here the Jefferson, Gallatin and Madison rivers unite to form the Missouri River. This is the famous "Three Forks" of the longest river in the United States, goal of Lewis and Clark and headquarters for fur traders.

Trident—A French way of saying "Three Forks."

Twin Bridges—Bridges crossing the Beaverhead and Big Hole rivers at this point made the name a natural.

Virginia City—Carefully restored pioneer Montana city. First called "Varina" to honor Jefferson Davis' wife, but Judge G. G. Bissell, a northerner, objected and refused to sign a legal document using that name. He scratched it out and substituted Virginia City, then signed. Second capital of Montana, it served as such from February 7, 1865, to 1875, when Helena took over.

West Yellowstone—Western entrance to Yellowstone National Park.

White Sulphur Springs—The town grew up around sulphur springs with the same chemical content as the famed "waters" at Baden Baden, Germany.

Wisdom—The old name of the Big Hole River was Wisdom River, from which the town was named. Lewis and Clark named the river for President Jefferson's wisdom.

Wolf Creek—Indian legend says that when buffalo were driven over a nearby cliff or "pishkun" to their death, a wolf went along for the last ride. They called the creek that flowed by the cliff "the creek where the wolf jumped too."

Bloody

Junction

Few men of consequence in the young West failed to leave their moccasin tracks at the headwaters of the Missouri, and tragedy and failure were among its frequent visitors.

Before the white men, the various Indian tribes fought over who was to control the three forks of the longest river in the nation, and Lewis and Clark arrived to find the contest still in progress.

First white man ever to see the historic "forks," which can be reached on Highway 286 from a junction about half way between Logan and the town of Three Forks on Highway 90, was Captain William Clark. It was July 25, 1805, and "a fine morning," Clark says. "We proceeded on a few miles to the three forks of the Missouri." Clark explored the west branch, or Jefferson River, decided this was the stream to follow and walked up it after breakfasting on the ribs of a buck deer killed the day before.

Clark commented on his return that his feet were sore from the prickly pears, that he had seen elk, deer, bear and many beaver in the neighborhood of what now is Willow Creek. He called that stream Philosophy River, but it didn't last.

Lewis came up shortly, concurred with Clark on the western fork, rather than the middle or Madison River, or the eastern or Gallatin. The explorers named the western fork for the president and the other two for cabinet members.

With the expedition when it landed on the gravelly beach at the junction of the rivers was John Colter, a man whose name forever will be linked with the Missouri and its headwaters. Colter fell madly in love with the West and interrupted his trip home with Lewis and Clark to come back upriver and help build Fort Lisa at the Big Horn's mouth in 1809.

Guided by Colter, trader Manuel Lisa started out in the spring of 1810 for the "forks." In April they began building a fort or trading post on a limestone table rock between the Madison and Gallatin, a place Lewis called "a handsome site for a fortification." The intent was to trap beaver in all the country above Great Falls.

However, the Blackfeet constantly harassed the party of 30, eventually killing eight of them, including Drouillard, Lewis and Clark's former hunter. The post was abandoned to the Indians, although its remains were there until 1870 and were known locally as the "Lewis and Clark Fort." Not far from there, and on the Gallatin River about a half mile above the forks, was old Gallatin City, long since rotted into the ground.

Lewis looked over the valleys from a cliff just above old Gallatin City. Although Lewis never came this way again, Clark visited the "forks" on his way back to St. Louis, coming through here on his way to Bozeman Pass and the Yellowstone.

It was 1821, after Manuel Lisa had died, that the Missouri Fur Company had John Pilcher for its president, and Pilcher yearned for the riches in furs on the Yellowstone and the Three Forks country. By 1822 Pilcher had 300 trappers working for him, including Robert Jones and Michael Immel, two of the best traders in the Northwest. They took $25,000 in furs on the Yellowstone, and a jubilant Pilcher sent them in the spring of 1823 to Three Forks to "use every effort to obtain a friendly interview with the Blackfeet . . ."

Trapping and trading were good. Jones and Immel left the "forks" with $15,000 in furs and headed for old Fort Benton at the mouth of the Big Horn on the Yellowstone, not to be confused with the Missouri River Fort Benton. The pair met 38 Blackfeet, camped with them and were pleased with the friendliness of the Indians.

Two weeks later, below the rimrocks downriver from the present city of Billings, Jones and Immel rode through a pass and into a Blackfeet ambush. Both were killed, and the Indians took furs, horses and equipment. The black luck of the Three Forks still held. With their deaths went Pilcher's hopes for a fortune on the Yellowstone.

In 1824 Alexander Ross of the Hudson's Bay Company assembled a band of his trappers at Three Forks, a band he earlier had dispatched through the country to seek furs. One of the returning groups embarrassed Ross by picking up a few American competitors guided by the pious and capable Jedediah Smith. Peter Skene Ogden, with his British trappers, used the Three Forks point in 1825. In 1828 Samuel Tullock built another fort at the "forks," but again Blackfeet drove off the white men.

From 1828 to 1832 Rocky Mountain Fur Company and American Fur Company traders battled over the area, adding their violence to that caused by the Blackfeet. In 1832 Blackfeet killed William Henry Vandenburgh, of American Fur, one of the original Pilcher traders, and in 1834 the Rocky Mountain Company was reorganized. The battle of the fur trade at the head of the Missouri was over.

Today's visitor to Three Forks will find the waters of three handsome rivers flowing together and a comfortable park marked for the benefit of those who come to see, largely through the efforts of Clark Maudlin of Anaconda, Montana's principal Three Forks "buff." There is little to indicate the blood that was shed to command this triangle where one of America's great rivers is born.

The Nervous Tree

Badge of distinction in all seasons, especially fall, is the brilliant aspen tree, nervously anticipating winter but gaily enjoying Indian summer while it lasts.

Biblical history tragically records the aspen as the tree from which Judas Iscariot hanged himself, a circumstance which forever doomed it to tremble in retrospect. However, I prefer my aspen as a golden flood of light across the mountain slopes, created by the mysterious chemistry of nature to delight the traveler before winter turns familiar things to photographic two-tone.

There is an affinity of aspen and water, and like the hen and the egg, none can say which came first, which deserves priority in this closest of friendships. Water, being the magic ingredient of all things living, undoubtedly locates the aspen, but, in turn, the heavily-banked snows around the feet of aspen groves restore the water for the springs that rise between the roots.

What mountain traveler, whether on foot or horse, or even rubber-tired, has been able to resist stopping by a clump of aspen to watch the wind worry the rich green or golden yellow leaves, occasionally flicking one from a twisted limb and tumbling it through the air. Under the tree will be the inevitable spongy ground, and far back beneath the tangle of grotesque trunks and the whitened ghosts of fallen aspen will be a spring or seep. It will be talking to itself, mumbling the same tune as the leaves above it, and working its way over the roots in tiny waterfalls as sparkling as the golden shower above it.

Softly padding through the ground tangle will be a ruffed grouse, hugging the water supply and taking advantage of the screen between herself and the sky, which could be full of hawks this fine day. The water pools will be covered with fallen golden leaves, swirling away on the water's surface like $20 gold pieces on a gaming table.

At a hunting camp in these southwest mountains each fall a part of the ritual of setting up camp is cleaning the leaves from the waterhole in the creek at the front door of the cabin. Leaves have clogged the pipe that pours out a silver stream for the waiting bucket, and the soggy mass of sunken leaves is a far cry from the color that clings above. But, even here, the gold remains in many a sodden leaf, and the pool beneath the pipe is covered with newly-fallen leaves, whirling off down the creek, turning the little stream into a molten flood in the afternoon sun.

A great, friendly mountain along Montana's eastern slope of the continental divide bases its limestone cliffs in solid evergreen all summer long, or at least so it seems to those who glance only. After the first frosts the springs and small creeks dropping off its slopes become yellow dots and lines in the darkening green. They are marked as on a road map, for only where the water is squeezed out between shelves of rock or pours down a stoney draw do the aspens follow and set up their fall guideposts.

There is so much aspen country in the mountains of Montana that no road is long enough to visit it all. Its very abundance is confusing. In the wide swing of the Big Hole valley above the junction of the Mill Creek road south of Anaconda with Highway 43 between Divide and Gibbons Pass, aspens trace their canary colors along every creek flowing out of the Beaverheads and the Pintlar. A hunter told me once this was a baffling country to him. The entire mountain base is a solid mass of dark timber, and each creek was marked by a splash of aspen, alike for miles along the west side of the valley.

If our friend was baffled, he no doubt also was inwardly pleased, for only the fall sunshine in the Big Hole could match such brilliance and contrast. He could have said the same of the Stillwater country south of Columbus, of the Gallatin Canyon south of Bozeman or the high Centennials east of Monida.

Probably the most spectacular aspens in Montana are those along Highway 15 north of Butte, just south of Elk Park Pass. This is all aspen country, etched against dark firs on both sides of Bison creek, but south of the pass the aspens take over completely. It is as though the mines of Butte had spilled out all their gold at once across the hills to flaunt their wealth at autumn's traveler.

The First Hooves

Three green Montana valleys a century ago felt the first hoofs of the state's range livestock industry, and descendents of those long-ago herds and flocks still nibble the bright grass in those same meadows.

Power-steering cowboys and sheepherders can take up the dust of the trailherd at Monida, for over these sagebrush hills came the lean cattle and tired sheep to be fattened and traded for gold in the mining camps.

Then as now the sheep were valued for their two crops of flesh and fiber and merited their pioneer nickname of "the golden hoof." Cattle were converted quickly to steaks, and even such famed builders of empire as James and Granville Stuart and Conrad Kohrs hacked out their first Montana dollars with a cleaver in a Bannack butcher shop.

But it wasn't the Stuarts or Kohrs who enterprised the first large cattle ranch in Montana, but Richard Grant, whose ranch house in the Deer Lodge valley was a landmark of the territory. The Missions at St. Mary's in the Bitter Root and at St. Ignatius in the Flathead had stock before Grant, and John Owen apparently bought the clergy's stock along with St. Mary's, when he took over the mission. However, Grant was the first to make a real business of turning Montana grass into beef.

He and his son John built up a profitable business of trading Oregon Trail pioneers out of trail-weary stock and driving it northward across the passes into the Beaverhead valley for winter fattening and spring trading back along the trail. Highway 15 from Monida to Dillon passes the first ranges grazed by Montana cattle.

By the early 1850s such practices were common, and the Stevens party found several herds in the Bitter Root. By 1856-57 the Grants had set up their ranch there, but by 1858 they had moved to the Deer Lodge valley and owned several hundred head of cattle.

Johnny Grant's became a legend in the Deer Lodge valley, just outside the town of Deer Lodge, and was known throughout the West. Any driver along Highway 90 through that valley today can see this site of one of the earliest cattle outfits.

Cattle came into the Deer Lodge valley from the Beaverhead country to the south by way of Deer Lodge Pass, a low pass which today carries Highway 15 from Dillon to Butte. The trio of valleys held an ideal position—in the midst of mining areas and blessed with grass and water.

In practice the cattle from the Deer Lodge valley were driven across the pass between what now is Anaconda and the post office of Fishtrap, 25 miles by blacktopped Highway 274 along the shoulder of craggy Mount Haggin, snow-topped to the west. Once in the Big Hole country they were in some of the finest summer range in the world, knee-high rich grasses, green as a great sea.

Just over Gibbons Pass, west of Wisdom by graveled road No. 43, is the head of the Bitter Root, third of the original livestock valleys. This is a beautiful drive, rising out of the Big Hole and the colorful cow town of Wisdom into the lodgepole pines and the country where Chief Joseph battled the U.S. Army and lived to fight another day.

At Sula the road meets paved Highway 93, and the way then is north and downhill into the rich Bitter Root valley, covered with grass a century ago but now squared neatly into orchards and prime acreages of sugar beets. To the pioneer cowman it must have looked like heaven, with its miles of grass back-dropped by the lofty barrier that splits Idaho and Montana.

At Hamilton turn east and follow the old road, Highway 269, north through Corvallis and into Stevensville. It's paved and good traveling, and more leisurely than 93. At Stevensville is old Fort Owen, where John Owen in 1850 was, without much doubt, the first real permanently located cattle rancher in Montana. When he bought St. Mary's mission he acquired a herd of cattle with the property, the animals apparently part of those brought to Montana by Father DeSmet, first in western Montana.

Eastern Montana soon became the great cattle country and still is. Populated by Texas herds, the grasses of the eastern benches spawned a massive industry, but the three valleys of the west hold the honor of its birth. In a leisurely drive it can be reborn.

Jim's Wagon Trail

Jim Bridger never needed a road map, and signs were scarce back when he picked out a trail over the mass of mountains that today bears his name and beckons the motorist.

Jim savvied Indians as few men did, and no one knew his way around the old West better than Bridger. When he set out in the last year of the Civil War to find a trail that woudn't annoy the Indians and would let the small wagon trains through, he marked out a road that is fun to follow a century later.

Jim's trail branched off the Oregon Trail west of Casper, Wyoming, crossed the Big Horn River at old Fort C. F. Smith south of Hardin, then cut northwestward across the Absaroka foothills and dropped into the Yellowstone valley. About two miles below Springdale, east of Livingston, the motoring pioneer can pick up the trail as it crossed the Yellowstone to the north side. A gravel road on that side from Springdale to Highway 89 practically follows the old trail.

Swing north up Highway 89 to Clyde Park in the Shields River valley. From here turn west again on gravel to follow Jim's wagons up Brackett Creek and over the divide into Bridger Canyon. For most of the distance from Wyoming to Virginia City the Bridger and Bozeman trails followed the same route, but for some reason, no doubt a good one, Jim picked Bridger Canyon in preference to Bozeman Pass, now used by Highway 90 and the Northern Pacific Railway.

Where the road over the Brackett divide joins the road down Bridger Canyon, historic trails were joined, too. From 1887 to 1893 bull teams hauled supplies through here to the roaring mining camps in the Castle mountains at Old Castle and Copperopolis. The canyon is on a direct line from Virginia City to old Carroll, the Missouri river port north of Lewistown, from the Judith Basin and Judith Gap country to the north. To the freighters this was the quickest way into the Gallatin valley from the upper Shields.

From this junction, the traveler who has time can backtrack northward along the road to the Shields valley through Wilsall. This road runs through historic Flathead Pass, one of the old passes known to the Indians from west of the divide on their buffalo hunts. Follow Flathead Creek downhill or eastward, and this is roughly the route of the old bull teams on their way to the Castle "diggins" north of Lennep.

About a mile and a quarter northwest of Wilsall is a weathered frame building that once was the Meyersburg community center and the postoffice until Wilsall took that honor in 1910. This building was headquarters for the bull team freighters, and its walls no doubt have absorbed much loud and coarse talk, for this gentry was never known for gentility or piety. Bulls were presumed to understand only the plainest language.

But, back to the Bridger Trail at the crossroads west of Clyde Park. Few pioneers have been treated to a more scenic trip, although most of them by that time probably were sated with scenery and would have settled for a warm meal and a roof over their heads in preference to any kind of magnificence.

Bridger is a great place for eagles, the big golden fellows, who no doubt glory in the uplift of the winds that sweep across the slopes of the Bridgers and provide free rides for aerial hunters.

Just outside Bozeman the wagon trains broke out into the Gallatin valley. At about this point the old Bozeman Trail came into view and the two trails met near where the canyon road now joins Highway 90. From here both trails headed southwestward across the tall grass of the Gallatin valley, through the Holland hills to the Madison and on to the Virginia City diggings.

Wealth Under the Alders

Indians were responsible for the discovery of Montana's most famous gulch. They didn't intend it that way, but when the savages turned back six prospectors headed for the Yellowstone from the Bannack diggings, Alder gulch, with all its riches, was ready to be born, and the year was 1863.

Grass was greening on the Montana hills when Bill Fairweather, whose name still is a household word in Virginia City, Henry Edgar, Barney Hughes, Thomas W. Cover, Mike Sweeney and Harry Rodgers set off to join James Stuart on his Yellowstone expedition. The sextet can thank the Indians. Stuart found no gold on the Yellowstone.

In was May 28 when the prospectors stopped in the little gulch above the Stinkingwater, now the Ruby, River. They weren't very happy about having to return, but Fairweather and Edgar decided to pan a little instead of help prepare something to eat. The rest of the party growled at them for their laziness, but complaints turned to wild joy when nuggets rattled in the pan.

They couldn't wait to get back to Bannack to get more supplies, and they, like all other prospectors, told everyone they saw about the strike. When they filed their claims they picked the name Alder for the new gulch. The party returned to the gulch, followed by a horde of wishful miners, and on June 4 the leaders and discoverers stopped at Point of Rocks, about 20 miles from the gulch and insisted on a code of rules to protect the newly staked mines.

The following Sunday the new rules were approved, claims recognized and a committee named to complete the governing laws. The area was called Fairweather district and the town was named Varina for Jefferson Davis' wife. However, Judge Bissell, a Republican, changed this to Virginia City, which he thought southern enough to please any Rebel.

Within two years 10,000 persons crowded into the gulch. By 1864 the town began to think of itself as permanent. Tom Cover and Perry McAdow built a sawmill, and a brick kiln and stone quarry were set up. Miners incorporated the town under Idaho territorial law January 30, 1864, but on May 26, 1864, almost a year to the day after the discovery, Montana Territory was created. So, on December 30 of that year the Montana territorial legislature at Bannack recognized the newly incorporated city. It also found a new seat of government for Montana.

Bannack had begun to decline sharply. Its placers were playing out, and on February 7, 1865, the territory moved its capital to Virginia City. Not for 10 years was it moved to its present home at Helena.

With all the gold fever, other nearby towns were inevitable. Summit, on the divide between Alder gulch and the Madison, and Nevada City, down the gulch from Virginia, were the principals. Pine Grove, Highland, Adobetown, Ruby and Alder burgeoned and then vanished, except for Alder. Virginia City, built where Daylight Creek entered the gulch, published the territory's first newspaper, the Montana Post, first printed August 27, 1864.

Helena and Butte business leaders supported Virginia City and gave it the flavor of a commercial capital as well as governmental center. After the quartz mines at Summit and other places gave out, dredges were set up in the lower gulches in the 90s. One of them even boasted Harvard University as a stockholder. Although several million dollars in gold was dredged out of the sands below Virginia, 1922 spelled the end of gold in Alder Gulch.

Today, Virginia City is the place where a visitor can see more detail of the mining frontier than anywhere else in the West. State Senator Charles Bovey and Mrs. Bovey have carefully restored the 1860s in architecture, atmosphere and decor. They hope to give the same restorative touch to Nevada City, complete with a pioneer railroad between the two towns.

Alder Gulch and Virginia City went through some of the worst throes of the mining west. It dealt with them, however, for it was a leader in organizing the Vigilantes, which made it safe for men to travel the roads and trails with their earnings in their pockets. It charged $25 as punishment for operating a house of ill fame and $10 for appearing on the streets in the nude. Public drunkenness was worth only $3 to $5, and a six-month dog license cost $3, an outrageous figure by today's standards.

Residents went without flour in the winter of 1864-65, but they settled what threatened to develop into a first-class "flour war." Without Virginia City Montana would not have found government by law so quickly or moved so swiftly into commerce. The little gold city in the gulch was a rough mother, but she raised a good son.

Lewis and Clark at the Beaverhead Forks. — C. M. Russell.

Day of Decision

August 10, 1805, was a day of major decision for Lewis and Clark, and Captain Meriwether Lewis made that decision where Red Rock and Horse Prairie creeks form the Beaverhead River.

It was here that Lewis knew they must abandon the boats that had brought them 3,000 miles from St. Charles, Missouri. This cold fact, forced upon the expedition by dwindling waters of the Missouri river system, also insisted that horses be found to get the travelers to the navigable waters of the Columbia River, across the Continental Divide.

In anticipation of this day, Lewis had obtained the services of Sacajawea, a Shoshone Indian and wife of Charbonneau, interpreter for the expedition. Sacajawea had been stolen as a child when her tribe was attacked near Three Forks by Minnetares or plains Indians. She had been sold to the Mandans, and it was at Fort Mandan the winter before that Lewis saw in this Indian girl a likely contact with owners of horses at the head of the Missouri. Now the day had come to test her ability and connections.

Lewis was ahead of Clark in their ascent of the Beaverhead River, and Lewis' day began by passing the mouth of Blacktail Creek and by sending Drewyer, the expedition's top hunter, off to shoot a deer which was grazing northwest of the Beaverhead valley just south of where Dillon now stands.

While Lewis and the rest waited for Drewyer to return they built a fire beneath what now is called Beaverhead rocks, just above Dillon. The expedition called them "rattle snake clifts" because of the large number of snakes there. Lewis also saw "several bald eagles and two large white-headed fishing-hawks," probably ospreys. The expedition took from the Indians the name of "Beaver's Head," for the bluff below Dillon now called Point of Rocks, creating confusion ever since.

About 15 miles above the "Beaverhead" rocks south of Dillon Lewis came upon a "handsome and open leavell valley where the river divided itself into two equal branches; here I halted and examined those streams and readily discovered from their size that it would be vain to attempt the navigation of either any further, here also the road (Indian trail) forked, one leading up the valley of each of these streams."

The expedition journal refers to Red Rock as the true Jefferson and what now is Horse Prairie Creek as simply "Prairie Creek." Drewyer was sent up one stream and Shields up the other, but Lewis soon found the main Indian horse trail was up Horse Prairie. He destroyed an earlier note left on a willow stick for Captain Clark and wrote another to tell him the party had gone up the west fork, which was "more in the direction I wished to pursue; I, therefore, did not hesitate about changing my route but determined to take the western road."

Lewis commented: "I do not believe that the world can furnish an example of a river running to the extent which the Missouri and the Jefferson's do through such a mountainous country and at the same time so navigable as they are." He foresaw a water route across the country, but this only partially came true, with navigation limited to below Fort Benton on the Missouri and to below Fort Walla Walla on the Columbia.

Just above the junction, where Horse Prairie valley opens out, the party camped that night, and Lewis called the spot Shoshone cove, expecting to contact Sacajawea's people at any time. The following day the leader had a nervous encounter with the first of the Shoshones, but the Indian escaped without any contact. Not until Monday, August 12, did Lewis come upon three thoroughly frightened Shoshone women, who, after gifts and persuasion, led the party to Chief Cameahwait and opened the door to the Pacific Ocean.

The party crossed Lemhi Pass, Lewis tasted the waters of the Columbia, and found them clear and cold. Not until August 17, when Clark caught up with Lewis, did Sacajawea meet her people, the Shoshone. She was warmly greeted by the chief, who instantly recognized her as his sister, and by a Shoshone woman who was captured with Sacajawea but who escaped and returned to her tribe.

A monument at the Forks of the Beaverhead honors the Bird Woman, Sacajawea, at the point where Cameahwait furnished horses to carry the expedition's supplies and equipment over the divide. There were troublesome days yet to come between here and boating on the Columbia, but now there were horses to carry the burdens.

Sterling in the Rough

Only the richest ores went through the smelter at old Glendale in the Big Hole country south of Butte, and their silver sheen made it known halfway around the world.

Glendale bore the burnish of civilization for the Hecla mining area, with its fabulous 40-foot ore pockets and its snowbound life among the 11,000-foot peaks of the Pioneer Range. It is Glendale today that still wears the dignity of the sterling silver economy that spewed out twenty million dollars for Hecla Consolidated before the great price break in the white metal.

Of all the towns strewn up the rough canyon of Trapper Creek from Melrose, the best preserved and easiest reached is Glendale, seven miles west of Melrose on paved Highway 15. The Melrose turnoff to Trapper Creek is 34 miles south of Butte.

It all began in the summer of 1873 when Jerry Grotevant, who was looking for lost horses, sat down to rest on a log and kicked over a small boulder. Underneath was the glint of native silver. He was literally sitting on the Trapper lode—on millions of dollars of the richest ore. The previous fall Jerry's partner, Bill Spurr, had found, while hunting in the Trapper drainage, an outcrop that later became the Forest Queen mine.

The rush from Jerry's discovery started Trapper City, which sprawled across Trapper Creek, but later discoveries spawned Lion City, at the foot of Lion Mountain. The ore from these mines snaked down the wild canyon in 10-ton wagons behind six- and eight-horse teams for freighting from Melrose to Corinne, Utah, then to San Francisco and halfway round the world to Swansea, Wales, for smelting. Glendale was yet to come. All the activity still was high in the pinnacles of the Pioneers.

By 1875 Charles Dahler and Noah Armstrong had built a small 20 ton smelter and the whole operation had taken on a new, progressive look. There was need for coke for the smelter, and this required wood for the charcoal kilns, largely over the ridge on Canyon Creek and operated by crews of jolly

Italians. By the 80s Glendale was in full swing, and the smelters continued to grow over the years and be improved. The 90-pound bars of bullion from the Glendale furnaces went to Omaha by Utah Northern's rails for refining.

There was a narrow-gauge railroad to haul ore from the Hecla mines to the concentrator between the two towns, a railroad with a real snow problem. Although Hecla was the principal town at the mining district at the head of Trapper Creek, and Glendale was the processing metropolis, there were other towns such as the suburbs of Greenwood and Norwood.

A few foundations and rock buildings remain at all the sites in the canyon, and even old Trapper City is remembered by a unique wooden-pegged cabin in good repair. At Hecla is the old office building and even a safe with lettering "Hecla Consolidated."

At Glendale the smelter which replaced the 1875 original still stands, a roofless shell. Best preserved at Glendale is the Knippenberg mansion, the cupolaed and carved home of Henry Knippenberg, superintendent of Hecla Consolidated. Built in 1881, the mansion had six fireplaces, sterling silver door knobs as benefitted a silver city mansion, blood-red draperies and ankle-deep Brussels carpets.

Mrs. Knippenberg, whose hospitality was widely known, had one social requirement. She permitted no smoking on the main floor and graciously suggested that the smokers repair to the big cupola room which still surmounts the massive home.

There was violence, too. The driver of the Glendale-Hecla stage was ambushed and shot dead from his seat on the stage at Point of Rocks between the two towns. His murderer was caught and hanged at Dillon. Justice quickly overtook the murderer of Dutch Jake Kruger, whose bones and coat were found in a campfire on a bitter December day in 1882.

Dutch Jake's companion, a 30-year-old miner, was found in a shack at Melrose, his feet frozen and his lips sealed as to Jake's fate. Jailed in Dillon, the frozen-footed man still refused to talk, but a delegation from Glendale decided the case. The jailer handed over the keys to the "liberators," and the miner's body swung from the jail door to avenge Jake's cremation.

Death House on the Ruby

Bloodstains on the aging floors of a two-story log house just off Highway 34 and about five miles south of Sheridan match the crimson of the garnets that visitors still can find in the sands of the Ruby valley.

In the early 60s the Ruby valley was the hoof-beaten trail between the feverish gold camps of Alder Gulch to the south and east and of Bannack to the south and west. Its level, grass-covered meadows were an ideal spot to headquarter organized crime that preyed upon the stagecoaches with their full strongboxes and lone riders with stuffed saddle bags.

Geography decided that Pete Daley's ranch house, a log, two-story, cottonwood-shaded building that fronted the old road between the gold camps would become famous as "Robbers' Roost." The robbers who roosted there were members of the Plummer gang, who cynically called themselves the "Innocents" while wiping from their hands the gore of miners who had given up their gold at the point of a gun.

The "roost" was, and is, the epitome of old West, with its second-story balcony facing the timbered Ruby Mountains and its dark windows opening on barnlike rooms. Upstairs the large, dormitory-like room recalls the violence that must have taken place under the sloping eaves, safe from the eyes of honest people. It is here that a dark bloodstain left a streak to the head of the stairs and spots down each step to the outside door. There were dark stains on the first-floor boards too, and only those who lie in the "boot hills" of Virginia City and Bannack know the names of those whose lives gushed out on these rough floors of the "roost."

Oddly enough, it was the brashness and complete cruelty of the gang led by the robber-sheriff Henry Plummer that stung the gold mining communities into action that eventually led to setting up a system of courts and indirectly to creation of Montana Territory in 1864.

The suave, gentlemanly Plummer, with his equally personable buddy, Jack Cleveland, had arrived in Bannack from Orofino, Idaho, with definite plans for profiting from gold without the effort of wielding a shovel. At that time the eastern counties of sprawling Idaho Territory might as well have been on the moon for all that most civilized people cared.

Plummer's manners (he reputedly was the only man in Virginia City who regularly washed his hands before meals) and his personality quickly earned him election as sheriff, an ideal set up for what he had in mind.

Plummer and Cleveland had skipped out of Orofino ahead of the law and soon had gathered around them in Bannack in the summer of 1863 a gang of steel-hard and lawless but charming young men such as Bill Moore, George Ives and Jack

Lyons. This was by no means all the road agents, but it was the nucleus, and Plummer was undisputed leader.

It was a bloody summer of terror for the gulches. A total of 102 persons were known to have been murdered, and uncounted others vanished without a trace. The loot was in the high thousands, including $3,000 in one holdup of the Caldwell and Peabody stage.

Idaho Territory was created March 3, 1863, and Chief Justice Sidney Edgerton was sent to Bannack in September of that year to establish justice. He had no court room, no bench and no way to enforce his decisions. Worse yet, the general feeling was that the gold camps were better off without law. There was open resistance to taxation to build a court house or any other governmental building. Taxes were looked upon as a detriment to development of the mines.

In this fertile atmosphere, Plummer's "Innocents" flourished. His gang plotted and planned at the "roost," using information obtained by the sheriff and from outposts in both Bannack and Virginia City. Several incidents, including the killing of a small boy on a ranch in the Ruby valley, outraged the residents, but nothing was done.

Finally, boldness, carelessness and the fortunate circumstances of a funeral in Bannack brought a swift end. Plummer had made it a practice to carefully avoid scenes of crime and to be seen elsewhere by prominent witnesses. The lure of $15,000 in gold reportedly on its way to Salt Lake City from Bannack in possession of Samuel Hauser and Nathaniel P. Langford lured Plummer into drawing a mask across his face and waiting in ambush for a Mormon wagon train on the Bannack-Salt Lake road.

Ned Ray, Ives and Plummer were waiting for the train in the moonlight, watching for a bright red scarf that Plummer had given to Hauser earlier in the day. The Mormons passed, and Hauser and Langford were not with them. Then Buck Stinson rode up to tell Plummer that the pair would be along shortly—delayed in leaving Bannack.

A lone, galloping horseman was stopped by the outlaws but allowed to go on when he was identified as Judge Edgerton's nephew, a youth named Tilden. This was the fatal slip that hanged the road agents. Tilden recognized Plummer by his brown-flecked eyes and told his uncle, who informed Colonel Wilbur Fisk Sanders, the territorial prosecutor.

At the funeral of William Bell, a prominent Bannack Mason, enough honest citizens gathered to form the Vigilantes, one of the outstanding volunteer law-enforcement groups in the West. The Masonic Lodge did not take the lead, although many were Masons. James Williams, who led the enforcement work in the field, was not a member of the lodge. Paris Pfouts, a Virginia City storekeeper, was president, and Mortimer Lott, Ruby valley merchant, was treasurer.

Once formed, the noose closed fast. Colonel Sanders was prosecutor, and on December 21, 1863, in Virginia City, George Ives was convicted on a robbery-murder charge. Two days later the Vigilante Oath was signed. January 10, 1864, Plummer and two others were hanged in Bannack, and January 14 five more necks snapped in Virginia City. By April 1, 1864, a total of 32 road agents were dead. No one knows how many fled the territory when law stretched out from Missoula on the west to the Gallatin valley on the east. The Vigilante sign of 3-7-77 meant business.

With this start, Justice Edgerton went to Washington, D.C., to split off the eastern Idaho counties and form a new territory. With the help of Congressman James Ashley, chairman of the Committee on Territories and an old friend of Judge Edgerton, Montana became a territory May 26, 1864.

With all its success, the Vigilante group never found the wealth that had been stolen by Plummer and company. It may be buried near the "Robbers' Roost" in the Ruby valley. Old legend says it was buried beneath a cabin on the middle of three tributaries to Sun River. Wherever it is, the ancient lode is no doubt Montana's greatest buried treasure.

Grasshopper Diggin's

Government by law in Montana began on a sagebrushy creek bottom where so many grasshoppers swarmed over the landscape that they gave a permanent name to the creek.

To Montanans, Bannack is the real birthplace of their state, yet, surprisingly, the record of early Bannack is sketchy, far more so than other places of less import. Apparently, the pressing urgency of affairs in the earliest days on Grasshopper Creek in Beaverhead County left no time for recordkeeping.

When John White found gold in a placer July 28, 1862, the creek was officially named Willard Creek, after Alexander Willard of the Lewis and Clark expedition. The rush began with White's discovery, but George Stapleton later found a richer bar higher up the creek, and here the first houses of Bannack were built. Stapleton tagged the name "Grasshopper" on the clear stream that flowed by town.

On October 19, 1862, the miners acted on a formal code of mining law, without much doubt the first written law in the Treasure State. By the next summer more than 2,000 persons lived and brawled in Bannack, including some of the most famous and infamous in the old West.

Most of the houses lined the single street and trailed off down-gulch for miles. Another small settlement across the creek to the south took the name of Yankee Flat. To the north Hangman's Gulch snaked its way back into the dry hills.

Bannack was not only Montana's first territorial capital but it also took a turn as seat of government for the eastern counties in Idaho Territory. In January of 1864 President Lincoln appointed Sidney Edgerton territorial governor of Montana, and Henry Plummer was elected sheriff. Montana was to hear a good deal more of both, but in different ways.

Hardly a lone rider or a stagecoach was safe on the road. Robbery and murder were common, and some even suspected Henry Plummer, the suave sheriff, of having a bloody hand. They were right. Vigilantes, formed by residents of Virginia City and Bannack, held quick trials, quicker arrests and immediate hangings.

Plummer's turn came on bitter January 10, 1864, when the Vigilantes seized Plummer and his deputies Ned Ray and Buck Stinson. Plummer as sheriff had built gallows in Hangman's gulch, and the three were taken there. Their necks snapped, and the leader of the "Road Agents" went to his death, but not without considerable tearful screaming of his innocence.

The rapidly feezing bodies were cut down, and Ray's taken to the home of his current mistress on Yankee Flat. Plummer's and Stinson's went to an unfinished two-story house across the street from the Goodrich Hotel. Probably in deference to his leadership, Plummer was laid out on a work bench and Stinson on the floor.

The following day Dutch John Wagner was tried and convicted in this room, then hanged from a rafter while the frozen bodies of Plummer and Stinson gave silent witness. Shallow graves were dug in the frozen ground January 12, and the four bodies laid away in Hangman's Gulch not far from Plummer's own gallows. F. M. Thompson charged $42.50 for putting the leader's bones in the ground. Some of the funeral party commented that the first cloudburst would no doubt wipe out the last traces of the four scoundrels.

What finally became of Plummer's remains is a mystery.

37

Legend has it that two drunks dug up his skull and, bouncing it on the bar at the Bank Exchange Saloon, demanded drinks. The skull supposedly remained there until the saloon burned several years later. Another legend is that his skull was sent east for medical examination. Plummer had a sloping forehead, amounting to a deformity, and he was known never to remove his hat except when absolutely necessary.

Even the gallows vanished. The town drunk, Davy Morgan, who was threatened with hanging, cut them down and destroyed them. The stumps are in the Masonic Lodge hall in Dillon, preserved as the last memento of Plummer's hanging.

Still standing in Bannack today are the venerable cottonwoods, what is left of the footbridge where Mrs. Edgerton met Plummer the day of the hanging, the old Goodrich Hotel and the next door Skinner's Saloon, the brick Hotel Meade with its sagging front porch, the jail with its floor rings for unruly customers and a score of dignified houses, including one that was used by Edgerton as Montana's first executive mansion.

The wind moans through the little graveyard above Hangman's Gulch, where tilting headstones poetically recall sorrow. Just above town are a few metallic remains of the Fielding L. Graves, first electric gold dredge in the nation. The mines above Bannack, on the hill to the south, are silent.

On a hilltop across Hangman's Gulch from the graveyard is a spot prepared for refuge for the women and children of Bannack when it was feared that Chief Joseph's Nez Perces would come this way in the summer of 1877.

To get to Bannack, drive south of Dillon on highway 91 to a well-marked turnoff just south of the Union Pacific overpass. Turn onto paved Highway 278 and follow this road about 15 miles to a marked turnoff to the left. Good gravel will take you to the town.

The Gold Gulches

Men who had fought each other in blue and gray sluiced the first gold from the gravels of the Big Belt Mountains and left their tailings as today's only evidence of the treasures they took out.

Modern travelers must look hard for a crumbled corner of a cabin or the rust-encrusted leg of a stove, but with only slight urging the imagination can still conjure the ghosts of ragged Civil war veterans washing the gravels for enough "color" to buy the fleeting favor of a dancehall girl.

The gulches that enriched or impoverished with equal disdain lie along the western slope of the Big Belts, the Missouri River side, across Canyon Ferry Lake from the stretch of Highway 12 that links Helena and Townsend. This is the gold country, as rich in history today as it was in yellow metal at the close of the war that left the South in ruins and the North with a burden.

To pan these historical nuggets get on the east side of the Missouri River and Canyon Ferry Lake either by turning east off Highway 12 at Louisville onto Highway 284 or off Highway 2 east of Townsend onto the other end of the same highway. It's a loop, so enter either end.

An improved graveled highway leads all along the lakeshore, and wooden signs point out the gulch turnoffs, dirt roads that wander off into the Belts.

Only two go clear over the top and into the Smith River valley. One of these is the Confederate Gulch road, one of the most famous both in that day and this, and the other is White's Gulch, the next gulch north of Confederate.

From the Townsend side turn your car into Confederate, southernmost of the gold gulches, for the greatest dredging up of lore of the gold country. A good way up the gulch are the piles of deserted gravel, long since left to leach away, both the gold and the goldseekers gone. In its midst is the ruins of a lone cabin, all that is left of what once was a roaring camp, alive with whiskey, frivolity and hopes.

The gravel piles straddle what in immediate post Civil war days was one of the greatest gold finds on earth, a placer that from one acre of ground yielded an estimated $4,000,000. What was even more amazing was that this horde of treasure lay in pockets behind slanted rock ledges that held it in exactly the same way the baffles on a sluice box held back the gold and let the lighter gravels wash away.

This was the site of Diamond City, which authentic legend states was named by four miners who wintered in adjoining cabins and found by spring that their trails from one cabin to another formed a perfect diamond in the crusted snow that covered the multimillion-dollar Montana Bar.

Your roaming of Confederate Gulch complete, you have the choice of the next gulch north, White's Gulch, where a lesser gold strike produced the town of White, now gone without a trace, or Avalanche Gulch, north of White. Avalanche produced some mineral, but its canyon-like walls, towering far above the road, are more spectacular than its history.

Hell Gate, the next gulch north of Avalanche, has both. Its mouth is pinched into a narrow slit in the limestone, but it opens out above into inviting meadows and parks only to narrow menacingly time and again. A few miles above its mouth is what is left of the Argo mine, a great copper producer in the early 1900s.

Bob Cooney, who was born and reared in this gulch country, recalls that in his boyhood he followed the six- and eight-horse ore wagons to pick up the brilliant "peacock copper" that the skilled horsemen hurled in chunks at the teams. Bob recalls, too, that the doubletrees on the wagons nicked each side of the narrow canyon mouth, a challenge to the reinsmen. Today dynamite has widened the slit.

This is the canyon where Indians, so ancient they had long left their mountain home before the days of either gold or copper, left a record in pictures scribed in ocher on the limestone walls.

If you wish, peek into Magpie Gulch, another gold gulch but one of less fortune and fame, or into Trout Creek, scene of bloody fights over claims, before you turn back across the Missouri and through the Spokane hills to Highway 12.

O. C. Seltzer

Colors in the Sage

Last Chance Gulch wasn't Montana's first gold discovery nor its richest, but it was spectacular, and the little gulch in the sagebrush became the home of the state's capital city—the latest and most permanent one, that is.

Two gold gulches before Last Chance had been similarly honored, but the one that nuzzled the pine-girt haunches of Mount Helena built a limestone and granite monument to government and surrounded it with administrative satellites that orbit a little farther each year.

Indians knew that the ground shook with earthquakes in the gulch and they moved through the area to hunt buffalo on the eastern plains, at times camping on the slopes above the valley. They knew nothing and cared less about the rich flakes in the gravel beneath their moccasins.

It was the far away blue-green Kootenai River, looping out of Canada into northwestern Montana and back north again, that brought gold diggers to Last Chance. When the hour glass of the Confederacy was fast running out in the winter of 1863-64 and the Alder Gulch diggings were well staked out, rumors crept into Virginia City about a rich new strike in the deep woods around the Kootenai, far to the north.

Among those hopefuls who set out in the spring of 1864 were Prospectors John Cowan, D. J. Miller, Reginald Stanley and John Crab, sometimes called the Four Georgians. They mounted the divide west of what is now Helena, but at Hell Gate Canyon, just east of what now is Missoula, the Georgians met a flat-broke party returning from the Kootenai. It was just another rumor gone sour.

On their way back east the Georgians tried the gravels of the Little Blackfoot valley, west of MacDonald Pass, then panned a little in Last Chance Creek at the foot of Mount Helena after they recrossed the divide. It was promising, but that was all. They headed their horses north, probably prospecting as far north as the Marias River, then, disappointed, returned to the little creek in Prickly Pear valley.

July 14, 1864, they dipped their pans into the Last Chance

sands again, and this time the magic worked. Cowan and Crab went back to Alder Gulch for supplies, and the usual rush of prospectors followed them back to Last Chance, for it was just that, the last chance for four tired prospectors.

Helena was born, and its main street keeps the name of the gulch which is buried under asphalt but loses much of its sophistication in its twists up the mountainside.

Of the four discoverers only John Crab received some temporary glory. The new shack town on the gulch was called Crabtown until the assembled citizens renamed it Helena, some say for Helen of Troy and others that John Somerville named it for his old home in Helena, Minnesota.

Gold camps eventually ringed the Helena valley, but only the city on Last Chance grew and prospered. It still likes to peek at its past and talk it over with strangers, although few residents of Last Chance could name any one of the Four Georgians. They will, however, proudly show you the old fire tower and a pioneer cabin at the head of the gulch.

It was the Gates of the Mountains, north of Helena, though, that made this area a landmark long before gold. It was July 19, 1805, when Lewis and Clark came up the Missouri canyon where the waters stretched from high bluff to high bluff and Lewis commented "the river appears to have worn a passage just the width of its channel." He added "From the singular appearance of this place I called it the gates of the rocky mountains."

The party camped at Meriwether landing on the east side, still a popular boat landing, and commented on the bighorn sheep, antelope at riverside, as well as playful otters along the shore. After this, commerce avoided the canyon, coming in from the north and northwest on less spectacular but more practical routes. By May of 1866 there was regular stagecoach service between Helena and Fort Benton, and Wells Fargo's Concord coaches rumbled over the hills until 1869, sharing the rutted Mullan road with strings of freight wagons pulled by oxen.

Peaceful Fort

Montana's best-preserved military fort never fired a shot in anger and was born of a fight over an Indian girl. To add another twist of fate, it was named for a man who opposed its creation.

Fort Logan's blockhouse, 18 miles north and west of White Sulphur Springs, represents the finest remains of a log fort in Montana and it stands as a reminder both of the bitterness of Indian warfare and the importance of the Smith River valley to commerce in the 70s. To go to Fort Logan, drive Highway 89 from north or south or Highway 12 from east or west into White Sulphur Springs. Anyone will show you the Fort Logan road.

What cinched Logan's establishment was Malcolm Clarke's death. A violent man who was married to Cutting-Off-Head-Woman, a Blackfeet, Clarke's Indian name was Four Bears. In a fuss over the Blackfeet wife of Owl Head, Clarke struck this Indian while he was unarmed, a great insult. In August of 1869, Owl Head came to the Clarke ranch on Highway 15 north of Helena and killed Clarke. There was a tremendous cry for a fort to protect the white settlers, for Clarke was a former West Pointer and American Fur trader, despite his bad reputation.

Logan was set up as Camp Baker on November 1, 1870, to protect freight moving up the Musselshell River, over the gap between the Little Belts and the Castle Mountains, then into Helena across the Big Belts. The southwestern gold camps also were getting their freight this way.

Major Martin Maginnis was the territorial delegate to Congress, and like his counterparts today, heeded the hue and cry from the voters. He saw to it that the war department protected the wagons, and soldiers were sent to the new fort from Fort Shaw on Sun River.

Major E. M. Baker of Fort Ellis, near Bozeman, for whom the fort was named, grumbled officially "in my opinion there is no more necessity for a company at Camp Baker than there is in front of the headquarters of the commanding general of the department." He felt forts Shaw and Ellis could handle the situation.

History eventually proved him right, although the soldiery at Logan narrowly missed glory when it was called to battle Sioux and Cheyenne on the Little Big Horn. They arrived in time to bury what was left of George Armstrong Custer's command.

After Chief Joseph stood off the U. S. Army on a late summer morning on the Big Hole River, the fort was moved and renamed after Captain William Logan, who died in the Big Hole battle. This was in 1877, and with the Indian power gone or at least fast fading, Logan was abandoned October 27, 1880, and its troops sent to Fort Maginnis east of Lewistown, another post that owed its existence to a busy Montana delegation in Congress.

Still standing on the tree-lined site are an old barracks, a clay-brick bakery, a store, quartermaster's quarters, a granary and the old officers' quarters, now doing duty as Nancy Berg's ranch home. Gone are the old hospital, tailor's shop and huge root house where the fort stored its vegetables. On the west end stands the old blockhouse, which did double duty as a guard house.

Don't miss the cemetery, which is some distance north of the buildings. Seven soldiers were buried there and some civilians, but later the soldiers' bodies were moved to the Custer Battlefield Cemetery.

As with most forts, there were cabins built around it by civilians, and families of married soldiers lived nearby. Indians came to the post to trade, and rocks still mark their campsites. Supplies for the fort came from Fort Benton by ox team through Millegan and up Smith River. There is a dirt road today that follows the old ox freighter road up the river, but it's a summer road.

Valley

of

Flowers

Indians called it the "Valley of Flowers" and held it as neutral ground, but winter's view of the Gallatin valley is that of a bowl of crystal sugar, held tightly in either season by encrusted summits of the Bridger and Spanish peaks.

This fertile namesake of President Jefferson's Secretary of the Treasury is beautiful around the calendar, a mountain valley whose acres are hardly for sale because they are so bountifully black and productive.

Indians agreed that here all could hunt, and the first white man to pass through this valley was Captain William Clark on his cut-through to the Yellowstone across what now is Bozeman Pass. This was in 1805, and from then until Montana found a use for its products of farm and range the Gallatin valley was a passageway, not a goal.

In 1808 John Colter crossed the valley on his way to the Three Forks, later to be stripped by the Indians on the Jefferson and forced to run for his life. A few settlers ventured into the valley in 1863, but most returned elsewhere to their gold pans, finding that more interesting and rewarding. In 1864 a few farmers began to work the soil along Bozeman Creek and John Bozeman first crossed the pass over the Bridger summit on Canyon Creek that now recalls his name.

That year Walter Cooper rode his horse to the summit of the hills west of the valley one August day and called its mountains "grand and imposing." Cooper's first impression of the valley was: "Bursting from every depression or gorge in the mountain sides flowed beautiful streams of water, cold and delightful to the taste. All the streams were fringed with a luxuriant growth of the smaller foliage, which, as a whole, made a picture the equal of which, it seemed to me, it had never been my good fortune to behold before, although quite familiar with many Montana lands.

"As I sat upon my horse and gazed upon this scene I wondered if it ever would be inhabited. Far to the north, east and south was one unbroken field of waving grass which came far up on the sides of my horse. Such a wealth of grass I had never before seen. Silence reigned everywhere, broken only by the startled bird, antelope or deer, many of which I disturbed as I came upon them unawares, hidden as they were by the tall, waving grass."

A year earlier James Steward in his diary praised the valley "as a grass country which far excelled the pastures west of the mountains (the Continental Divide). It was well watered, there being many beautiful streams teeming with trout and grayling hungry and eager for any sort of bait offered. Surely nature had provided well for the children of the plains. No wonder they guarded it jealously and well."

Even to those flint-hard mountain men the valley was rich and pleasing to the eye. Wagons from the east to west coasts passed over its face. The summit of Bozeman Pass, to the east, marked the boundary between areas that could be settled and Indian country, where whites passed at their peril. But gold tempted east of the Bridgers, while emigrants came across the pass and down Bridger Canyon to the north, into the valley.

In July of 1864 Bozeman brought a train of emigrants to the valley and Jim Bridger brought in a wagon train from the Platte River in Nebraska. In the next few years mines were opened in Emigrant Gulch, 1864; Cevis Gulch, 1865; Bear Gulch, 1866, all placer workings, and in 1867 coal was found at Chestnut, just west of the summit of Bozeman Pass.

That same year Indian raids made the Gallatin residents nervous, and Fort Ellis, just east of the city of Bozeman, was established. Crow Indians, usually friendly to whites, killed John Bozeman on the Yellowstone side of his pass. Still the east side diggings beckoned, and in 1874 a huge wagon road expedition with 147 men in 22 wagons left for the Yellowstone, but returned in two months, harrassed by the Sioux and short one man.

Still determined, the Gallatin pioneers sent an expedition down the Yellowstone in boats in the spring of 1875 to set up Fort Pease just below the mouth of the Big Horn. Sioux killed most of the party of 33, and the soldiers had to relieve the post.

Nelson Story, who pioneered cattle raising in the Gallatin, was fortunate enough to bring in his herds before the Army closed the Bozeman trail to travel and thus barred competition. He likewise was a good enough businessman to run these herds into plenty of money by selling beef to the gold miners.

In 1876 and 1877 the Indian problem was resolved for good in Montana, the Montanans found there was more gold in Gallatin grass and grain than in the gravels of the Yellowstone. Today's traveler in the Gallatin on Highway 90 will roll through the center of the valley of flowers and agree with the Indians.

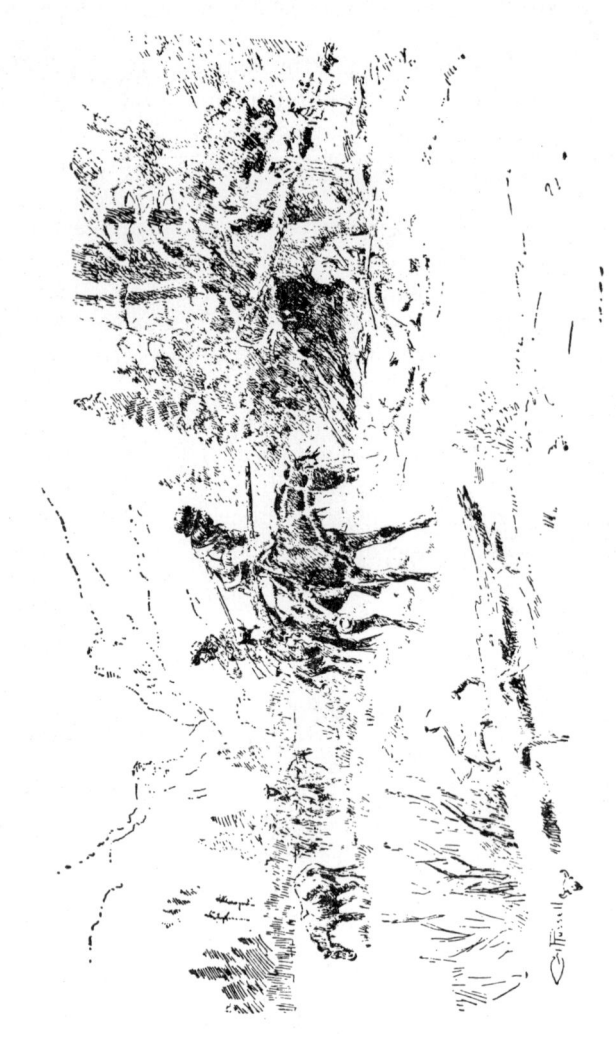

Northwest — Tamaracks and White Water

This is the country of great rivers, white-water rapids and deep, quiet forests of tamarack, pine and fir, growing to the very edge of the bluest of lakes and the tops of snow-tipped mountains.

It's a country of firsts, for here the white man first bowed his head in worship inside the borders of Montana, here the first gold was discovered, the first Catholic mission was established and the first herds of cattle raised.

It's as much the backdrop as the show itself that pleases the eye in this northwest corner, west and north of the "dogleg" that the Continental Divide makes as it drops southward out of Glacier Park and snakes itself southwestward to separate Idaho and Montana.

The divide would have been Montana's western boundary had it not been for a surveying party's understandable error. Confused in the tangle of mountains around Lost Trail Pass, the rod-and-transit men followed the Bitter Roots north instead of the Anacondas. Not until they reached the waters of the Clark's Fork of the Columbia, rolling green and deep through Cabinet Gorge, did they realize their error. Idaho was shortchanged quite a chunk of gorgeous real estate.

The first human residents of this country were the Indians, the Kutenai of the big tree country on the Kootenai and Yaak rivers, the Kalispells and the Flatheads farther south. It was the Flatheads or Ootlashoots who greeted Lewis and Clark when they entered the Bitter Root valley and who gave the explorers horses to send them on their way to the Pacific.

Montana's rugged northwest greeted David Thompson on his way to the western sea, Father Ravalli on his grim Jesuit task of teaching the word of God, Francois Finlay on his chore of discovering Montana's first gold at Gold Creek and the MacDonald's on their fur-buying missions for the Hudson's Bay Company.

Kutenai and Flatheads no longer rule this country, but their descendants are here, and when you meet them you may be surprised that they are ranchers or businessmen. Fur and gold have been replaced by logs, copper, cherry orchards and sugar beets, but over all are the same glistening summits that have dominated these valleys as long as the waters have run down to the sea.

How They Got Their Names — Streams and Lakes

Tobacco River—Flows into the Kootenai River at Rexford. Named for plants found in Tobacco valley used as pipe tobacco by Indians and pioneers.

Kootenai River—Flows into Montana's northwest corner from Canada, forming a loop between the Purcell and Ural mountains, then flanking the Cabinets on the south. Named for Kutenai Indian tribes (still spelled this way in Canada). Lower Kutenai lived outside Montana and downstream, middle Kutenai around Libby and upper Kutenai in Canada and out on the Montana and Canadian plains. One of the oldest tribes in Montana and lived mostly on deer. Where the Kootenai flows out of Montana is the state's lowest point, less than 1,800 feet.

Fisher River—Flows out of the Kalispell or Flathead Range into the Kootenai at Jennings. Named for the large number of fisher, a large, fur-bearing member of the weasel family, found here.

Yaak River—Clear, fertile stream that drains the Purcell Mountain in extreme northwestern Montana, running into the Kootenai just above the Idaho boundary. Yaak is an old Kutenai Indian name for the river.

Silver Bow Creek—Heads just east of Butte on the Continental Divide. Extreme headwater of the Clark's Fork of the Columbia, named by Lewis and Clark after Captain Clark. According to the best accounts, four prospectors in January, 1864, Bert Barker, Jim Ester, Joe Ester and P. Allison, stood on a rise looking at the little creek in the basin below them. The day was dark but as they argued about a name for the creek the sun burst through the clouds and made the creek, as it flowed around the shoulder of the mountain, shine like silver. That settled the argument, for it looked like a burnished silver, curved bow.

Clarks Fork of the Columbia River—Drains all of western

Montana except that portion in the extreme northwest drained by the Kootenai. Flows northwestward from Butte to just below Heron, where it flows into Idaho, eventually draining into the Columbia River and Pacific Ocean.

Thompson River—Rises in Thompson Lakes on Highway No. 2, then flows southward to join the Clarks Fork of the Columbia just above Thompson Falls. All three are named in honor of David Thompson, who explored this area and built Saleesh house at the mouth of the river in 1809, second permanent fort in Montana.

Flathead River—Longest tributary to the Clark's Fork. Flows from three branches or forks which meet just above Bad Rock Canyon east of Columbia Falls. Below this point the river flows through a wide valley, which gave the river and the Flathead Indians their name. Other Indians referred to them as the Indians who lived at the "flat head" of the river as distinguished from the deep canyons below.

Flathead Lake—Took its name from the river, which enters it just below Kalispell. The lake is 28 miles long and the largest in Montana west of the divide. The river flows out of the lake at Polson, then south and west to join the Clark's Fork at Paradise.

Jocko River—Runs westerly from the Jocko Lakes at the south end of the Mission Range to join the Flathead River at Dixon. Named for Jacques Finlay, Hudson's Bay Company fur trader and trapper, commonly called "Jacco."

Little Bitter Root River—Flows out of the Little Bitter Root Lakes west of Marion on Highway No. 2 and southward to join the Flathead River west of Charlo. Named for Montana's state flower, the Bitter Root, which named another river, a mountain range and a valley.

Whitefish River—Feeds Whitefish Lake north of Whitefish, flowing out of the Whitefish Mountains, then into the Flathead River just above Kalispell. Named for the big whitefish that used to live in the lake.

Stillwater River—Parallels the Whitefish River on the west and runs into the Flathead River near Kalispell. Largely a river of still, deep pools, unusual in a country of white water rapids.

Swan River—Flows into Flathead Lake at its northeast corner. Heads just north of the town of Seeley Lake and flows northward through the Swan Valley and Swan Lake. Named for number of swans that used to live on the river and lake. Enters Flathead Lake at Bigfork.

South Fork of the Flathead River—Heads just north of Ovando in the mountains between the Continental Divide and the Swan Range and drains an extensive wilderness country. Flows through Hungry Horse Lake into the junction of the North and Middle forks to form the main river.

North Fork of the Flathead River—Heads in British Columbia northwest of Glacier National Park, then flows southward along the western edge of the park to join the Middle Fork of the Flathead below West Glacier.

Middle Fork of the Flathead River—Rises along the Continental Divide south of Glacier Park, flows around the southern edge of the park to join the North Fork and then the South Fork.

Pablo, Kicking Horse and Nine Pipes Reservoirs—In Flathead valley, all named for Flathead chiefs.

St. Regis River—Flows eastward out of the Bitter Root Range near Saltese on Highway 90 to enter the Clarks Fork at St. Regis. Only eastward-flowing river west of the divide. Named by the Jesuits for a Catholic saint, St. Regis de Borgia. Jesuits early lived among the western Indians.

Bitter Root River—Flows northward from near the Idaho boundary, draining the Bitter Root and Sapphire Ranges, to join the Clarks Fork just west and south of Missoula. Named for Montana's state flower, which has a pink blossom and an edible root, relished by the Indians.

Skalkaho Creek—Flows into the Bitter Root River south of Hamilton, flowing westward through the Sapphire Mountains. Name is Flathead Indian, meaning "muddy hole" or "beaver hole" and recalling days when beaver were plentiful on the stream. At its head is Skalkaho Pass, only automobile pass across the Sapphires.

Rattlesnake Creek—Flows southward out of the Stuart Peak area northeast of Missoula and into the Clark's Fork inside

Missoula city limits. Named for its winding course down the canyon, resembling a rattlesnake.

Big Blackfoot River—Rises in the Continental Divide country east of Lincoln and flows into the Clarks Fork River at Milltown, just east of Missoula. Flathead Indians, who once lived in the Bitter Root valley, called this river Cokahlarishkit or "river of the trail to the buffalo," because they used that valley to cross the divide either by Lewis and Clark or Cadotte's Pass to go to the Sun River country west of Great Falls to hunt buffalo. Captain Lewis of the Lewis and Clark expedition followed this trail in the summer of 1806, crossing the mountains by Lewis and Clark Pass northeast of Lincoln on Alice Creek, a tributary of the Big Blackfoot. The Big Blackfoot name came from the habit of Blackfoot Indians or "Blackfeet" from the eastern plains crossing by that trail to raid Flathead camps.

Clearwater River—Drains the Clearwater chain of lakes, including Seeley, Placid, Salmon, Alva, Inez, Rainy and Summit. Flows southward to join the Big Blackfoot at Clearwater Junction on Highway 20. Formerly named Werner's Creek after Private Werner of the Lewis and Clark expedition.

Monture Creek—Named after George Monture, pioneer and prospector in the Big Blackfoot valley who rounded up the settlers to protect them from a feared attack by the Nez Perce Indians in 1877. Runs into the Big Blackfoot River just east of Clearwater Junction.

North Fork of the Blackfoot—Heads in the Cooper's Lake country northeast of Ovando, and runs into the Big Blackfoot south of Ovando. Called Salmon Trout Creek by Lewis and Clark.

Nevada Creek—Heads in the Continental Divide country southeast of Helmville and flows through Nevada Reservoir into the Big Blackfoot southeast of Ovando. Pioneers called this stream the Nile because of the fertile valley it waters, but later prospectors called it Nevada Creek after their home state.

Rock Creek—Drains the east side of the Sapphire Mountains, entering the Clark's Fork just above Clinton. Drains a rocky, canyon-type area.

Flint Creek—Drains the Georgetown Lake country of the Flint Creek Range and flows into the Clark's Fork at Drummond. Named for the flint found in the formations, which also have plenty of mineral.

Little Blackfoot River—One of the early pioneer routes over the Continental Divide followed the Little Blackfoot, as did the Mullan road. Heads on the divide west of Helena and flows westward to join the Clark's Fork at Garrison.

How They Got Their Names — Mountain Ranges

Anaconda Range—From Anaconda southwestward to Lost Trail Pass on Highway 93. Named for the city of Anaconda. Includes Pintlar wilderness country. Highest mountain is Mount Evans, southwest of Anaconda at 10,635 feet. Forms Continental Divide from Mount Evans southwest.

Bitter Root Range—Longest range in western Montana, extending from Lost Trail Pass to Cabinet Gorge on the Clark's Fork River. Takes its name from the Bitter Root valley and the state flower which grows there. The western slope of this range is all wilderness country. Highest mountain is Trapper Peak, west of Sula, 10,131 feet.

Historic passes in this range include Thompson's, west of Thompson Falls, used by David Thompson, famed British-Canadian explorer, on his way to the Pacific Coast, and Gibbon's, which General Gibbon used in his pursuit of the Nez Perce in 1877. At the foot of this pass on the Big Hole side, Gibbon's infantry and Joseph's Nez Perce fought a bloody battle in the summer dawn. Through Lost Trail Pass, west of Gibbon's, Lewis and Clark re-entered Montana after turning back from the impassable Salmon River canyon at what is now North Fork, Idaho.

Cabinet Mountains—South of Troy from the Idaho boundary to Thompson River. Highest peak, Mount Snowy, southwest of Libby, 7,621 feet.

Coeur d'Alene Mountains—From Lookout Pass on Highway 90 to just west of Paradise. Named for the French term for chain of lakes in Idaho. Highest peak is Goat Mountain at 5,597 feet, just south of Thompson Falls.

Columbia or East Range—Between the upper Flathead

valley and the South Fork of the Flathead valley. Shares the Columbia name with rivers and towns such as Columbia Falls. Called East Range because it arises abruptly from the east side of the Flathead valley. Three Eagles Mountain at 7,445 feet is highest peak, just east of Bigfork.

Flint Creek Range—Between Philipsburg and Deer Lodge. Named for Flint Creek, which drains its western slope. Old and productive mining country. Lone Tree Hill at 6,270 is highest mountain.

Garnet Range—North of Highway 90 from Avon to Bearmouth. Named for the garnets frequently found by early miners. Old Garnet, a mining town, lies on its western slope, north of Bearmouth. Mount Baldy, northwest of Bearmouth, at 6,930 feet, is highest.

Lewis Range—Named for the explorer Captain Meriwether Lewis. Extends from the northern boundary of Glacier National Park south to Helena and is the main range of the Rockies separating eastern and western Montana. The geological upheaval which caused it is called the Lewis overthrust. From Marias Pass south of Glacier Park to Rogers Pass east of Lincoln on Highway 20 is the longest stretch of major mountains in Montana with no highway or rail pass. Just west of Helena, on a dirt road, is Mullan Pass, used by Captain John Mullan for his military wagon road from Fort Benton, Montana, to Fort Walla Walla, Washington. At the summit of this pass was held the first Masonic ceremony in the state of Montana. Highest peak is Cleveland in Glacier Park, 10,448 feet.

Mission Range—Separates the main Flathead drainage from the Swan valley and takes its name from St. Ignatius Mission at its feet on the western slope. Highest mountain is Harding, east of Charlo, at 10,000 feet.

Ninemile Divide—North of Alberton on Highway 90. Named for the Ninemile drainage on the old river road.

Purcell Mountains—in extreme northwestern Montana, north of the Kootenai River. Probably named for Henry Purcell, noted 17th Century composer in England. The major portion of the mountains lie in British Columbia. Northwest Peak at 7,700 feet is highest mountain.

Sapphire Range—Separates Bitter Root from Rock Creek

valley. Named for sapphires found in old "diggings." Quigg Peak at 8,450 feet is the highest point.

Swan Range—Separates Swan valley from South Fork of Flathead. Named for Swan Lake and Swan River. Highest peak is Evans, northeast of Ovando, at 8,950 feet.

Ural or Flathead Mountains—From Rexford south to Marion. Ural from resemblance to Urals in Europe and Flathead from the Indian tribe. Highest point is Elk Mountain west of Whitefish at 6,581 feet.

Whitefish Range—Separates Stillwater and North Fork of Flathead River drainages. Named after Whitefish Lake, which once produced huge Rocky Mountain whitefish. Highest mountain is Poorman Mountain, 7,800 feet, just south of the boundary.

Squaw Peaks—Northwest of Missoula. Name originally paid tribute to the fact that the principal peak resembled a squaw's breast, but later mapmakers subdued this earthiness.

How They Got Their Names — Towns and Cities

Alberton—After Albert J. Earling, president of the Milwaukee railroad at the time the town was born.

Anaconda—Mike Hickey named his mine Anaconda because he was an admirer of another Irishman, General McClellan. Horace Greely had commented that McClellan's Civil War army would surround Lee's "like a giant anaconda." Both the mine and the city profited from this Hibernian admiration.

Arlee—The Flathead chief for whom this town was named was the first chief of these Indians in the Jocko valley, where the tribe was moved in small numbers in 1873 from the Bitter Root valley as a result of the Council Grove treaty west of Missoula in 1855 and of the 1872 Garfield treaty.

Bonner—E. L. Bonner, early businessman, lumberman and president of the Missoula and Bitter Root Valley Railroad, gave his name to this lumber town.

Butte—Mining always has dominated this city, and the name itself comes from Big Butte, the most prominent landmark, almost on the School of Mines campus.

Camas Prairie—Indians called the small onion-like plants

that grew all over this valley "Camas." Both this town and nearby Camas took their names from the wild bulbs.

Charlo—Capable Chief Charlo, or Charlot, of the Flatheads steadfastly refused, as did his father, Victor, to leave the Bitter Root valley for the Jocko and Mission valleys just to please the white man. He earned a town named after him.

Columbia Falls—Early residents combined the name of the nearby Columbia Range of mountains with the name "Falls." There really aren't any falls in the Flathead River nearby, but there could be. Flathead river steamboats used to come this far upstream.

DeBorgia—Jesuits brought some of the first religion to a raw Montana, and among these was Father De Smet. He named the town for St. Regis DeBorgia, a member of his order.

Deer Lodge—A cone, 30 feet high and formed by a hot spring, attracted many deer in the winter time, so the Indians called it the Lodge of the White-Tailed Deer. In 1831 Warren Ferris called the whole valley Deer Lodge Plains during his trapping expedition here. The name eventually became attached to a town, county, river and valley.

Dixon—Namesake of former Governor, Joseph M. Dixon of Montana.

Drummond—Hugh Drummond, a trapper who sought beaver in the Flint Creek valley, gave his name to this town that later grew up at its mouth.

Eureka—First called Deweyville, but later changed by a vote of the residents. There must have been a reason.

Frenchtown—The Frenchtown valley surrounding the town was populated early by farmers of French descent.

Galen—Montana Supreme Court Justice Albert J. Galen gave his name to this town where the State Tuberculosis Sanitarium is located.

Garrison—Early admirers of William Lloyd Garrison, pre-Civil War foe of slavery, wanted a Montana town named for their hero.

Gold Creek—After nearby Gold Creek, on which, in 1850, Francois Finlay or Benetsee, as he was nicknamed, found Montana's first gold.

Hamilton—J. W. Hamilton sold the right of way for the Northern Pacific to enter the town, and J. T. Hamilton surveyed the townsite. Take your choice.

Hot Springs—The hot springs here drew the Indians and still draw Montanans and their visitors.

Hungry Horse—A skinny, slab-sided horse, left over winter on the South Fork of the Flathead, inspired this one. Both the dam and the town took the name.

Kalispell—After the Kalispell or Kullyspell Indians.

Lincoln—President Abraham Lincoln left his name with this town in the pines.

Lolo—In September, 1805, Lewis and Clark camped at this spot, then ascended what they called Travelers' Rest Creek on their way to the Pacific. Early maps show the creek as Lou Lou Fork of the Bitter Root, probably a corruption of the French name Le Louis.

Milltown—From the nearby Anaconda company lumber mill, one of the oldest in western Montana.

Missoula—Duncan MacDonald, factor of the Hudson's Bay trading post in the Mission valley, interpreted the Salish "In-mae-soo-latkhu" as "Sparkling River." In conversation this came out "Nm-i-sule." Another version is that the word meant "place of fright or terror," referring to the Hell Gate just east of the City, where the Blackfeet regularly ambushed the Flatheads on their way to the buffalo hunting grounds east of the mountains.

Moiese—A Flathead Indian sub-chief gave this reservation town his name.

Pablo—After Michel Pablo, Flathead Indian chief and the man who saved the American bison as a species. Descendants of the Pablo bison herd still live in the National Bison Range at Moiese.

Paradise—Two versions on this one. One is that it was adapted from the "Pair-o-Dice" saloon or roadhouse on the old Clark's Fork road or trail. Another is that the beautiful surroundings reminded early residents of a celestial existence.

Philipsburg—Philip Deidesheimer was the first superintendent of the St. Louis-Montana Gold and Silver Mining Company, which put life into the town and gave it a name.

Plains—Even before there was a town, Indians called this broad meadow in the Clark's Fork valley Horse Plains, because horses were wintered here. Half the name stuck.

Ravalli—Father Anthony Ravalli, one of the first Jesuit missionaries in Montana, left his name with this town.

Ronan—After Peter Ronan, first Flathead Reservation Indian agent.

Saint Ignatius—Jesuit Fathers founded the old mission in 1854 and named it after Ignatius Loyola, founder of the order.

Saint Regis—Named for the St. Regis River, in turn named for a Jesuit saint.

Saltese—Corruption of the name of Seltisse, oldtime Flathead Indian chief.

Seeley Lake—Both the town and lake took their name from the old Seeley ranch at the south end of the lake.

Silver Bow—After Silver Bow Creek, named because it looked like a silver bow as the sun struck its surface where it curved around the mountain.

Somers—Lumber town named after George O. Somers, assistant to the vice president in charge of traffic for the Great Northern Railway at that time.

Stevensville—After Governor Isaac I. Stevens of Washington Territory, which then included western Montana.

Superior—Probably a namesake of Superior, Wisconsin.

Swan Lake—From nearby Swan Lake, named after the swans that used to cover the lake on spring and fall migrations.

Thompson Falls—Named for the Thompson falls in the river at the south edge of town. Thompson was a British explorer who discovered the river and the falls on his journey from British Columbia to the Pacific. He spent the winter of 1809-10 at the mouth of Thompson River just east of Thompson Falls.

Victor—Chief Victor of the Flatheads was leader of his tribe during the Hell Gate treaty negotiations with Governor Isaac I. Stevens.

West Glacier—Near the western entrance to Glacier National Park.

Triple Divide Mountain—Water from this mountain flows into the Atlantic Ocean, Pacific Ocean and Hudson's Bay, through creeks named for each of the final destinations. Atlantic creek flows into Cut Bank Creek.

Running Crane Lake—After a chief of the Pikuni, about 1880, when he led some of the last Blackfeet buffalo hunts.

Eagle Plume Mountain—After a Pikuni chief, father of one of the most beautiful Blackfeet girls, Otter Woman, wife of Black Elk.

Mad Wolf Mountain—After Mad Wolf, the Pikuni who recovered the tribe's sacred albino otter skin bowcase from the Crees. A cree had stolen it and robbed the Pikuni of the power which the bowcase gave them in war.

White Calf Mountain—After a Pikuni chief, one of the last of the tribal leaders in the 1880s.

St. Mary Basin

St. Mary Lakes—Named by Father De Smet, the Jesuit who erected a wood cross at the foot of the lower lake in the 1830s. The Blackfeet called the lakes Puhtomuksi Kimiks or the "Lake Inside." St. Mary River was the "Lakes Inside River."

Red Eagle Pass, Mountain, Glacier, Lake and Creek—After Red Eagle, uncle of Fine Shield Woman, wife of James Willard Schultz, famed author who lived with the Pikuni. Red Eagle was a medicine chief, possessor of a medicine bundle and an elk-tongue medicine pipe. George Bird Grinnell claimed Red Eagle's prayers helped him discover the glacier that bears his name. Red Eagle Pass was one of the main passes used by Indians traveling from the Missouri to the Columbia drainage.

Mahtotopa Mountain—After the chief of the Mandans, who was so admired by George Catlin, pioneer artist. Mahtotopa was the father of Earth Woman, wife of James Kipp, who built the first trading post in Blackfeet country—Fort Piegan near the mouth of the Marias River.

Little Chief Mountain—Named by George Bird Grinnell for Captain Frank North, "Little Chief," who led Pawnee Indian scouts in campaigns against the Sioux. Another version is that the namesake is Little Chief of the Small Robes clan of the Pikuni, who was trampled to death in the 1860s when his horse fell in a buffalo hunt.

Almost-a-Dog Mountain—For the Pikuni warrior who was one of the few survivors of the New Year's Day, 1870, massacre of Blackfeet by Colonel E. M. Baker of Fort Shaw on the Marias River south of Chester.

Citadel Mountain—Named by George Bird Grinnell for its "fantastic and spired summit."

Blackfoot Glacier—Largest glacier in the park, named for all three tribes in the Blackfoot confederacy—Blackfeet, Bloods and Pikuni—by William Jackson and James Willard Schultz.

Mount Jackson—For William Jackson, one of General Custer's scouts, who also scouted for General Nelson A. Miles and for the Royal Northwest Mounted Police during the Riel rebellion.

Divide Mountain—Named by James Willard Schultz in 1883 because this was the last mountain on the Atlantic-Arctic watershed.

Curly Bear Mountain—After a Pikuni whose principal distinction was that he was buried with a suit of Spanish armor, brought north from the Always-Summer-Land (the southwest) by one of his ancestors (who no doubt was horse-stealing when he picked up the armor).

Mount Logan—For William Logan, soldier with Custer at the Little Big Horn and one of the discoverers of Blackfoot Glacier. Logan was the park's first superintendent.

Gunsight Mountain, Lake and Pass—All named by George Bird Grinnell on an exploration trip in 1890 to the head of the St. Mary valley. Grinnell thought the pass at the valley head looked just like an old-fashioned rear iron sight on a rifle. It does, too.

Fusillade Mountain—In 1888 William Seward III, grandson of President Lincoln's Secretary of State and Alaskan advocate, and Henry L. Stimson, who was to be President Hoover's Secretary of State, reportedly fired 27 shots to kill one young mountain goat on this mountain. William Jackson, on hearing the shots, called the mountain "fusillade." Seward and Stimson didn't appreciate the humor, but the name stuck.

Going-to-the-Sun Mountain—In December of 1887 James Willard Schultz and his Pikuni friend Tail-Feathers-Coming-Over the Hill butchered a bighorn ram on Red Eagle Mountain and sat looking at Going-to-the-Sun, across the lake, while they smoked. The Pikuni said it was the most beautiful mountain he had ever seen, and if he were younger and it were summer he would climb that mountain and lie on its summit to fast and pray the sun for a vision. Both agreed to give the mountain its present name, honoring the sun as chief god of the Blackfeet.

Baring Creek and Falls—After the Barings, English bankers who hunted bighorns with James Willard Schultz in the park in 1889.

Goat Mountain and Lake—Schultz was intrigued with the large number of goats on this mountain. It was one of his favorite hunting spots.

Yellow Fish Mountain and Creek—Named for a Pikuni who, when hunting, fired 29 shots without killing any game, although normally he was an excellent shot. Yellow Fish later found his mother had died the morning he failed in his shooting, and he claimed the bad marksmanship was an evil omen. The creek now is called Roes and the mountain Whitefish.

East Flattop Mountain—Another Flattop is west of the divide. James Willard Schultz named the mountain in the fall of 1882 when he shot a bighorn on top of it. He was looking for what trappers called a Rocky Mountain ibex, which proved later to be the Rocky Mountain goat. No white man had seen one at that time, but Stony Indians had brought their snow-white skins into Fort Benton for trade.

Singleshot Mountain—In the fall of 1883 George Bird Grinnell killed a large bighorn ram on top of this mountain with one shot from his Sharp's rifle. The name came easy after that, and it stuck.

Napi Rock—After the sacred Old Man of the Blackfeet. Napi created the world, then put all the pretty women in Cut

Bank valley and the men in the rough, rugged country south of Two Medicine Lakes.

Swiftcurrent Basin

Lake Sherburne—After a pioneer white family in the country east of Glacier Park.

Swiftcurrent Lake—White water all through this drainage made the name a natural. There also is Swiftcurrent Falls at the end of the lake and Swiftcurrent Ridge north of Lake Sherburne, as well as Swiftcurrent Pass and two Swiftcurrent glaciers. The Blackfeet called the lake Jealous Woman's Lake. Two sisters loved the same warrior and decided to settle the dispute by swimming the lake side by side from its head to the falls at the outlet until one of them drowned. The elder sister lost, sinking beneath the waves of the wind-ruffled waters.

Mount Siyeh, Siyeh Glacier and Siyeh Pass—Siyeh is the Blackfeet name for Mad Wolf, a great warrior of long ago who led many successful raids against the enemy. Recovered by him was the sacred Blackfeet albino otter skin bowcase from the Assiniboine.

Altyn Mountain—After the old copper-mining town of Altyn, now partially covered by Sherbune Reservoir.

Morning Eagle Falls—After the Blackfeet chief who was killed in a successful Blackfeet attempt to recover the sacred white otter bow case from the Assiniboine.

Cracker Lake—Prospectors Hank Norris and L. C. Emmons cached a lunch of cheese and crackers at a nearby mine, giving both the mine and the lake a name.

Grinnell Lake, Mountain, Glacier and Falls—Named for George Bird Grinnell, professor and naturalist who discovered the glacier in the summer of 1886. Grinnell killed a bighorn ram on the glacier the day he discovered the ice field, one of the largest in the park.

Mount Gould—George Gould, a Californian, was a hunting companion of James Willard Schultz and George Bird Grinnell.

Mount Wilbur—After Ray Lyman Wilbur, Secretary of Interior in President Hoover's cabinet and onetime president of Stanford University. Blackfeet called this Heavy Shield Mountain. Heavy Shield was a powerful Pikuni warrior who was attacked and nearly killed by a Kutenai named Cut Nose. The incident nearly brought war between the tribes until it was found the Kutenai tribe had banished Cut Nose for killing his wife in a rage.

Appekunny Creek, Falls and Mountain—James Willard Schultz' Pikuni name was Apikuni or Far-off White Robe. Other interpretations make it Spotted Robe or even Scabby Robe. Lieutenant Beacom of Fort Shaw on Sun River named the three after Schultz, but the geological survey misspelled the name when mapping the area.

Bullhead Lake—Probably after Colonel MacLeod of Fort MacLeod, Alberta, whose Blackfeet name was Bull's Head. He was a friend of Schultz and fur trader Joseph Kipp.

Fishercap Lake—After George Bird Grinnell, whose Pikuni name was Fisher Hat or Fisher Cap.

Iceberg Lake, formerly Ice Lake—Named by Rising Wolf (Hugh Monroe), who discovered the lake in the 1850s, complete with floating ice cakes.

Kennedy Creek Drainage

Kennedy Creek—In 1874 John Kennedy, great uncle of Michael Kennedy, built a trading post where what now is Kennedy Creek enters the St. Mary River. This was the first trading post anywhere near the park and the post furthest inside Blackfeet territory. Later he moved it to the Sweet Grass Hills, then to Fort Benton. The exact site is near the junction of highways 89 and 17.

Seward Mountain—After William H. Seward III, grandson of Lincoln's Secretary of State. Grandson Seward hunted in the park in 1883 and returned in 1902 to climb Chief Mountain with George Bird Grinnell.

Sherburne Peak—After a pioneer family of the area, same as the Sherburne Lake namesakes.

Chief Mountain—Probably the best known mountain in the park. Stories vary on how buffalo skulls used in long-ago Indian medicine visions on the peak were discovered. It is agreed Henry L. Stimson was one of those who climbed the rugged east face, previously thought unclimbable. He probably was accompanied by William Seward III and a Pikuni guide named "Comes-with-Rattles," and the year very likely was 1902. It is assumed that Pikuni climbed the mountain with buffalo skulls for use as "pillows" during their sleeps to obtain visions to make them strong in war and the hunt.

Belly River Drainage

Belly River, Lakes—Named for the Gros Ventre or "Big Belly" Indians, called the Entrails People by the Blackfeet.

Mount Cleveland—After President Grover Cleveland. Highest peak in the park at 10,448 feet.

White Quiver Falls—After the famed warrior of the Pikunis, long successful against his enemies and the man who went into the camp of the "Red Coats" or Canadian Mounted Police and took back the horses impounded there as property of the Crow Indians. White Quiver originally had stolen them from the Crows, but this didn't count. Horse stealing was an honorable pursuit among Indians.

Ahern Glacier, Pass, Creek—After Lieutenant George P. Ahern of Fort Shaw on Sun River, who was ordered in the summer of 1890 to explore the mountains south of the Canadian boundary. His party included a professor from the University of Wisconsin, Indian guides and a detachment of Negro soldiers, probably the first colored persons in the park. He reached the park on Cut Bank Creek, then turned north to Belly River, thence up the Belly and its South fork to Ahern Pass. The party had great difficulty getting into the Flathead drainage. Once there it moved up McDonald Creek, crossed to Camas Creek and followed that stream down to the North Fork of the Flathead, thence into the Flathead valley. It was a tough, long pack trip under the worst kind of weather conditions.

Wachcachak Pass—Origin obscure. Could be after the legendary ruler of the world whom the Cree Indians claimed gained supremacy over another legendary figure "Round Man" by surviving atop the Sweetgrass Hills (Sweet Pines Mountains) east of Glacier Park for 50 years.

Mount Kipp and Kipp Creek—After Joseph Kipp, proprietor of Fort Conrad, southeast of Glacier Park. Kipp and

James Willard Schultz were associated at the trading post. Fort Conrad was on an island in the Marias River, just above where the Great Northern Railway now crosses that stream and east of the Highway 91 crossing of the Marias.

Kootenai Creek, Pass—After the Kootenai (also spelled Kutenai) Indians of northwestern Montana who came into the park to hunt, even crossing to the eastern side.

Logan Falls, Glacier—After Will Logan, Indian service official, soldier with Custer at the Battle of the Little Big Horn and first superintendent of Glacier Park after its creation on May 11, 1910.

Dixon Glacier—After U. S. Senator Joseph M. Dixon, who helped push through Congress the bill creating Glacier Park. Significant assistance also came from his colleague, Congressman and later Federal Judge Charles N. Pray.

Carter Glaciers, Mount Carter—U. S. Senator Thomas H. Carter of Montana introduced the bill to create Glacier Park.

Lake McDonald Drainage and North to Park Boundary

Lake McDonald and McDonald Creek—After the pioneer hotelkeeper on the upper lake shore. For years before creation of the park the Kutenai Indians called this largest of the west side lakes Sacred Dancing Lake, a tribute to observance of their rites at this spot.

Cannon Mountain—For many years called Old Man Dog Mountain by the Kutenai Indians.

Logan Pass—Also after William Logan, first superintendent of the park.

West Side of Park South of Lake McDonald

Mount Stimson—After Henry L. Stimson, former Secretary of War.

Mount Pinchot and Pinchot Creek—After Gifford Pinchot, pioneer American forester.

Eaglehead Mountain—After Eagle Head, Pikuni friend and buffalo hunting companion of James Willard Schultz.

Tinkham Mountain—After A. W. Tinkham, who in 1853 led an exploration party on the west side of the park.

Little Dog Mountain—After one of the last of the Pikuni chiefs who accompanied the buffalo hunts of 1879-80 in central Montana.

Three Bears Lake—This lake, just north of the John F. Stevens memorial at Summit, is named for old Three Bears, who claimed the bad Pikuni god—Red Old Man—had hidden the buffalo in a cave, then the good god—White Old Man—brought them out again. Now (1882) he said the white man again had hidden all the buffalo to starve the Indians to death, but powerful Sun—the greatest god—would bring them back. All the Blackfoot nation believed Old Bear's prediction, but the faith didn't bring back the buffalo.

John F. Stevens Canyon—All along the southern border of Glacier Park. Named for the civil engineer who, on December 11, 1889, located Marias Pass for the Great Northern Railway, which planned to build west from Havre, Montana, to the Pacific coast. The pass is the lowest (5,216 feet) Continental Divide crossing north of New Mexico. Indians and white men both shunned the pass, believing it to be guarded by spirits.

Loneman Mountain—Named for a Pikuni member of the Blackfoot Confederacy or nation. The mountain was named by Writer Emerson Hough, Indian Scout William Jackson and James Willard Schultz on a goat hunting trip in midwinter, 1885. They slept in a lean-to on Nyack Creek in 33-degree-below-zero temperatures and five feet of snow. They dined on ruffed grouse, shot through the neck by Hough, who also shot some bigger game.

Running Rabbit Mountain—After a noted chief of the Kainah or Blood tribe, part of the Blackfoot nation. Running Rabbit was one of the chiefs who took part in the battle on Point-of-Rocks River or Sun River in which the Pikuni killed a war party of Crows to avenge the death of Big Snake, a Pikuni killed by Crows. A dog brought Big Snake's scalp into the Pikuni camp and started the rumpus.

Sign of The Cross

Old print by Sohon

Flathead Indians picked the site for Montana's first "Black Robe" mission, then marked the spot under the gleaming summits of the Bitter Root Mountains by felling two huge trees to make the sign of the cross on the banks of the Bitter Root River.

It was 1841 and Father DeSmet, the great inspiring priest, was on his second journey to Montana. The previous year he had met the Flathead Indians in the Gallatin valley, more than 200 miles from the Bitter Root, and had left them there to journey down the Yellowstone River and back to St. Louis to get money for his mission.

Now he had returned when the leaves were yellowing in the Bitter Root valley, and the Flatheads had come to Fort Hall, Idaho, to tell him that the tribe awaited him in the Beaverhead. The Indians had halted here on their fall buffalo hunt, waiting to take Father DeSmet to the sign of the wooden cross.

Iroquois who had married into the Flathead tribe had told the western Indians of the Black Robes, and the Flatheads believed the Catholic priests would give them strong medicine to whip their enemies, the Blackfeet, into submission. This desire gave them a practical reason for their thirst for religion.

On a bright September 24, 1841, the mission was established and named St. Mary's for the day of "Our Lady of Mercy." St. Mary also gave her name to a mountain to the west in the Bitter Root Range. Cottonwood logs were felled for the mission and a 25 by 33-foot chapel, together with two houses, soon rose on the river bank. Walls were chinked with riverbank clay, roofs were of poles and windows of deer skin, scraped and dried to make them translucent. In the bitter winter of 1841-42, Father Mengarini blessed the windows' small size, for he said later that even thinking of that winter brought a chill to his bones.

Late in October, 1841, Father DeSmet left for Fort Colville, Washington, and returned in 42 days, a round trip of 600 miles, carrying with him potato, wheat and oat seed and driving livestock. St. Mary's became Montana first real farm.

The next spring the Flathead Indians sat on the mission fence and watched patiently for the seeds to sprout. That fall and summer they enjoyed vegetables from the mission garden, but they shunned onions and "greens." These were all right for white men but not good enough for Indians.

Life at the mission followed a routine of prayers, mass, teaching, canticles in Flathead with Latin translations, generously sprinkled with work details. Brother Natalio Savio entertained the Indians with his Italian puppets, and an Indian band played eight instruments, all by ear. A church organ from St. Louis furnished religous music.

Indian boys relaxed after catechism by shooting arrows at a ball of cotton or a stick thown into the air. They seldom missed. There were three buffalo hunts a year, spring and fall for meat and midwinter for the heavy, warm robes. The priests tried to keep the Flatheads from fighting their enemies on these trips, but soon gave up in disgust and stayed at the mission, instead of going along on the hunts.

July 29, 1842, Father DeSmet left St. Mary's for the east after traveling to Fort Vancouver in Washington for supplies. Father Mengarini was left in charge, along with two other priests. By 1845 the little mission had its own flour mill, built around stones brought from Antwerp, Belgium, and run by water power. Wagon tires were used to make a sawmill, and both were the first such mills in the state.

The year 1846 saw both a larger mission and an open break between Father Mengarini and the Flatheads, caused largely by promises made by DeSmet which couldn't be carried out by his successor. The Flatheads openly suspected the Black Robes of being liars, the same as other white men. Things went from bad to worse. Indians threatened the little mission, and when Father Mengarini left in the summer of 1850 for his yearly consultations at Coeur d' Alene in what now is Idaho, the mission was closed.

That fall the priests found a buyer for their mission. Major John Owen had come over the Oregon trail looking for a trading post, and here was one ready made. He bought it for $250 and moved in November 5, 1850.

The fathers fondly hoped to revive their mission, but it was a forlorn hope. Father Ravalli and Father Giorda returned in 1866 and built a new church which was dedicated October 28 on a site west and south of the fort. Father Ravalli remained here until he died in 1884, administering to the sick and bringing to the frontier a lavish supply of European education plus a lively personality that endeared him to everyone, white and red.

In 1891 the church was closed when the Flathead Indians were moved to the Jocko reservation, but the parish church of Stevensville, since replaced with a modern building, still bears the name St. Mary's. So does the mountain which looks down on the white church with the cross and the small row of faded rooms that are all that is left of Major Owen's fort.

The old fort is partly restored on a ranch just north of Stevensville, its building outlines marked, sagging roofs bolstered and old fireplaces reminiscent of the flames that once warmed the Black Robes and Major Owen during lonely winters in the Bitter Root.

Stone

Writing

Flathead Lake delights all visitors to its shores, but in a long-lost time an unknown Indian looked out upon its blue waters and saw a vision that some strange faith compelled him to picture in ocher on solid rock.

If he possessed words he doubtless would have been unable to express his feelings, to explain why he drew in native red clay or powdered rock the parallel lines, dots, pictures of animals and men that he left on Flathead's shore.

There are many other spots in Montana where these paintings have escaped years of erosion, rain and freezing, but the sites on Flathead, six in all, are among the best in the state. They deserve a visit, these primitive shrines.

Any guess as to what symbols mean is purest speculation, and many have speculated. Present Indians share the speculation with the whites. One of the best sites on the lake is about two miles east of Rollins on Highway 93 and four miles south of Flathead Lake Lookout.

Thain White of Flathead Lake Lookout, who has studied these paintings for years, leans to the red man's explanation, and the word passed along is that the spirits made the paintings, that they were messages to other Indians, or that the ghosts of extinct tribes scribed the walls. Thain says the Painted Rocks drawings, near Rollins, are in the best Indian tradition, "a good place to have vision."

This Rollins country was important to the Indians, even in historic times. The "Big Lodge" of the Kootenai was about one mile west of Rollins. On the nearby ridge or divide there was a Treaty or Medicine Rock on which Indians left offerings as late as 1910.

On Finley Point, at the southeastern corner of the big lake, are other paintings. These probably are later than the others, for they include symbolic turtles, the sign of the Iroquois, although the Iroquois could very well have added their art to more ancient symbols. Iroquois were brought to western Montana in the early 1800s to teach the Kootenai to trap beaver, their traveling expenses paid by the fur companies. History indicates the Iroquois, an eastern woodland Indian, were far more interested in frolicking with the Kootenai than in teaching them anything, and apparently they found time for art as well as fun.

Across the "narrows" from Finley Point are the Little Bull Island paintings, and Indian tradition indicates these were made in a good place to record visions and to wait for other visions to come to the red men. Most paintings in the Flathead Lake area are made with natural red pigment found in the rocks or in the ground. There are no petroglyphs, in which the stone has to be chipped, carved or chiseled.

Thus, the days of the paintings are numbered. Already many are dimmed and blurred, as are the true meaning of these symbols. In other countries, around the globe, primitive men painted such symbols, whether to insure themselves a lasting memory, to express an embryo of religion stirring within them or to assure success in the hunt, no one can say.

There are legends in the Flathead that some of the paintings were made by the water monster spirit or some other spirit that dwelt in the lake country or the mountains.

The technique is unusual. Some appear to have been made by the fingers of the artist. Others have excellent lines, as done with a brush. Again, who knows? Some even have black paint or color, instead of the nearly ubiquitous red.

Trail to the Buffalo

Meriwether Lewis' trail up the river of the road to the buffalo is 156 years old, but the journal Lewis kept of his trip is as clear as the Big Blackfoot River in midsummer.

Cokahlahishkit, the Indians called it, the "buffalo river road" from the west side valleys to the broad Missouri and Medicine River plains where buffalo dotted the hills like stars in the sky. To the meat-hungry Lewis and Clark party, fresh from the game-barren Bitter Root Mountains, the prospect of roasted buffalo-hump drew them magnetically to the divide at the head of Cokahlahishkit.

The pass that opened the way at the continental summit to the grassy hills of the Dearborn and Medicine rivers is named for Lewis and his partner in discovery. Ironically, it is one of the few good passes in the northern Rockies still passable only to foot travel, horses and rugged vehicles. Its trails still are those of elk and deer.

For the first time in their journey, Lewis and Clark separated at Travelers' Rest at the mouth of Lolo Creek in the Bitter Root valley, Lewis to explore the Marias River and Clark to go down the Yellowstone. To follow Lewis up the Big Blackfoot take the "buffalo river road" by driving Highway 10-12 eastward from Missoula to the turnoff at Bonner onto Highway 20. Stay with Highway 20 eastbound for the rest of the journey.

There is no mention in the journal of the nation's birthday when at 6 a.m. the morning of Friday, July 4, 1806, Lewis said an emotional farewell to the Nez Perce Indians who had guided him across the rugged Bitter Roots. The parting was at the mouth of Rattlesnake Creek, now inside Missoula city limits, and was preceded by instruction from the Indians on how to reach the Missouri headwaters.

Lewis commented on the mosquitoes and complained how he had wet his chronometer in crossing the Clark's Fork River, matters of more import than the national holiday.

Turn left on blacktop through town of Bonner on Highway 20 between the hills covered, as Lewis noted, "with longleaf pine and fir." The party camped eight miles upstream from the mouth on the north side of the river in a "handsome and timbered bottom." Two squirrels were killed as specimens, one of them apparently the Columbian ground squirrel.

Thus passed Independence day for the Lewis party, and July 5 Lewis made note of a "gang of antelopes here of which we killed one" just below the mouth of the Clearwater, about 37 miles out of Missoula. Lewis called this stream Werner's River, after Private Werner and commented "saw two swan in this beautiful creek."

Lewis' trail clings closely to Highway 20, passing the mouths of Cottonwood Creek and Monture Creek, probably the Seamon's Creek referred to in the journal. Highway 20 crosses Kleinschmidt Flat, which Lewis call the "prairie of knobs" and which later was called first Stevens' Prairie for Governor Isaac I. Stevens of Washington Territory, who explored it in 1853-54, and later Blackfoot Prairie.

Lewis noted the North Fork of the Blackfoot, which for a time was called Salmon Trout Creek, probably after the Dolly Varden trout which spawned in its waters. Highway 20 crosses the North Fork just east of Ovando.

Lewis wrote of seeing "Curloos (curlews), bee martains (martins), wood peckers, plover, robins, doves, ravens, hawks and a variety of sparrows common to the plains, also some ducks" on the prairie. He was worried about a Minnetares party, whose horses' hoof prints were still fresh in the trail ahead of them.

Noted also is a "large crooked pond," either Kleinschmidt or Brown's lake, and more mosquitoes in the Blackfoot Canyon west of Lincoln. At Alice Creek, just east of Lincoln, the exploring party took the north trail up that stream.

Highway 20 swings further south, over Rogers Pass. Nearby Lander's Fork is the namesake of a surveyor in the 1853 Pacific railway survey.

Lewis observed in his journal that high on the drainage the "deer are remarkably plenty and in good order" and that Rueben Fields "wounded a moos (moose) deer" which had bothered Lewis' dog.

At the summit of this pass Lewis first sighted Square Butte south of Fort Shaw, a familiar landmark which he named Fort Mountain when he saw it from near Great Falls on his 1805 journey upriver at about the same time of year. He joyfully noted "sighn of buffalo" where the party camped, high on the headwaters of the Dearborn River.

From Highway 20 east of the Rogers' summit today Haystack Mountain is a purple cone on the horizon to the north. This is Lewis "Shishequaw Mountain." As the driver descends to the forks of the Dearborn he may even see Lewis' "barking squirrels" and be "much rejoiced at finding ourselves in the plains of the Missouri, which abound with game."

Disaster Falls

Known and respected by the earliest travelers on the great rivers of the north were the Kootenai Falls, a treacherous symphony of green water on red rock just west of Libby on Highway 2.

For centuries the Kutenai Indians had moved upstream past these falls, risking their lives on the slippery trail that followed the northern bank, a trail pioneered by white-tailed deer, Rocky Mountain bighorns and other four-footed predecessors of the Kutenai.

These mountain-wise Indians knew the vagaries of this glacial-fed river and had a great respect for its eddies and swirls in the canyons both above and below the falls. It was David Thompson, who came down from Canada as the first white man ever to guide his canoe down the big river, who discovered the falls for the civilized world.

In 1809 he struggled along the old Indian trail on the north bank and commented in his journal on the "rude path 300 feet about the river, and the least slip would have been sure destruction." Still in existence along the north side is the old trail that Thompson and the Indians took. The Forest Service tells a story of a packtrain that years ago slid into the river from this trail, with all animals perishing in the icy waters but one trembling horse that stood, terrified, on a mid-river rock until rescued.

It was 35 years after Thompson that Father Pierre DeSmet, the Jesuit who knew his way around the West so well, passed this way, again on the old portage trail. He called it a "defile of precipitous and frightful rocks" and added the area was one of "livid gashes of ravines and precipices, giant peaks and ridges of varied hue, inaccessible pinnacles, fearful and unfathomable chasms filled with the sound of ever-precipitating waters . . . many times have I been obliged to take the attitude of a quadruped and walk on my hands."

Although conceding the rock walls were "heaven-built" Father DeSmet still spoke in awe of the "cataracts and whirlpools engulfing crags and trees beneath their angry sway."

It was this sort of impression left by the falls and their leaping rapids above that caused early traffic to go southward along the Clark's Fork River instead. Cabinet Gorge was far less frightening than the old portage.

Not until 1892, when interest was shown in the falls as a power site, did Great Northern rails penetrate the canyon with the aid of considerable blasting powder.

Just above the falls are Chinese Rapids, tricky as the falls themselves. The story goes that in the 60s a party of Chinese miners from the Wild Horse country in British Columbia rafted down the river with a load of gold dust. They feared ambush by white miners and took this route rather than go overland. At the rapids the gold shifted, upended the raft, and only one Chinese made it ashore. He long afterward told the story of his lost gold and drowned companions after he had reached safety in San Francisco.

This was only one of the drownings at the falls. A party of hunters, minus one who took to the shore to shoot grouse, rafted confidently into the falls, but only one came ashore. It was great sport in the late 19th century to dynamite the big sturgeon which gathered in the plunge basin below the falls. In the 80s one of these parties blew up raft, fishermen and all with a misplaced firing of their own powder charge.

One fisherman, believing he had snagged an all-time record sturgeon, hauled out a body he had hooked under the chin. There were plenty of chills at the falls, with unpredicted bodies constantly showing up in the canyon below.

Today Kootenai Falls is a beautiful sheet of water and well worth a quick pull-off from Highway 2 to visit it.

Council
of Peace

A grove of cottonwoods in the green-meadowed Grass Valley west of Missoula revives a century of history and the council fires that sent blue plumes of smoke against the bluer Bitter Root Mountains.

It was in 1855 that the three Salish tribes, Flathead, Kootenai and Kalispell or upper Pend d'Orielles, gathered in the Grass Valley to meet for the first time as a nation with the United States of America. Representing the white man's nation was General Isaac I. Stevens, governor of Washington Territory, who wanted to put all three tribes upon a common reservation. Facing the general were Victor, head chief of the Flatheads; Alexander, head chief of the Pend d'Orielles, and Michael, head chief of the Kootenai.

Selected for the negotiations was a pleasant spot known as Council Grove. To reach it turn off Highway 90 just west of Missoula at the sign which reads "Mullan trail." This is a paved route and follows the tracks of the military wagons through the valley. Eastbound, turn just east of Frenchtown.

The grove itself is about nine miles west of Missoula and today is unmarked, but watch for the huge boles of the cottonwoods on the north side of the highway, where they form a rough enclosure. Many of the big trees have been cut down, their stumps lining the highway, but some still stand, reminders of the solemn proceedings that went on beneath their twisted limbs.

General Stevens had in mind a treaty that would place on one reservation all the tribes represented. This would be either the Bitter Root valley to the south, or the Jocko, first valley to the north over Evaro Hill, now traversed by Highway 93-10A. The tribes were willing to unite to strengthen themselves, but each was unwilling to leave its ancestral home.

The Bitter Root was home to the Flatheads, for Lewis and Clark found them there a half-century before. For eight days the emissaries of two great nations bargained, Victor and Alexander being unable to reach an agreement despite the diplomacy of General Stevens. Michael indicated he would accept whatever Alexander decided.

On the eighth day, Stevens, taking a hint from Victor, wrote the famed 11th article of the treaty, known today as the Hell Gate treaty, after the Clark's Fork River gap just east of the grove. This article promised a presidential survey of the Bitter Root valley south of the mouth of Lolo Creek, the spot Lewis and Clark called Travelers' Rest.

If this survey, the treaty promised, found that lush valley to be better for the Indians than the Jocko valley offered them, then it would be set aside as a reservation. In the meantime, white settlers were to be barred from the Bitter Root. All agreed and signed.

As did many other white men's agreements, the Hell Gate treaty languished, while Congress considered it for five years. No move was made to make the promised survey, and whites drifted into the valley while Washington looked the other way.

Finally, in the summer of 1872, James A. Garfield, then a congressman and later President of the United States, was sent by the Secretary of Interior to the valley to persuade the Flatheads to move to the Jocko. He met with the chiefs at old Fort Owen, near Stevensville on Highway 93, and again at Arlee, in the middle of the Jocko valley, also on Highway 93.

On August 25, a Sunday, Garfield wrote in his journal: "Held a long conference with the Flathead chiefs and, after almost failing, succeeded." Garfield wrote of the Jocko, "It is a country of wonderful beauty. All the varieties of mountain, valley, prairie and woodland combined."

He could have written the same of the grassy valley on the old Mullan trail where the two nations treated with each other and pledged their words.

Ice-Locked Waters

Get our your imaginary snorkel and take a submarine ride in western Montana's forested valleys.

You'll be a few thousand years late to navigate under the water, but your whole journey will be on the bottom of a lake so huge that even its memory makes Flathead Lake look like a duck pond.

Drive Highway 90 out of Butte or Highway 12 out of Helena, and your car will slip beneath the prehistoric waters of Lake Missoula somewhere between Clinton and Bearmouth. The dam which held back this huge lake, 300 feet deep at Missoula, was a block of ice which had pushed southward down to Sand Point, Idaho, then bulged back up the Clark's Fork River to what now is Noxon.

At this point it was met by a 2,000-foot thick block of ice which moved southward up the Bull River, then across a trench in the Cabinet Mountains and down Lake Creek. The two filled the Clark's Fork River channel with ice from Lake Pend Orielle to Noxon and backed water up the Clark's Fork valley past Missoula, up the Bitter Root valley and many side channels.

Another huge ice sheet, or more properly a block, flowed into the Flathead valley, and where Kalispell now stands the ice was 3,000 feet thick. Its pressure forced ice across Marias Pass out onto the plains, and the moraine or mountain of dirt pushed out by the Glacier now holds back Flathead's water south of Polson.

This mass of ice was known as the Cordilleran Glacier, and while it covered western Montana, most of northern Montana's plains, as far south as Great Falls, were in a deep freeze known as the Keewatin Glacier, born near Hudson's Bay.

To continue your imaginary submarine voyage, drive into Missoula and look at the ridges on the slopes of Mount Sentinel and Mount Jumbo, at each side of the Hell Gate entrance to the valley. Waves lapping at these mountainsides left parallel ridges all the way down. This is only one of hundreds of boldly-scribed records the lake and its glaciers left for motorists to read as they drive.

Cross the Squaw Peaks Range at Evaro west and north of Missoula on Highway 10A and 93, and just as you break into the Jocko valley look eastward against the mountains. There is a huge washed-out alluvial fan at the mouth of a small creek. This is the first of dozens of these fans, which are deposits of gravel and dirt dropped by melting ice waters as they coursed down these slopes and flowed out into the lake. You can chart the lake level by the flat surfaces of the tops of these fans or deltas, since the silt-laden waters dropped their burden as they entered the still waters of the lake.

From the road they resemble railroad or highway fills or grades, but built on a mammoth scale that would baffle any bulldozer.

As you drive westward stay on 10A at Ravalli Junction and you bore deeper and deeper into the long-gone waters of Lake Missoula. Stop at the town of Dixon and look north. A huge moraine marks the place where the glacier that covered Kalispell's plain stopped and deposited its load.

From here to Noxon there are deltas or terraces of long-exhausted streams all along the cliffs above the road. Below Arlee beach lines are easily seen along the cliffs. Just west of Dixon there is another landmark of later date, two circles and a cross on a slope of slide rock south of the bridge across Magpie Creek. Not even the oldest Flathead Indians know its origin, proof of its age and construction by a people long forgotten.

At Paradise is a delta whose flat surface is nearly 400 feet above the road. There is another at the mouth of Vermillion Creek near the town of Trout Creek. In glacial days this now small creek was a raging river of melted ice.

West of Trout Creek where the river bends west, the horizonal beach lines are 1,200 feet above the river, for you are nearing the dam that held back these waters. When this dam gave way, fading under the warming sun of long ago, the torrent must have been one of the most terrifying sights in the formation of the world, but no man lived in western Montana to view the terror.

Slim's Lake

In the golden fall of 1927 Montana joined America's wild enthusiasm over a slim, quiet young man from Little Falls, Minnesota, shared it so deeply that it named a mountain lake after him and invited him to visit the glories of his namesake in the timber-carpeted Swan valley.

"Slim" Lindbergh earned this devotion by piloting alone a single-engine plane from New York to Paris, a pioneering feat, and Montana always has loved and admired pioneers. Today's traveler in a car with more horsepower than the City of St. Louis can retrace on blacktop most of the journey that the fabled flier traced among Montana's peaks and pines.

After Charles A. Lindbergh startled and delighted the world with his April, 1927, flight, all America wanted a first-hand look at this Minnesota boy who had become a global hero. In NX-211, the plane that now hangs venerably from the ceiling of the Smithsonian Institution in Washington, D.C., he traveled the nation, accompanied by his aide, Lieut. Donald E. Keyhoe, in another ship.

When Lindbergh arrived in Butte that bright September day he had a plan in his agile mind, a plan to ditch the schedule and take a quick look at Glacier National Park. He always had wanted to see Glacier from topside and confided to Lieutenant Keyhoe they would "bend the course a little" on their way from Butte to Helena, the next scheduled stop.

Soon after sun-up the two planes took off, circled to the west and flew the gamut of the gleaming Missions and the pointed Swans, along the green trough of the Swan and Clearwater Lake country that in those days hardly knew the ring of an ax. To follow the route today drive Highway 90 from Butte to Garrison, 10-12 to Drummond, 271 to Ovando, 20 to Clearwater Junction, then north on the Swan River blacktop to Bigfork. Follow Lindbergh to Glacier if you wish.

The flying colonel cut across the south end of the park, rendezvousing with Keyhoe above the Glacier summits. Lindbergh was in ecatasy as he darted through the white clouds around the summits of such giants as St. Nicholas, Triple Divide, Rising Wolf and Citadel. He slipped down into the mists along the battlemented valleys and skimmed across the lakes, watching the shadow of his plane chase him in the water below, not an unkown medium to Lindbergh.

He was fascinated by the park, by the mountains all across Montana's face, and he turned reluctantly toward Helena when he had run the course of his time. He had played hookey and couldn't afford to be caught, but he had taken with him the marvelous memory of rocks and clouds, water and timber.

Particularly he had been drawn to a blue angle of water held tight in blue-green forest, a lake unimaginately known as Elbow in those days. It lay in the Swan drainage, in a fold in the mighty Mission Range's eastern slope. Obligingly, the name was changed to Lindbergh Lake to honor the hero.

As fall touched the aspens and gilded the massive-boled tamaracks of the Swan valley, Lindbergh visited the lake which bore his name, hosted by J. R. Hobbins of Butte and other noted Montanans. He watched at first hand the blue water that had fascinated him from the air, patted the head of a friendly camp dog, smelled the sweet smoke of the campfire and saw the mists vanish from the lake under warmth of a rising September sun. Someday he may wish to come again.

When Men Feared Gold

Montana's first commercial wealth—furs—and its second—gold—blended their eras at the southernmost post of the fabled Hudson's Bay Company, a tiny fort in the shadow of the giant Mission Mountains.

Fort Connah, named for an old Scottish river, lived only in the twilight of the fur trade west of the Rockies. East of the divide the slaughter of buffalo kept profit in this trade for several years after it had declined in the west.

But, back to Fort Connah's story, a story that can be relived by a casual drive. Fort Connah was built on Post Creek or Crow Creek, as it was then called, because Flathead Indians were reluctant to come to the Flathead Post, an 1824 Hudson's Bay post at Eddy, on Highway 10A between Plains and Thompson Falls. The year was 1846.

The Fort Connah site, well marked by a state highway sign, is about a mile east of where Highway 93 rises into the hills north of St. Ignatius in the Mission valley.

Hudson's Bay had long been interested in the American fur trade, and Alexander Ross wintered in Ross's Hole south of Sula when he was caught there in the blizzards of 1823-24. Ross later led an expedition through the Big Hole, then fell into disfavor and ended up as the factor at Saleesh House or Flathead Post.

By 1831 the great Hudson's Bay Company had decided to abandon the upper Snake River country, and its last large-scale effort there was John Work's expedition of that year. American competition was too keen.

Francis Ermatinger, factor at Flathead Post, had a good trade, but by 1836 he left the post, and clerks operated it until 1845, when Neil McArthur took over. It was McArthur who began building the new post in the Mission valley. He thought the old fort was too far west for a brisk trade with the Flatheads, who then filled the Jocko and Mission valleys.

In 1847, even before the fort was finished, trade began at the new post, but McArthur had trouble getting along with the Indians. To correct this, Hudson's Bay replaced him with Angus MacDonald, father of Duncan MacDonald, who named the post after the river Connen, near his old home in Scotland. Later the name was corrupted to Connah.

Because the Oregon treaty of 1846 barred British and Canadians from land west of the divide, Canadian trade was politically as well as economically ruined. Even so, the fort hung on for several years, enough to see the dawn of the gold era, and this is Fort Connah's greatest story.

The whole fabric of the yarns about the first discovery of gold in Montana is woven in legend, but Francois Finlay, or Benetsee by nickname, has support of the Fort Connah MacDonalds in his claim to triggering the gold industry of Montana.

Duncan MacDonald signed a statement that his father in 1850 at Fort Connah saw a teaspoonful of gold in the hands of Finlay, who told him he had placered it in Gold Creek, just west of the present Garrison on Highway 90. Finlay gave the gold to MacDonald, who was suspicious and asked Finlay to get him some more, which Finlay did, always in small quantities.

MacDonald, fearful of the effect a gold rush might have on the dwindling fur trade, wrote his superiors, who cautioned him about utmost secrecy, since a rush of miners would be bad for the fur business. Major John Owen, who established Fort Owen in the Bitter Root valley, picked up the rumor and shared the fears of Hudson's Bay.

However, some of Owen's white employees, according to Duncan MacDonald, tipped off the Granville Stuarts, and the gold secret was out.

The death of one era spawned another, and here, under the glistening point of Mount MacDonald, named for the factor, a white man for the first time in Montana fingered the yellow flakes of destiny.

Finan's Winter Tents

Snow already had powdered the peaks of the Selkirk Mountains and the gentle rolls of the Purcell Range when fiery Finan McDonald pulled his canoes against the north bank of the Kootenai River and put together the first white man's building in western Montana.

It was the fall of 1808, and McDonald was the trusted right arm of gentle, diplomatic David Thompson, first scientific explorer of the upper Columbia. The two traders from the Northwest Fur Company had crossed the Canadian Rockies at Howse Pass north and west of Calgary. Thompson had stayed at the new Kootenae House on the Columbia River north of Lake Windermere in British Columbia, second fur trading post west of the Rocky Mountains, while McDonald paddled down the Kootenai into Montana.

The pair parted the last day of October, 1808. There is some discrepancy in the date, since Thompson's Narratives show it as 1807, but his notebooks and other documents show 1808. This puts the tiny camp near the mouth of Pipe Creek on the Kootenai across the river from Libby a year later than Fort Manuel Lisa, at the mouth of the Big Horn River, first trading post in Montana.

Western larch or tamarack along the Kootenai were prime in their golden glory when McDonald left Thompson and crossed Canal Flats linking the headwaters of the Columbia and Kootenai in British Columbia. McDonald and his party had trade goods for the Kutenai Indians. They had no intentions of establishing a trading post. This was to be a winter "camp-out" as a base for trading among the Indians.

With their axes the McDonald party trimmed out small trees and built a log enclosure, possible a lean-to type or "hangard" with a roof, a rude shelter for the goods they had brought to trade for the rich furs of these virgin woods. McDonald was no green hand, for he had come across the ridge of the Canadian Rockies in the spring of 1807 with Thompson and helped to build Kootenae House, where Thompson now was wintering.

Now, McDonald had built the first commercial establishment in western Montana. Along with the "hangard," McDonald and his men set up two "leathern tents." In this crude outpost the tiny party of traders prepared to brave out the harsh cold and deep snow of a Kootenai winter. Not for three years would there be a permanent trading post on the Kootenai, and Thompson set it up at Jennings, a few miles up the river from McDonald's camp and at the mouth of the Fisher River.

Not until October of 1809 did Thompson travel up the Fisher River. He was on his way up the Clark's Fork of the Columbia and down the Kootenai in a circle tour from Pend Orielle Lake and crossed the divide between the Fisher and Thompson rivers. Thompson, whom the Indians called "The Man Who Looks at the Stars," didn't think the stream important enough to give it a name.

Thompson's journals are silent on how the McDonald party fared along the frozen Kootenai. Anyway, Thompson was far upriver in his own camp at Kootenae House, two tiny specks of civilization cut off even from the wild prairies of Canada by miles of impassable snow and the highest mountain range on the continent.

It was April and the ice was beginning to break up in the blue-green river when Kutenai Indian furs were stowed in the canoes, and Thompson and McDonald again joined their parties. The products of the winter's trading were on their way to the far-off markets of the Northwest Fur Company, the first furs from western Montana to go into the European trade. Thompson packed them out across Howse Pass and to Fort Augustus, now Edmonton, Alberta. The great era of the fur trade west of Montana's mountains was underway.

Medicine Tree

Ancient in the Indian legends is a tree by the side of the road, a road now paved with asphalt but worn deep by the feet of men both white and red.

Another traveler, on a bleak late winter day in 1824, first saw the now-famed Ram's Horn Tree at the edge of Highway 93 between Darby and Sula. Fur trader Alexander Ross, on his way to the Snake River in Idaho, found the big yellow pine worthy enough to note in his journal.

Although he camped by the tree, now marked by a Forest Service sign, he remarked on the "gloomy" character of the spot, comparing it with the grisly Hell Gate east of Missoula, famous Indian ambush. Here by the trail on the east fork of the Bitter Root River, was a tree with a Rocky Mountain sheep ram's horns and skull embedded in the trunk.

The Flathead Indians with Ross explained the legend of the tree as the spot where an early Flathead had wounded a huge bighorn ram which turned to attack him. As the ram rushed toward him, the Indian ducked behind the tree, so the ram struck the trunk and was killed. The Indian then cut the body from the head, leaving horns and skull in the tree.

Even more fanciful is another legend which credits the mythical and symbolic Coyote of Indian lore as having encountered a huge bighorn ram at this spot, that the ram attacked and suffered the same fate as in the Ross account. With the years the legend grew, and a later version pictures

Coyote as being warned by a small bird that a huge ram would kill him if he approached the Medicine Tree.

The alerted Coyote, challenged as a trespasser by the ram, taunted the sheep into boastfully showing his strength by butting the tree. When the ram became fast to the trunk, Coyote drew his knife and killed the ram, throwing the severed body high on the slope above the tree, where it left the mark of a human face. Coyote then declared the tree forever a Medicine Tree for all Indians.

Whatever the cause, natural or otherwise, there remains a hole in the tree where the ram's horn became imbedded many years before Ross. Visitors have long since carried off the extruding horns, as well as the beads and other trinkets left by Indians at the tree's base.

Great powers were ascribed to the tree, and the Flatheads tell of a Nez Perce who defiled the tree by firing a shot into its trunk while he was on his way to hunt bison east of the divide. On this hunt the Nez Perce fell with his horse and was killed, a misfortune laid by legend to his disregard for the sacred tree.

There is some argument among old-timers as to whether this was the original Ram's Horn tree. There may have been several, and in other places in western Montana such trees are known to have existed, all with a certain amount of legend woven about their aged trunks.

Anyone can speculate about their origin. Early hunters, white or red, may have hung the ram's head in the trees so that years of growth surrounded the bone, as a tree grows around a rock or other foreign matter. It is unusual, though, that only ram's horns figure in legend or fact, never elk or deer antlers or buffalo horns.

Since the scar on the tree is about as high as a man's head, a sheep could hardly have butted the tree, unless sheep at that time were much larger than at present, which isn't likely. The tree itself is estimated to be more than 300 years old, and aged Indians tell of seeing it when they were children.

Flat-Tailed Monarch

Crouching across the Clark Fork valley about 25 miles east of Missoula is a thousand-year-old beaver, or so the Indian legend goes, and the beavers themselves told the story to the Indians.

To the whizzing motorist on Highway 90, it is Beaver Tail Hill, between Clinton and Bearmouth, and here in late winter and early spring the mule deer gather to nibble the first green shoots of alfalfa on the valley's meadows.

On a long-ago day, though, the hill was all a level meadow, and only the beavers lived in this vast country. The great king of all the beavers, named Skookum, lived at Big Warm Spring Mound (now Warm Springs in the Deer Lodge valley.)

The great king had received word that his subjects down river were going to rebel and set up their own government. He gathered all his loyal followers from the Little Blackfoot, Tincup Creek, Dog Creek and all the other tributaries and met the rebels at the plain where Beaver Tail Hill now rises. He demanded the usual tribute plus renewed allegiance to his sovereignty.

The rebels refused, saying they owned the whole river below, to the great sea, that the river below was longer than the river above, and the downriver beavers were more numerous than the upriver beavers. This forced the old king to play his aces, and sent for all beavers living under his reign.

When they arrived he directed them to scoop out the hillside, creating the deep gulch which lies northwest of Beaver Tail Hill and in one night damming up the whole flow of the Clark's Fork. The king vowed he would run the waters across the divide to the Missouri.

The rebels saw their big river dwindle to a trickle, then

dry altogether, and they repented their defiance of the king. They quickly made peace with their ruler, meekly paid their tribute and reavowed their allegiance.

King Skookum then ordered his beavers to remove the dam and let the waters of the Clark's Fork rush on to the great sea. They tore out the southwest end of the dam, creating a narrow canyon for the river, and piled the dirt so it resembled a crouching beaver for all to see up and down the river, even to this day.

When first the Indians settled in the Clark's Fork valley they heard this legend directly from their cousins, the beavers, for in those long-past days the Indians could talk to the beavers. Not long afterward some young and reckless Indians killed their cousins, the beavers, for their furs, and the animals solemnly vowed never again to speak to an Indian, and they have kept their vow.

Today, Highway 90 crosses where the crouching beaver's tail meets his body, and two transcontinental railroads bore underneath.

Tommy's Nuggets

Sprawled across the Continental Divide like a saddle blanket thrown across a bronc's back is a chunk of historic gold country that manages to keep up its reputation and social standing even after a century of ups and downs.

To relive this high life of the high gold country drive Highway 15 out of Helena to the north, then turn left on highway 279. About 12 miles west on 279 is the Marysville turnoff. Close by is Silver City, where Silver Creek, which you have been following, lured Tommy Cruse, the sparkling, energetic Irishman, to search diligently through the surrounding hills for the great lode he knew in his warm, old Irish heart must be there.

It was, and in 1876, when he broke the lode that eventually spewed forth $20,000,000 in gold and silver, he named it the Drum Lummon after his native parish in Ireland.

To visit Tommy's hillside town, which devotes most of its time to hosting skiers, keep on the dirt road for only a few miles, passing the dredge cuts made by placer seekers below Marysville. The town still is intact, and you can visit the rotting timbers of such famed mines as the Bald Mountain, Gloster, Empire, Penobscot, Bald Butte and Shannon, as well as the Drum Lummon, which is virtually in the streets. Proud local people will show you where to look.

In the late 80s, Marysville really felt its oats. Great Northern and Northern Pacific raced for the privilege of serving the mines with transport, and what is left of the old NP trestle still can be seen. In this heyday, Marysville could furnish home folks and visitors with the facilities of six hotels, three churches, a fancy opera house, two newspapers, a Masonic Lodge which still is active, and, most important of all, 27 saloons, all in good working order.

Tommy Cruse's life was filled with tragedy, but he left behind him St. Helena Cathedral in Helena, a stately mausoleum for his family and more memories than most men ever achieve.

When you have finished checking out this colorful town and have looked out from its streets onto Silver Creek valley and across to the summits of the Belts far away, it's time to tackle the Continental Divide. Ask any local resident to point out the Ophir Gulch road, which is dirt, but good in fair weather. Take it slow and watch for rocks or an occasional wandering mountain spring.

Stop at the summit for a good look at all this gold country, then drop to Ophir Creek and Blackfoot City, a town which won't yield one drop of color to Marysville. A rowdy contemporary of Marysville, the town lay along Ophir Creek below Cemetery Ridge, a name that smacks of the Civil War and Gettysburg.

It was one year after the war ended that the first gold strike was made in Blackfoot City, probably by Dave Johns and his Indian squaw. By the middle of that year the town was going strong along Ophir Creek. Fire was the nemesis of Blackfoot City, for it was partially destroyed in 1869, again in 1875 and nearly wiped out in 1882. When rebuilt the last time, it was named Ophir.

In 1876, year of Custer's defeat, the town celebrated Independence Day with a whingding that brought in 6,000 people, and Asa Brown, Blackfoot City's silver-tongued spellbinder, gave the principal oration. There were plenty of saloons to care for the thirsty, and a few graves on the ridge testify that some arguments at least ended in bloodshed.

This was placer country, and the gravels gave up more than $5,000,000 in gold, plus some additional in later dredging along the creeks.

From Blackfoot City, drive downhill to the three-mile junction with Highway 272 and blacktop. It's only a few miles south to Avon and Highway 12. Returning to Helena watch the north side of the highway for the turnoff to Snowshoe Gulch, where one nugget worth $3,200 was placered from the creek, bigger than anything at Blackfoot City or Marysville.

To Map an Empire

One hundred years ago a Welshman died in poverty in Montreal, blind and forced to sell even his overcoat to keep himself and his wife from starving in his last few months of pitiful existence, even though his name is one that never can be erased from Montana's amazing frontier history.

The trail of David Thompson, whose accurate pencil drew the first surveyed charts of the gleaming peaks, churning rivers and forested mountains in the Northwest, is a challenge to the traveler. Whether the trail follows the still-virgin timbered shores of a Montana lake or river or lies buried forever beneath a slab of asphalt highway, its memory is as brilliant as the mind of the man who traveled 50,000 miles by moccasin, dogsled, horseback and canoe for 27 years to map this mountain country.

With only a pocket watch, a sextant, a candle and the cold fire of the stars in a black sky, Thompson set the first white man's foot upon mile after mile of the country of green trees, green waters and blue skies. To roll a rubber-tired wheel across his country-old trail is to honor his vision and enrich your travel experience. The road map that guides your way was sired by the hand of him whom the Indians called "The Man Who Looks at the Stars."

Apprenticed to the Hudson's Bay Company from a charity school for boys in England, he came as a youth to the firm's York Factory post on Hudson's Bay itself in 1784. Fascinated by the rugged land of Canadian and American northwest, he traced the geography of everything from Lake Superior to the Pacific Ocean in a canoe, only to find an American trading post at its mouth and thus deny him the privilege of claiming its drainage for England.

But to follow his trail of exploration and geography. He left a heavy hand in Montana, and his landmarks are easily visible from the blacktop. Thompson explored Montana's northwest corner in 1809, guided by a handful of Indians and French adventurers, meeting the Salish and Kalispell Indians. That same year he built Salish house for the Northwest Fur Company—which he had joined after leaving Hudson's Bay—about opposite the mouth of Thompson's River and about a mile and a half east of Thompson Falls on Highway 10A. Thompson wintered here, leaving his name on the falls of the Clark's Fork River and on Thompson's River, which flows into the Clark's Fork from the north.

West of Thompson Falls on a road hardly passable even in summer, is a gap in the Bitter Root mountains called Thompson's Pass, just east of Murray, Idaho. The same year that he made history with Salish House in Montana he built the first building in Idaho, a log post on the east shore of Lake Pend Oreille, east of the present town of Sand Point.

The traveler on Highway 10A west of Thompson Falls will about follow Thompson's water route between the forts, a dangerous rapid-filled excursion for the geographer.

Thompson left his tracks along Highway 2 as well, for he traveled the length of the river which bears his name and rises in that shining necklace of timbered lakes known as Upper, Middle and Lower Thompson. This is one of the finest forest highways in America, summer or winter, and the Thompson lakes are its highlight.

Thompson, busy as he was with his surveying and mapping, created a map which served all the civilized world for years and brought to them a picture of the face of this new wilderness. He cannot have helped but be enchanted by the same land that binds Montanans to their home.

The trading posts have crumbled, and even the ruined chimney at Kullyspell (Kalispell) House on Pend Orielle, which revealed his work in later years, has sunk into the forest floor. Every year, though, adds to the lustre of his achievements, new light to his adventuresome spirit, his vision and his ability.

The British government for which he risked his life in the rapids of the Columbia, rejected even a small pension for his remarkable explorations. He sold his precious mapping tools with which he put a million and a half miles of geography on paper; sold them so he could eat.

Today he is known as the "Builder of Canada" and the explorer of northwestern Montana's forests and streams. To follow his trail is to find adventure and to honor Thompson as he deserves.

The Scouts — O. C. Seltzer

Deer House Plains

High grass flowed like water before the wind in the Deer Lodge valley when western Indians crossed it to reach the great hunting plains east of the mountains where the buffalo were fat.

No tribe called the high valley home, but trails of travois and Indian horses crossed it in all directions. Game was scarce in the western mountains before the white man, and the red men who lived in Montana's western valleys and even west of the Bitter Roots in Idaho and Washington, came this way to find the passes to the buffalo country.

The wide valley between the Continental Divide and the Flint Creek Range opened up before the eyes of Angus Ferris, a trapper, on a summer day in 1831. Ferris was lured to the valley by a hundred lodges of Pend Oreille Indians, headed for the buffalo hunt, and their 3,000 horses, grazing knee-deep in the meadows.

Ferris named the valley after a high cone, formed by a hot spring, which attracted the white-tailed deer, especially when other water was frozen. He called the valley Deer House Plains, which soon became Deer Lodge.

That same fall a party of Canadian fur traders crossed the valley from north to south, headed for the Three Forks of the Missouri, but it was 10 years before Father DeSmet rolled into the valley in the first wheeled vehicles, headed north and west to Hell Gate and the Bitter Root valley.

Jacques Faquaere, free trader and squaw man, brought the valley's first cattle in 1850 from California, but not until 1865 did William Thomas build a ranch on Warm Springs Creek below what now is Anaconda. In partnership with Jim Purdy he ran 500 cattle and half that many horses in the upper valley.

French and Spanish herds dotted the valley until 1857, when the clash between Mormons and the Army in Utah drove ranchers from the Beaverhead into the Deer Lodge valley. The Army sent Lieutenant Ficklin to buy beef, and he returned with 300 cattle and 100 horses from Deer Lodge ranches.

Gold discoveries across the west side mountains on Gold

Creek in 1852 had stirred adventurers, and Captain John Mullan was approaching from Fort Benton with his military road down the Little Blackfoot. At the junction of that river with the Clark's Fork or Deer Lodge river, which flowed down the valley, Johnny Grant calculated would be a good place for same cabins. He finished these in 1859, a year before Mullan arrived, and on the site of the present town of Garrison.

Johnny Grant, whose father had become wealthy by trading for Hudson's Bay Company at Fort Hall and later with the Mormons and Montana Indians, was a landmark in the Deer Lodge valley. In fact, an ancient sign at a road fork on the Beaverhead once mentioned only two destinations, the Grasshopper diggins' at Bannack and Johnny Grant's, as worthy of frontier note.

First located at Grantsville, in the lower valley, he later moved upward to Cottonwood and built a two-story home, the showplace of Montana Territory. With his fair trading and his Indian wives he had little difficulty adding to the family fortune, and Grant was estimated in the early 60s to be worth from three to four hundred thousand dollars. Cottonwood later became the town of Deer Lodge.

The valley was becoming settled. More stock was pouring in, and Grant was ready to leave. He sold to Conrad Kohrs, the pioneer butcher who became a cattle king, and the town of Deer Lodge began to grow up around the Cottonwood Creek cabins. Mining in nearby gulches, water in ditches for mines and ranches, plus lumber mills, combined to make a city of Deer Lodge. Johnny Grant even put up a grist mill and brought in a thresher to be sure the mill had grain.

By 1869 the new town had a court house and the valley was proud of its 279 miles of ditches, worth nearly half a million dollars. Montana's 1865 territorial legislature established the Hell Gate and Deer Lodge Wagon Road through the valley, and by 1883 Union Pacific from the south and Northern Pacific from the east had joined at Garrison. The valley where the Indians camped on their way to the buffalo had grown up, and cattle and sheep were eating the grasses that had fed the hunting ponies.

Buffalo – At Home on the Range

Montana's senior citizens are at home to you anytime you care to call at their magnificent dwelling—the National Bison Range at Moiese, in the morning shadow of the Mission Mountains.

The American bison, or buffalo, as he is known to those who have viewed him on the nickel, traces his ancestry back at least as far as the ice age in Montana. Such established seniority entitled him to dignified manner and respect of his human neighbors. He has both, in large quantity.

Home for Montana's bison is the 18,540-acre preserve between highways 10A and 93 and northwest of the town of Ravalli on the Jocko River. It's an estate of mountain, forest, grass and water, with the Flathead River washing its western side. For all its wildness, the range is one of the easiest spots in Montana to visit, for there are highways all around it.

On Highway 10A, going westward, turn off to the north just before you reach Dixon, drive a few miles to the town of Moiese. This is headquarters for the range, and arrangements can be made here for trips through the preserve. For advance arrangements, the headquarters can be telephoned from St. Ignatius, north of Ravalli on Highway 93.

If you can arrange to arrive at about lunch time there is a good picnic ground on the banks of Mission Creek, and from your table you can watch the buffalo in an exhibition pasture close by. A few white-tailed deer likely will wander by your table, looking for a lettuce leaf, and there should be a few elk grazing with the buffalo. Antelope are in a nearby pasture.

There are mallards on Mission Creek and pheasants in the lower draws, and against the blue sky of afternoon there could be a golden eagle. Clark's nutcracker and Lewis's woodpecker, commemorating two illustrious names of the West, are as much at home here as the bison. So are the bighorn sheep, but they are harder to see.

Besides being a pleasant place to visit and to view the crests of Red Sleep Mountain and Red Man's Ridge against the white clouds and blue sky, the bison range is a sort of American shrine. On these grassy hills the bison as a live and real animal was jerked back from the brink of extinction.

To no one man can go the credit for saving the buffalo. Of an estimated 60 millions of bison on the plains of the West at the beginning of the 19th century, fewer than two dozen were left at its end. It was Walking Coyote, a Pend Oreille Indian hunting in the Milk River country of north-central Montana, in 1873, who brought back a few bison calves to the Flathead valley, probably a half dozen.

Walking Coyote very likely stopped at the Jacob Schmidt ranch near Haystack Butte on Sun River and just north of Lewis and Clark Pass with the calves on his way west. Schmidt was the grandfather of Ory Armstrong of Kalispell and a friend of Flathead Chief Michel Pablo, who, with Charles Allard, bought for $250 each the entire Coyote herd. In 1884 the herd totaled 13 animals.

Enjoying his new wealth, Walking Coyote shortly was found dead under a bridge in Missoula, but his good work outlived him. Kalispell's Conrad family had a hand in this buffalo herd, and soon the American Bison Society bought 34 buffalo from the Conrad estate. These 34 were augmented by seven donations—two each Montana and Texas and three from New Hampshire—of all places—to start the bison range herd.

Teddy Roosevelt in 1908 created the range, and $10,000 of American Bison Society money plus $40,000 federal funds went into the new range. Today a healthy herd of 300 to 500 bison needs annual trimming to keep it from growing out of house and home. The buffalo and other residents are not only an amazing sight—they are the raw material for dozens of research projects.

St. Ignatius Mission in the 1850's — Sohon

Chapel of the Snows

Eternal snows of the Mission Mountain crests backdropped the valley which Chief Alexander of the Kalispell Indians picked in the summer of 1854 for a new Jesuit mission, handy to his tribe as well as the Kutenai and the Flatheads.

The valley was home to the Flatheads, known by that name since this was the "flat" head of the river as contrasted to the deep canyons below. Father Adrian Hoeken, a grim Jesuit with a decade of life among the Kalispell already behind him, was to head the mission, known as St. Ignatius.

Soft gold was on the tamarack needles in the fall of 1854 when Father Hoeken arrived at the mission to find a "beautiful region" of woodland and prairie, lake and river "the whole crowned in the distance by the white summit of the mountains and sufficiently rich withal in fish and game." Father Hoeken was similarly delighted with the response of the Indians to his open air mass under a clear fall sky. He commented simply "the place was utterly uninhabited." Apparently Indians didn't count.

Within weeks the industrious Jesuits had seen to erection of several frame buildings, two houses, some shops and a chapel. The site was picked by Chief Alexander because all three of these northwestern Montana tribes gathered here regularly for a "sinielman" or rendezvous. There had been a St. Ignatius mission on the Pend Oreille river in Washington, but floods threatened it in favor of the new site near Flathead Lake.

Indians busily erected lodges around the site, and by Easter of 1855 Father Hoeken rejoiced in the thousand Indians of different tribes who gathered for mass at the little log chapel. He boasted of having bapitzed 150 adult Indians whom he thought docile and artless. He optimistically hoped they would give up gambling, the greatest vice of the Flatheads.

St. Ignatius was the second Catholic mission in what now is Montana, following on the heels of St. Mary's in the Bitter Root valley, a mission sought by the Flatheads. Captain John

Mullan, while cutting his wagon road across the Coeur d'Alene Mountains and the Bitter Roots, wintered at St. Mary's, and his help with St. Ignatius is shown in the praise given him by Father Hoeken, who invoked God to bless the Captain's generosity.

In his stern way Father Hoeken was fond of the Flatheads and admired them. He spoke of their brotherly qualities, of their family love, respect and obedience for their chiefs. He lauded their honesty, their abhorrence of theft and the fact that slander and lies were severely punished. Polite, jovial and helpful to each other, the Flatheads impressed Father Hoeken as they did Governor Isaac I. Stevens of Washington Territory.

The mission grew, and in 1864 four Sisters of Providence came to the mission by way of Frenchtown from Montreal and opened a boarding school for Indian girls. In 1884 Ursuline sisters, the first in Montana, joined them. By 1888 the Jesuits had a boarding school for boys at St. Ignatius and a branch school at Arlee in the Jocko valley across the hills.

A printing press at the Mission, probably the first in Montana west of the divide, printed a Salish-English dictionary, now a rare volume. A water-powered whipsaw cut lumber, and power from the same creek ground flour for the mission. Indian boys learned trades.

St. Ignatius is a history of churches. The first chapel of logs still stands across the highway from the Holy Family Hospital and is used as a shed. The second church, built of lumber from the whipsaw mill, came in 1864. In 1891 the present brick church was built, complete with the religious paintings of J. Carignano, a Coadjutor Brother of the Society of Jesus. It still stands, its doors open to all comers.

At Arlee the old branch church still looks out on the valley where the Flatheads were moved by treaty from their beloved Bitter Root.

Evergreen Pulpit

Montana's first religious services were conducted in a cathedral of pine trees by a Nez Perce Indian, who made up in fervence what he lacked in formal ecclesiastical training.

The day was September 20, 1835, and the place was a mountain park on West Creek in the upper Bitter Root valley southwest of Darby. For the Reverend Samuel Parker, who had come with Dr. Marcus Whitman to the Sweetwater country in Wyoming, it was a great day spiritually but a disappointment physically. He was ill and wanted desperately to reach the Idaho gold camps, the closest civilization in the West.

To see this place of religious beginning, drive Highway 93 south from Hamilton and turn west on the West Fork turnoff near Conner, just south of Darby. Just past the West Fork ranger station keep the left-hand road past Painted Rocks Lake and up to Alta. West Creek flows into the West Fork of the Bitter Root at Alta, and it was on West Creek that the Indian minister brought the word of God to his uninitiated flock under the trees.

But back to Parker, who had left Dr. Whitman at Sweetwater when that renowned missionary turned back to bring a larger force of followers to the West in 1836. Parker went on with a large band of Nez Perce. He was foreign to the West and to outdoor living, and he soon become ill and stayed that way. His journal, possibly due to his ill health, has gaps which make tracing his path somewhat difficult.

Idahoans claim Parker stayed in their state all the time on his journey from Pierre's Hole to Lewiston, Idaho, which began August 29, 1835.

There is, however, some pretty good evidence to the contrary. This points to the well-accepted fact that Parker's party crossed the divide by coming up Crandell Creek and following down Hughes Creek to the present Alta. This was very likely on September 18, 1835, and from here the party wound westward through the pines along an old Indian trail up West Creek.

Because Parker's health was getting worse and worse, he

wanted to make better time than was possible with his big Indian camp. Hence, he selected 10 Indians and set out ahead of the main party. Parker said of Charlie, the Indian leader, that he "prays each morning and evening with his men and asks a blessing whenever they eat."

On September 20, a bright September Sunday, Parker sat beneath a redolent pine and proudly wrote in his journal: "We continued in the same encampment. I expressed the wish to the chief that the day should be spent religiously, and that he should communicate to his men, as well as he was able, the scripture truths he had learned. This was faithfully done on his part, and he prayed with them with much apparent devotion. I was interested to see how readily they were disposed to obey to the extent of their knowledge. . . . After they had closed their worship, I sang a hymn and prayed and conversed with them."

Without much doubt this was not only the first Christian service in the state of Montana but the first observance of the Sabbath as well. It is a strange twist of ecclesiastical fortune that an Indian, not a white missionary, conducted the service, but Parker's journal indicates this was by design. Certainly, nothing could have been more appropriate with a tree trunk for an altar and pine boughs for a nave.

What tabs this location so accurately, for all the dispute about the exact area, is that on September 21, when the party was moving westward but still in Montana, an unusual rock formation was sigpted and noted in the journal. Castle Rock, the only such mountain in central Idaho or western Montana, was described so perfectly by Parker that there is little doubt of the site of the religious service the previous Sunday.

By the next Tuesday, September 22, Parker and his Indians were on upper Deer Creek in western Idaho, headed downriver in the Selway drainage toward the Idaho settlements and help for the ailing leader. Even so, he had satisfied his heart with the religious fervor of his Indian followers, although he probably cared less that he had witnessed Montana's first formal services than that he had brought Christianity to the wilderness—that the word of God had been spoken by the red man to his fellows.

Justice by Rope

Montana's first hanging was prompted, in the best old western style, by a horse theft. Equally fitting was that two strangers rode up from Elk City, Idaho, to offer the evidence that stretched the hemp.

The state's most famed exponents of justice by rope, the Vigilantes, had not even been thought of that hot August day in 1862 when Bill Arnett, B. F. Jermagin and C. W. Spillman rode their handsome mounts into American Fork, the old camp on Gold Creek, where the Stuarts mined Montana's first gold.

The three men were harder looking than their horses by a good bit when they arrived, and they drove before them three fresh mounts. Arnett wore a Navy revolver. Itching to take a few dollars away from the miners, the trio set up a monte bank of $200, which they promptly lost to James Stuart.

A day later two strangers rode in from Elk City, a mining camp on the Clearwater River in Idaho a good 200 miles by trail from American Fork, and came to Stuart's cabin. They were seeking stolen horses, and a description of the suspected thieves convinced Stuart that the unlucky gamblers were the wanted men.

The Elk City men, with the unlikely names of Bull and Fox, found Spillman in Worden's store, and Bull swung his 10-gauge shotgun on Spillman, who wisely surrendered. The Idaho pair found Arnett and Hermagin in a nearby saloon, trying their luck at gambling again.

Arnett was dealing when Bull stepped in and had just

111

picked up his pasteboards. Arnett swore, grabbed for his Navy revolver and fell over backwards as Bull's shotgun drove a charge of lead into his chest. Fox backed Jermagin into a corner, where he surrendered meekly.

Arnett was buried, still clutching his cards and Navy revolver, for the miners thought he might need them where he was going. Spillman and Jermagin faced trial for one of the West's most serious offenses.

Under August's golden sunshine Jermagin swore he had taken up with the others after the horses had been stolen, and Spillman backed up the statement. James Stuart testified that Jermagin arrived without a saddle and rode the horse with his own blankets over the animal's back. This got Jermagin off with a six-hour limit to get out of American. He had no trouble meeting the deadline.

Spillman had no defense, and hanging was his sentence. The frontier court gave him half an hour to make his last requests. He carefully composed a letter to his father, blaming his associates for his troubles and sad end, then gave the letter to James Stuart for dispatch. The letter never left Stuart's hands, for one of the wisest men in Montana's infancy felt it was kinder to keep from Spillman's father the last hours of his son.

At 2 o'clock the afternoon of August 26, 1862, the dead body of Spillman hung from the butcher's scaffold, and it was cut down to be buried beside Arnett. Thieves were together again in death. American Fork paid for its action of justice. For years it was marked on territorial maps as Hangtown.

To visit the scene of Montana first capital punishment drive Highway 10-12 east from Missoula or west from Helena. Cross the river on the Gold Creek turnoff bridge west of Garrison about nine miles. The town of Gold Creek, successor to American Fork, is just across the river from the turnoff.

It isn't hard today to visualize the hanging on the old scaffold and the burial of Arnett and Spillman along the creek bottom. Somewhere in the sod by the river both of them sleep.

Cruel Christmas – 1813

Not holiday happiness but bitter revenge was in the hearts of most of those who gathered for Christmas, 1813, "at the junction of a bold mountain torrent with the Flathead River."

History clouds the exact location of Saleesh House, but recent investigations show it on the O. J. Murray ranch about two miles east of Thompson Falls and on the banks of the Clark Fork River just below its junction with Thompson River, named after explorer David Thompson.

It was here a large band of Flathead Indians had gathered for the white man's holy day, bringing with them several Blackfeet captives taken in battle.

Factor at the North West Company post, recently purchased from John Jacob Astor's Pacific Fur Company, was James McMillan and his assistant was youthful Ross Cox, newly arrived from England by way of Cape Horn and Astoria, Oregon. It was Cox who recorded the horror of the day.

Supplies were newly arrived from Astoria, so Cox on Christmas eve distributed tea, coffee, rice, flour and 15 gallons of rum to his red guests. Hunters had brought in a bighorn sheep, and there was tobacco for all the pipes.

The stage was set for a holiday celebration, but the Flatheads had other ideas. They had picked this day to torture their Blackfeet prisoners, a common practice among Indians of that day.

Cox's eyewitness report of the torture of the first victim, a Blackfeet warrior, says the Indian was tied to a tree "after which they heated an old gun barrel red hot, with which they burned him on the legs, thighs, neck, cheeks and stomach. Then they commenced cutting the flesh from about the nails, which they pulled out, and next separated the fingers from the hand, joint by joint.

"During these cruelties, the captive never winced, and instead of suing for mercy, he added the most irritating reproaches. Said he: 'My heart is strong; you do not hurt me; you cannot hurt me; you are fools; you do not know how to torture; try it again; I do not feel any pain yet; we torture your relatives much better; because we make them cry out like little children. You are not brave; you have small hearts!' Addressing one Flathead, the captive said: 'It was by my arrow that you lost your eye.' Upon which the man darted at him and with a sharp knife scooped out one of the prisoner's eyes, at the same time cutting the bridge of his nose almost in two.

"This did not stop him; with his remaining eye he looked at another and said, 'I killed your brother and I scalped your fool of a father.' The warrior to whom he spoke instantly sprang at him and separated his scalp from his head. The raw skull, the bloody eyesocket and the multilated nose presented a horrible appearance, but by no means changed his note of defiance. Addressing the chief, the prisoner continued: 'It was I that made your wife a prisoner last fall—we put out her eyes, we tore out her tongue, we treated her like a dog.' The chief then seized his gun and a bullet passed through the brave fellow's heart and ended his suffering."

When the Flatheads led out a 15-year-old girl to be tortured next, Cox seethed in anger and, through an interpreter, ordered the torture stopped. The Flatheads objected that the Blackfeet treated Flathead prisoners the same way, but Cox insisted, through the interpreter, that, much as the traders valued Flathead friendship, they would leave the valley forever if the torture did not cease. He promised the Flatheads guns and ammunition to fight the Blackfeet and defend themselves.

The Flathead chief then promised to end the tortures, and Cox was convinced he kept the promise, at least for that winter. Later, Cox persuaded the chief to release his Blackfeet prisoners and paid for horses and meat to send them back to the plains.

This peaceful valley in winter has little to remind the traveler of this violence of 1813. The meadow lies quietly beneath the winter fog where the old post stood and the broad waters move on their way to the Pacific.

Lewis and Clark — Von Schmidt

Traveler's Rest

Up from the pleasant, grassy camping spot by the "bold, clear-running stream" led the trail that was to give Lewis and Clark their severest trials on their way to the Pacific.

When the captains arrived September 9, 1805, at this point in the Bitter Root valley where the Indian trail turned westward up the little creek, they wearily laid down their baggage, turned the horses to graze and Lewis wrote in his journal, "We called this creek Travellers' rest." It is now Lolo Creek, but the name has clung to the spot beside the river.

The legends of the Lolo trail above Travellers' Rest are even less strange than its long history, fading far away before Lewis and Clark first recorded its usefulness. How many centuries the Indians, the Nez Perce of the Walla Wallas or their predecessors, traveled the Lolo trail to hunt buffalo on the eastern slopes of the Rockies, no one can tell.

It was this trail that the Ootlashoots or Flatheads of the Bitter Root valley pointed out to Lewis and Clark as the way to the Pacific and warned them of its difficulties.

To follow the explorers, drive southward from Missoula on Highway 93, and at the town of Lolo you come to the old Travellers' Rest at the mouth of Lolo Creek. Turn west on Highway 9 to follow the old trail to the Montana-Idaho boundary.

The travelers stopped here twice, once on June 30, 1806, on their return from the Pacific, nearly a year after the first stop September 9 and 10, 1805. It was here the captains parted in 1806, Lewis to follow the Big Blackfoot River to Lewis and Clark Pass and the Missouri drainage, Clark to explore the Yellowstone.

On that bright September morning of 1805, with frost white on the valley floor, the explorers set out at 7 o'clock for the pass between the Bitter Root and the Clearwater or Kooskooskee. They soon found the way rough and rocky and the trails tangled with brush and fallen trees. It was only a taste of the hardship to come.

The explorers saw a sweat house used by the Indians on upper Lolo, and Lewis put his finger into a hot spring where he "could not bare it in a second." Soon afterward the party crossed Lolo Pass into the Glade Creek drainage and what now is Idaho.

Both elk and Indians used the hot springs on the Montana side, just across the meadow from Lolo Hot Springs near the top of the 5,100-foot pass is a rock used for years by the Indians to check the movements up and down the canyon trails. Old signal fires charred its summit. Another nearby rock bears a cross, apparently a marking made by man, but its origin is lost.

Many rocks all along the road resemble Indians' heads or the bodies and heads of animals, giving rise to scores of legends. Indians believed the spirits which were locked in these stones showed themselves when the shadows fell across the rocks and brought the facial features into relief.

Just above the town of Lolo is what is left of an old railroad grade, the remnants of a dream of a steel highway to the Pacific. In several places the old grade can be seen fairly easily on the south side of the highway.

It was through this pass in the summer of 1877 that Chief Joseph of the Nez Perce led his retreating warriors, women and children. Joseph cleverly avoided the trap of Fort Fizzle set at the mouth of Lolo Creek for the Indians and left the defenders from Missoula embarrassed.

Ranger Station No. 1

Under big yellow pines, Montana's state tree, the axes of Montana's first pair of forest rangers—and America's too—built the nation's first ranger station—a construction free of both red tape and government money, a novelty in this age.

The year was 1899 and the place was deep in the felds of Montana's geographical dewlap where the Bitter Root River heads hard against the Idaho border. The Bitter Root's West Fork flowed by the door of the little cabin where Hank Tuttle and Than Wilkerson ran the Bitter Root Forest Reserve, 300,000 plus acres of timber, grass, rock and water.

Today this same acreage is little more civilized than it was when this pair of rangers for the newly-created Forest Reserve borrowed a horse from a friendly neighbor and snaked in the logs to build their station. In two weeks they had a comfortable cabin, even though they had to squeeze out of their $50 monthly pay the money to buy door hardware, a few nails, windows and even a flag to fly from the end of the ridgepole. Without a flag the station wouldn't have been official.

Hank and Than had no uniforms and no mimeographed directives, but they did know the woods, and their job was largely to keep trespassers from stealing government timber. In 1891 Congress had authorized the president to set aside

117

"forest reservation," and in 1897 these were placed under the Land Office of the Department of Interior. This was the department that put Hank and Than to work for $50 a month.

Not until 1905 were the forest reserves consolidated and transferred to the Department of Agriculture. In 1907 they became national forests, and in 1909 Than's and Hank's domain became part of Region No. 1 of the forest service, with headquarters at Missoula.

But all of this was in the future. Lacking instructions and having only a few letterheads and envelopes as official word from their chief in Washington, D. C., the new rangers decided on some forest trail improvements, probably also the nation's first. For some reason known best to the rangers, Wilkerson and Tuttle, along with Frank Overturf and Al Osborne, also rangers from the upper Bitter Root, built 20 miles of new trail from Medicine Springs on the East Fork to the head of Hughes Creek.

The only tools these men had were their personal axes, and they lived under a wagon sheet in the woods. Wilkerson gained the title of "King of Rangers" and, since he kept a journal or diary of what took place, he appears to have been the leader. It was the custom to lay off all rangers during the winter except one man, and there is no record of who the fortunate fellow was.

The year after the cabin was built, prospectors began to work the country around the little ranger station. At the time the cabin was finished only P. B. Bennett, a prospector, shared the whole West Fork of the Bitter Root with the rangers.

By 1900 more cabins were built and soon the town of Alta surrounded the station. As more gold was discovered, the town increased to include a post office, store, the inevitable saloon and frontier hotel and even an assay office. Mining claims were patented all over the surrounding timbered mountains during the early 1900s, but soon the gold played out and left Alta a ghost town.

To visit the cabin and what is left of Alta, drive Highway 93 south from Missoula to the West Fork turnoff south of Darby and keep left past Painted Rocks Lake and soon you'll come to the old mining town where national forestry was born.

Silver Dollar Summit

For a silver dollar or less the traveler of the late 70s could pass the toll gate and wearily cross the Continental Divide where today's driver follows in high gear and cushioned comfort.

The same mountains which yielded gold and tempted journeyors threw a giant of rock and forest across their paths. In these early days of commerce between eastern and western Montana two names, MacDonald and Priest, stand out as conquering pioneers with a true sense of individual enterprise.

There was, of course, Captain John Mullan, who found the way for the soldiers' pay wagons and the surveyors who plotted the first rails across the northern rockies, but MacDonald and Priest pioneered the wagon passes.

R. Alexander MacDonald and Valentine Thomas Priest were out to open a way across the divide and make a profit in the process. They succeeded gallantly in the former and very satisfactorily in the latter. The blacktop of Highway 12 now follows approximately the old route of MacDonald pass, while Priest Pass road is gravel surfaced but easily travelable to the north of MacDonald.

To turn the clock back on both MacDonald and Priest, drive Highway 12 west of Helena about 10 miles, then turn right at a white board sign marked Priest Pass. It was across this decomposed granite flat on September 16, 1879, that workers for Priest carved with pick and shovel the beginnings of the toll road to the top.

Priest had come to the divide country with Jim Bridger in 1864, and in 15 years of prospecting and other work had determined to find a new way across the mountains. His crews, working fast against early snows and little noticing the golden aspens along Ten-Mile Creek, in less than eight weeks had punched through to the Little Blackfoot drainage a road good enough for buggies to travel.

Priest pointed out in a Helena Herald interview that his route was shorter than MacDonald's to the Deer Lodge valley and the grade "very light." By next June there were railroad surveyors across the ridge to the north from Priest's pass, looking for a way for the Utah Northern to reach the west slope from a Crow Creek valley approach near Townsend, then down the Missouri River to Helena and up Seven-Mile Creek.

These surveyors took note of Priest's work and commented on his "infinitely better approach" by way of Carbon Moor, just below the divide headwall. Also noted was that "freighters frequently travel the route over which the railroad line is surveyed (Mullan's Road) in preference to MacDonald's toll road."

Priest was acquainted with timber because he ran a sawmill in Colorado Gulch, a few miles down Ten-Mile Creek from the Priest turnoff, before going into the toll road business. He built for that time a fine, two-story house with a porch at the edge of the timber and overlooking Ten-Mile valley. His daughter Millie, in what appears to have been "casing the competition," was paid $10 a month to collect tolls for MacDonald at his nearby toll gate.

At the new Priest home, a community social center, daughters Millie and Alice Priest soon were collecting tolls from horsemen, freighters with multiple teams and heavy wagons, as well as ranchers driving cattle to new pastures in the Deer Lodge and Blackfoot valleys.

The Priest girls collected $1 for a horse and wagon, while wagon trains paid up to $3 to use the road. A saddle horse and rider was priced at 25 cents and a horse and buggy 75 cents. MacDonald charged similar prices. Loose stock went through at a dime a head, presumably including horses and riders, a sort of wholesale deal.

After you have driven across the summit of Priest Pass, drift down the western slope until you come to the lime plant and intersection with Highway 12. Turn east on Highway 12 and you're on your way up the western slope of MacDonald. At the summit, just as you break over into the valley, look at the right of the road, on the south, and you can see traces of the old MacDonald toll road. From here it runs below Highway 12, or south, all the way to the bottom.

About halfway down, the old road ran into swampy going, and corduroy of lodgepole pine was laid to keep the wagon wheels out of the mire. Maintenance of the corduroy was difficult. The old road wound around the timbered knobs, now on the south of Highway 12, then dropped into the creek bottom where Highway 12 makes the horseshoe curve at the bottom of the hill.

Where this little creek breaks out into the Ten-Mile valley, at the right of highway 12 by the point of rocks, is the old MacDonald toll gate and station. The station still stands, its logs covered with stucco but in daily use as a ranch house.

There was a big stable nearby for the horses used in changes on the daily stage. The stage left Helena on Park Avenue just across the street from the old Payne Hotel, which stood where the post office now stands. Light teams were used at the start, or 7 a.m. every day. By noon the stage had reached the MacDonald toll house, now a drive of 10 minutes from downtown Helena. Travelers lunched with the MacDonalds, the light teams were changed to heavier teams for the long haul over the divide.

At a stop called the Frenchwoman's on the west side, horses were changed again, dinner served, and the travelers overnighted. The next morning they took off for Deer Lodge for about a noon arrival. On the return trip the stage stopped overnight at MacDonald's and arrived in Helena at noon.

On the flat just below the old MacDonald toll house, where the Carson ranch now stands, Flathead Indians camped in the fall on their way to hunt buffalo in the upper Musselshell. At this house the late Mrs. E. M. Hall of Helena was born, and she recalls Indians asking for bread at the old toll house.

By 1883 Northern Pacific had laid its rails across the divide at the summit of Mullan and changed the whole freighting picture as well as blasted the hopes of any rail competitors in that field. In 1892 Priest sold his toll road to a man named Jamison, apparently getting out just in time.

For years Priest was the automobile road across the divide, but in the late 20s MacDonald came into its own again as the main highway. It still is, but minus the rough locks and dust that made it famous in the 70s.

121

Northeast — The Long Skyline

Nowhere across Montana does the sky arch so far to reach the plains as in that old cow country of the Missouri and Musselshell, goal of the trail herds from Texas and mother of the buffalo.

Its head is in the clouds of Glacier Park and the long, rough backbone of the Continental Divide north of Helena. Its feet are in the clay of the "breaks" of the Missouri River which winds along its full length below the Canadian border and above the low ridge between the Musselshell and the Yellowstone.

No country in Montana is bigger. It is big with ranches, and isolated mountain ranges, with strip-cropped wheat fields running their ribbons miles on end, with flat-topped buttes and rolling hills and badlands that drop away into contortions that end in the muddy waters of the Missouri.

Up this Missouri came the dugout boats of the Lewis and Clark expedition, followed by the boats of the fur traders bent on luring the Blackfeet to trade, and finally by the steamboats of the companies who hauled supplies up and furs and gold down. Theirs was the first real commerce of Montana, and they amassed riches or lost all they had, depending upon the fortunes of the journey and the shifting sandbars of the river bed.

There was gold here, too, in the Little Rockies between Milk River and the Missouri, and the gold lent color to one of the most colorful ranges of mountains in the old West. Montana's first commercial petroleum was produced in this country, at Cat Creek, and wells still pump oil and gas along the front range of the Rockies.

Mostly, however, this is grass and grain country. It is a country of antelope and deer, of mallards on potholes beside the road. To take in its broad sweep is impossible on one journey across it. It must be explored, and savored, and its people met and understood. Over the angle of an auto hood the plains unfold like an ocean of waves, giving easy rise to an illusion that no progress is being made at all, though the speedometer may stand at a figure that does justice to the powerful engine and straight roads.

So clear is that air that a mountain seems to hang on the horizon for miles before it is passed and headlights at night approach interminably. It is a country where storms gather like tiny patches in the broad sky and the winds whip them away, out into North Dakota and the Canadian prairies, leaving the plains alone in the sunlight.

Where They Got Their Names — Lakes and Streams

Missouri River—Although the Missouri heads at Three Forks in southwestern Montana, it becomes another river below Great Falls, the thundering drops that told Lewis and Clark they were on the right river, that they had not taken the wrong fork in their way west. This longest river in Montana drains more acreage in the state than in any other and flows across its eastern border to join the Yellowstone in North Dakota. Named for the Missouri Indians, who lived at its mouth, where it joins the Mississippi at St. Louis.

Big Muddy Creek—Flows out of northeastern Montana in a southerly direction to join the Missouri River above Culbertson. Captain Clark of Lewis and Clark named the creek Martha's, but didn't identify Martha. This was April 29, 1805, shortly after the expedition first stepped on what is now Montana soil. Near here the expedition saw its first grizzly bears and bighorn sheep.

Poplar River—Flows from the north into the Missouri River at Poplar. Named for the poplar trees on its banks. Lewis and Clark, passing here May 3, 1805, called it Porcupine River after those animals found at its mouth. The Porcupine now is a creek flowing into the Milk River from the north, entering at Nashua.

Milk River—Enters the Missouri from the northwest, flowing in just below Fort Peck. This river rises in Glacier Park, flows northward into Canada, then back into the United States and all across northern Montana, making the longest Montana tributary of the "big muddy." May 8, 1805, Meriwether Lewis named this river, commenting in his journal that its water "possesses a peculiar whiteness, being about the color of a cup of tea with the admixture of a tablespoon full of milk." The Milk River valley was one of the principal pioneer ways west, since it is level and straight, while the Missouri is crooked and winds through tortuous "breaks."

Fort Peck Lake—Largest reservoir in Montana. Named for old Fort Peck, a trading post whose location was just above Fort Peck Dam, about where the Big Dry runs into the lake. At full pool level, the lake is 175 miles long.

Musselshell River—Drains a large portion of central Montana, rising in the Castle and Crazy mountains, together with the Little Belts, flowing eastward to Melstone, then north to join the Missouri straight south of Malta at the U L bend of the Missouri, named after the old U L ranch here. Minnetares Indians gave it the name from the mussels found at its mouth, or in Minnetare "Mahtush-azhah." Lewis and Clark called it "a handsome, bold river" and named a nearby creek Blowing Fly Creek because of all the trouble they had with flies there May 20, 1805.

Judith River—Drains the Belt and Judith mountains and flows into the Missouri from the south slightly west and north of Lewistown. Its mouth was an important commercial and military point during the early days of Montana Territory, when goods came that far by steamboat on the Missouri and were reloaded onto wagons for freighting all over central Montana. Lewis and Clark named the river after Clark's girl friend, Julia or "Judy" Hancock of Fincastle, Virginia, whom Clark later married. She was only 13 years old when the expedition reached the Judith on May 29, 1805. Lewis first called the river Bighorn before yielding to Clark's choice, making three rivers in all that the party named "Bighorn."

Marias River—Called by the Minnetares the "River that scolds at all others," it flows almost due east after being formed by the junction of Cut Bank and Two Medicine creeks south of the town of Cut Bank. It enters the Missouri just below Loma. Captain Lewis named the river June 8, 1805, after his cousin, Maria Wood. For a time the explorers confused this river with the main stem of the Missouri, but they took the correct stream by turning south. The mouth of the

Marias was an important point in early fur trading, Indian fighting and steamboat history of Montana.

Teton River—Flows into the Marias just above where that stream enters the Missouri at Loma. Rises in the Teton-Sawtooth Range just west of Choteau. The river was named Tanzey by Lewis and Clark but later changed to Teton, French for woman's breast or nipple after the Teton peaks.

Sun River—Rises in the Continental Divide and Teton-Sawtooth ranges west of Augusta and flows directly east to join the Missouri at Great Falls. Named by the plains Indians as Medicine River for the mineral springs near its head. Sun and medicine were somewhat interchangeable words among the Indians with health in mind. At the mouth of Sun River Lewis and Clark found many buffalo and large, white grizzlzy bears, usually known as "silvertips." Blackfeet called it "Point-of-Rocks" river.

Smith River—Heads in the Belt Mountains around White Sulphur Springs, with some drainage from the Castles. Flows northward through a deep, limestone canyon to join the Missouri at Ulm. Lewis and Clark named the river July 15, 1805, after Secretary of the Navy Robert Smith in Jefferson's cabinet.

Dearborn River—Rises on the eastern slope of the Continental Divide in the Rogers and Lewis and Clark pass country, then flows southeast through a rugged canyon into the Missouri River just north of Craig. July 8, 1805, Lewis and Clark named the "handsome, bold and clear stream" for Jefferson's Secretary of War, Henry Dearborn. As a general, Dearborn ordered construction of Fort Dearborn, around which Chicago was built. This was in 1804.

Duck Lake—Lies a short distance southeast of the bridge over St. Mary River at the outlet of lower St. Mary Lake. Good trout fishing lake. Named by James Willard Schultz, famed old western writer and explorer, who camped on its shore in October, 1882. Schultz shot a dozen or more ducks that rose from the lake and commented "to my surprise and delight found that they were all canvasbacks and redheads and very fat from feeding upon the wild celery beds of the lake. I named the sheet of water Duck Lake."

Cut Bank Creek—Flows out of Cut Bank valley in Glacier Park and flows eastward to join Two Medicine Creek and form Marias River. Named by the Indians for its high, steep banks.

Belly River—Rises in the northeast corner of Glacier Park, flows through a wilderness valley and out into Alberta's Waterton River, eventually draining into Hudson's Bay. Probably named for the Gros Ventre or Great Belly Indians who lived in this area and eastward.

Lake Frances—Southwest of Valier. Noted for waterfowl hunting. Named for the daughter of a pioneer family, the Peter Valiers.

Tiber Reservoir—Named for the town of Tiber to the north on Highway 2. The town was named for the famed Italian river.

Gibson Reservoir—On Sun River west of Augusta. Named for Paris Gibson, founder of Great Falls.

Frenso Reservoir—West of Havre on Milk River. Named for the town of Fresno nearby.

Nelson and Bowdoin Reservoirs—North and east of Malta. Noted for ducks and geese.

Medicine Lake—South of Plentywood. Named by plains Indians and known for large numbers of waterfowl.

Where They Got Their Names — Mountains

Little Belt Mountains—From Monarch south and east to Judith Gap. A belt of light colored rock around Belt Butte at Belt town is responsible. Judith Gap, at their southwestern end, is a famous pass for Indians and pioneers into Judith Basin from the south. Joseph used it in his 1877 flight from the Army. Highest peak is Big Baldy, 9,191 feet.

Mountains of the Bear's Paw—South of Chinook. Indians who climbed to the summit of this medium-altitude range saw in the shape of the ridges sprawled out beneath them a huge bear's paw. In the foothills of these mountains to the east General Miles accepted surrender from Chief Joseph of the Nez Perce in the fall of 1877, forever ending the Indian wars in the United States.

Castle Mountains—Between White Sulphur Springs and

Martinsdale. Named for the many stone turrets or "castles" throughout the range. Old mining and ghost town country.

Highwood Mountains—East of Great Falls. Lower slopes are grassy and higher ones timbered, hence, "high woods."

Judith Mountains—Northeast of Lewistown. Named by Lewis and Clark after Clark's girl friend, Judy Hancock of Fincastle, Virginia.

Larb Hills—South of Saco to Fort Peck Lake. Probably named for the larb, which grows in these rugged, dry hills and was one time used for pioneer tobacco.

Moccasin Range—Northeast of Moccasin. One of the few ranges in Montana that honor the Indian. Old mines in these hills, too.

Piney Buttes—South of Fort Peck Lake. Rough buttes covered with gnarled yellow pine timber. In these buttes lived the new extinct Audubon sheep, a type of bighorn sheep, and the Sun bear, a small yellow-haired bear.

Little Rocky Mountains—These were the first "rocky" or "stony" mountains seen by Lewis and Clark on their way west. This is gold country, and the mountains hid not only yellow metal but many notorious outlaws, including the Kid Curry gang of train robbers.

Big Sheep and Little Sheep Ranges—South of Circle. In these rough hills lived the Audubon sheep.

Big Snowy and Little Snowy Ranges—South of Lewistown. Their bare slopes showed snow much plainer than the forested mountains on the other sides of the Judith Basin, hence "snowies" for distinction. Old Baldy at 8,600 feet, north of Harlowton, is the highest.

Sweet Grass Hills—North of Chester. Named for Sweet Grass Creek, which took its name from the "sweet" or nutritious grass on the surrounding ranges.

Teton-Sawtooth Range—From southwest of Bynum to west of Augusta. A spur of the Lewis range, it is separated from the Continental Divide by Sun or Medicine River. Teton means squaw's breast and Sawtooth refers to a sawtoothed mountain west of Augusta. This range includes Shishequaw, or Haystack Butte, the prominent landmark south of Augusta used as a checkpoint by Captain Lewis when he recrossed the divide from the Blackfoot River drainage into the Missouri over Lewis and Clark Pass in the summer of 1806.

Where They Got Their Names — Towns and Cities

Antelope—This one didn't take much thinking. Look around, even today, and you'll no doubt see a few antelope on the nearby hills and prairies.

Augusta—Augusta Hogan was the daughter of the first rancher in this upper Sun River valley country, where free grass was for the taking, and only the Indians stood in the way.

Browning—This Blackfeet Agency town honors oldtime Indian Commissioner Browning.

Box Elder—Trees of this name made shade for the early cowpunchers in this Bear Paw foothill town. The name came easy after that.

Buffalo—Pioneer rancher Edwards, greeting a Great Northern Railway surveyor who rode his horse up to the Edward's sheep band, told the surveyor he was on Buffalo Creek. The surveyor said, "There is going to be a town here, and its name will be Buffalo." He was right.

Cascade—Great Falls of the Missouri, 25 miles north, are the only cascades in this part of the river. Both county and town get their name from them.

Cat Creek—Cat Creek, which flows into the Musselshell River, gave its name to the town where the first commercial oil production in Montana began. Plentiful wild or bobcats no doubt gave the creek its name.

Chester—A homesick Great Northern Railway telegrapher named this county seat of Liberty County after Chester, Pennsylvania.

Chinook—Warm winds melt winter snows along the Milk River valley, the Chinook winds which blow all along the eastern slope of the Rockies on both sides of the Canadian border. The only other place in the world such winds are found is in the Alps of Europe.

Choteau—Fur-trader Pierre Chouteau left his mark several places in Montana, but this old town on the Teton River left one "u" out of his name. Chouteau founded the Missouri

129

River Fur Company, and his son, Pierre, Jr., headed the American Fur Company.

Circle—Nearby Circle ranch, named for its brand, gave its identification both to the town and thousands of cattle.

Coffee Creek—One look at nearby Coffee Creek in flood time gives away this name. Java with cream in it is a dead ringer.

Conrad—One of the town's founders was W. G. Conrad, a pioneer businessman and financier.

Culbertson—One of the most accomplished fur traders in western history gave his name to this town in historic fur-trading country. Alexander Culbertson was factor for the American Fur Company at Fort Union, just east of here at the junction of the Yellowstone and Missouri rivers. He established many other trading posts for his company, and he and his wife, the handsome Natawista Iksana, a Blackfeet princess, were hosts to John James Audubon on his Missouri River journey in 1843.

Cut Bank—This town takes its name from Cut Bank Creek, named for its sheer high banks, especially near the town. Blackfeet called it the "river that cuts into the white clay banks."

Devon—A town in Scotland gave this Montana prairie town its name.

Dodson—A Milk River fur trader and saloon keeper gave his name to this town.

Dupuyer—Audubon, in describing an 1843 buffalo butchering in Montana, says: "The shoulders are taken off, as well as the hindquarters, and the sides, covered by a thin portion of flesh, called the depouille, are taken out." The present name of the town is a corruption of this French word "depouille" and recalls the buffalo hunting days of the Blackfeet Indians on these grassy slopes.

Dunkirk—A wandering Scotsman is supposed to have named it after Dunquerque, France, one of the landing points during the World War II assaults on the French coast.

Fairfield—Center of an irrigation project whose green fields inspired the name.

Fairview—From all sides a pleasing view of the lower Yellowstone valley and its bluffs.

Fort Benton—The old fur or trading fort on the site of this town was named on Christmas night, 1850, when Alexander Culbertson, who had charge of the post, proposed a toast to Senator Thomas Hart Benton of Missouri. Senator Benton had saved the American Fur Company's license when it was charged with selling liquor to the Blackfeet Indians, and Culbertson was properly grateful.

Fort Peck—The fort which gave this town its name is now on the bottom of Fort Peck Lake, just above the dam. Built in 1867 by Abel Farwell, a veteran Indian-fighting frontiersman, the fort in 1871 became an Indian agency to serve the Lower Assiniboines and four Sioux tribes. It was abandoned in 1879. The fort was named for Colonel Campbell Peck of Troy, N. Y.

Fort Shaw—The namesake fort for this town still is in somewhat good repair. One of the forts built to guard against hostile Blackfeet, it was established in 1867 as Camp Reynolds. The fort was named for Colonel Robert G. Shaw of the 54th Massachusetts Volunteers, a Negro who was killed in Civil War action in 1863.

Fresno—In frontier words, a wide place in the road. It probably was, way back then.

Frazer—A grading crew foreman on the Great Northern Railway left his name here.

Galata—A suburb of Istanbul, Turkey, inspired this name, which probably also is associated with Galatia, where St. Paul preached. David McGinnis, a Great Northern Railway immigration agent, probably named the town.

Geraldine—Took the name of Geraldine Rockefeller, wife of a director of the Milwaukee Road.

Glasgow—Some pioneer Scotsman, lonesome for his Clydeside city of Glasgow, Scotland, was responsible for this one.

Grass Range—All around the town are grass ranges which have been used for nearly a hundred years to produce beef cattle. This is still a real ranch community.

Great Falls—From the great falls of the Missouri, just

northeast of the city. Lewis and Clark were the first white men to see these falls, on June 13, 1805. Lewis saw them first.

Harlem—After Haarlem, the Netherlands, but Montanans dropped the extra "a."

Havre—At first the name was Bull Hook Siding, after Bull Hook Creek, which enters the Milk River here. Later it was changed to Havre after France's LeHavre, birthplace of Simon Pepin and Gus DesCelles, whose homestead made a townsite for Havre.

Heart Butte—Plenty of Indians still live in this town, named after a heart-shaped butte or mountain in the nearby Rockies.

Highwood—After the nearby Highwood Mountains.

Hingham—A Plymouth County, Massachusetts, town sent its name west.

Hinsdale—After a New Hampshire town.

Hobson—One of two prospectors in the Belt Mountains west and south of here left his name on the town. Frank Hobson and J. S. Hobson found some gold in Yogo Gulch in the Belts, along with the first of the famed Yogo Gulch sapphires ever seen. Their reaction: "What in hell is a sapphire?"

Homestead—There are hundreds of places in Montana that could have this name, but this is it.

Inverness—Scotty Watson, a pioneer cowman, named it for his old home town in Scotland.

Jordan—This town offers three choices of namesakes— A. A. Jordan, its first postmaster; W. B. Jordan of Miles City, or the Jordan family of Dawson County.

Judith Gap—Captain William Clark left his girl friend's name on plenty of places in central Montana. The town sits in a gap between the Belt Mountains on the west and the Snowies on the east.

Kremlin—Russian settlers in this area named the town for the Russian name for fortress.

Kevin—After Thomas Kevin, superintendent of the Alberta Rail and Irrigation Company.

Landusky—One of the west's roughest characters, "Pike" Landusky, left his name on this old mining town in the Little

Rockies. Pike was killed in a saloon fight with Kid Curry on New Year's eve, 1894, and his grave is on Boot Hill, just outside town.

Malta—This colorful old cow town is a namesake of the island of Malta in the Mediterranean Sea, a British naval station made famous in World War II. There still is plenty of color around Malta.

Moccasin—From the nearby Moccasin Mountains.

Melstone—Probably named for Melvin E. Stone, an Associated Press official.

Musselshell—After the Musselshell River, which Lewis and Clark named for its Indian designation noting the mussels found at its mouth.

Neihart—One of the first prospectors in the mining country of the Belts was J. L. Neihart.

Oilmont—A combination of oil and Montana gave this early petroleum town its name.

Outlook—Probably because early residents wanted to promate the favorable outlook of this wheat-farming community.

Plentywood—Back in the open range days several cowpokes from the Diamond outfit nearby were trying to build a buffalo chip fire along a little creek. Rough old Dutch Henry finally growled: "If you'll go a couple of miles up this creek, you'll find plenty wood." They did, and the town got a name.

Portage—Commemorates the Lewis and Clark expedition's portage around the Great Falls of the Missouri in late June, 1805.

Roundup—Early cattle outfits maintained a big roundup corral here on the banks of the Musselshell.

Ryegate—Probably for the heavy cover of rye grass on the river bottom when white men first saw the area.

Saco—Probably after a Maine Indian tribe, but there's an outside chance that it took the first syllable from Sacajawea, Lewis and Clark's Indian woman interpreter.

Sandcoulee—A geographical landmark named this one, a nearby sandy coulee.

Scobey—Major C. R. A. Scobey, agent for the Fort Peck Indian reservation, left his name here.

Shawmut—Named by a resident from New England after

the site of Boston, Mass., which was called Shawmut by the Indians.

Shelby—After Peter O. Shelby, manager of the Montana Central Railway.

Sunburst—Probably because the rising sun "bursts" over the Sweet Grass hills to the east.

Sweetgrass—From the Sweet Grass hills to the south.

Valier—Probably after Peter Valier, an early resident.

Vaughn—After Robert Vaughn, lower Sun River valley pioneer.

Westby—The suffix "by" means town in Danish. Before the Soo Line Railroad built its tracks through this wheatland, Westby was the westernmost town in North Dakota. When it moved across the boundary, it kept the name.

Whitetail—White-tailed deer were plentiful in this area, and still are.

Winnett—After Walter J. Winnett, rancher and owner of the townsite.

Wolf Point—On the Missouri riverbank near here "wolfers" or wolf hunters stacked a huge pile of wolf carcasses one winter. Steamboat captains, passing this point in the spring, hung this name on the town.

Zortman—After Pete Zortman, pioneer prospector in the Little Rockies.

Zurich—Named after the city in Switzerland.

The Agony at Bird Tail Rock

The mission of St. Peter the Apostle was born in agony and died by fire, its stone walls as grim as the determination of the Jesuits who defied the government to save men's souls.

For all its struggles and disappointments, and they were as numerous as stars in a Montana sky, St. Peter's Mission was a crowning glory of Jesuit fervor. Indian agents, bureaucracy on the Potomac, congressional misunderstanding, tragedy and misfortune failed to bring it to its knees. Today it nestles serenely under the shadow of the Belt Mountains, a small white chapel against the rock-crowned hills.

All the turmoil of Blackfeet Indians against the white man marked the course which led to St. Peter's establishment. Its predecessors were a trio of log huts on the Teton River, a cluster of log cabins near what is now Fort Shaw on Sun River, an ill-fated cottonwood compound on the Missouri River six miles above what now is Great Falls and also called St. Peter's.

The last of these was established and named according to instructions which Giorda and Imoda and Brother de Koch received at Fort Benton in October of 1861, or at least they had such instruction when they arrived at the steamboat town. The Jesuits took possession of the riverside mission February 12, 1862, and Father Kuppens remarked on its "interior peace and consolation in poor surroundings."

The good father hadn't seen anything yet as far as poverty and trouble was concerned. Indians stole horses constantly, and each bedroom had a tiny corral by the window for all-night vigilance against the raiders. Father Giorda nearly drowned in the frozen Missouri and was rescued by a Blackfeet who kept a spare woman in his tent. Father Giorda ignored this immorality and was forever dedicated to the tribe for this act of kindness.

Giorda suffered further indignities at the hands of fate. On a visit to the Gros Ventre tribe to the north these Indians stole his horses and provisions, stripped him of all his clothes, including his red flannel shirt which was appropriated by a Gros Ventre. Stark naked in 40-below weather, Father Giorda finally was given a lousy garment. He made his way to Chief Bull Lodge's camp nearby, and this chief recovered his horse and clothes and gave him a buffalo robe but promptly kicked him out of camp.

With all these troubles, the Black Robes continued to baptize Blackfeet, but little help and pratically no encouragement came from Rome. Even less came from official Washington. There were some redeeming events. In August of 1864 Father Ravalli, kindly and brilliant, arrived from across the mountains, and Father Kuppens, a fiery youngster of 26, came up-river from St. Louis.

The young man was soon in trouble. A Blackfeet buck tried to steal his horse, and the Father whacked him across the face, a serious insult to an Indian. The Blackfeet promptly shot Father Kuppens in the calf of his right leg with an arrow, and it fell to Father Ravalli to take out the shaft and restore good relations.

Then came the bitter winter of 1865 and a gold stampede on Sun River. Many frozen miners came to the little mission and the government, as was its habit, went back on its word to furnish seeds, farm implements and tools to the Indians. The Blackfeet moved away to the north, back to the buffalo which were far more dependable than Uncle Sam.

This was the final blow to the little mission in the bend of the river. A conference on April 26, 1866, settled the issue— the mission would move to its last site, on a pleasant slope near Bird Tail Rock on the old Mullan Road, where today's visitor can see what is left of the old buildings. Giorda left the river mission with tears in his devoted eyes.

Even though construction at the site already was underway with lumber from Helena, the priests had heavy hearts, for the Jesuit Superior already had ordered the new mission abandoned until whites and Indians had ceased fighting. Father Giorda ordered his men to St. Ignatius mission in the Flathead valley and himself returned to Helena. Giorda called the next eight years of St. Peter's a "prolonged agony," for the Jesuits visited it carefully to hold legal title to the ground.

Father Giorda's health failed, and he was replaced temporarily by younger Father Grassi, who, in a year, ordered the mission closed. Its fate hung precariously, neither open nor closed, for two more years, then the government, which had taken over the old Missouri Bend mission, struck another blow. On December 5, 1870, President Grant turned the Blackfeet country over to the Methodists and barred both Black Robes and Missions from contact with these Indians.

But Father Giorda would not give up. He had assumed the office of superior in 1869 and in 1874 he sent his old comrade, Father Imoda, to reopen St. Peter's as a school for both white and Indian boys. On April 5 of that year Congress ordered the Blackfeet Reservation line moved 60 miles north of St. Peter's. It was a crushing blow, atop all the others.

Joining the staff at St. Peter's was Father Rappagliosi, a wealthy and refined Italian, whose health broke under the harshness of the frontier, and he died in February, 1878, the mystery of murder hanging over his death. Rome was shocked and enraged. Three priests came to take his place, including fiery Father Peter Prando, who promptly got into a bitter personal battle with Major John Young, Blackfeet Indian agent and a Methodist, over Prando's hard-pushed efforts to convert Blackfeet right on the reservation.

Father Cataldo, the new Superior for the Rocky Mountains, backed Prando by establishing the Birch Creek mission far north of St. Peter's, as an official Jesuit residence, further infuriating Young. Cataldo ordered St. Peter's expanded to offer schooling to more Blackfeet boys. The war was on, and Young was further needled when the mission hired rebellious Louis Riel as a teacher. Louis had a price on his head and in 1885 was executed in Canada for his rebellion. Pressure from Washington caused Father Prando to be moved to St. Ignatius.

Meanwhile, more boys enrolled at St. Peter's, and the Ursulines, led by Mother Amadeus Dunne, on October 30, 1884, set up a school for girls amid the same poverty that had plagued St. Peter's from the start. Thirty little Indian girls attended, and Catherine Drexel of Philadelphia, patron of the Holy Family mission which grew out of the Birch Creek mission, put up some money.

In 1891 the girls moved out of log cabins into a new stone

building, but poverty and privation moved with them. An Indian education contract with the government breathed some life into the operation, but a typical federal change of heart in 1895 cut off the funds and ordered all Indian children into government schools. The end was not far away.

The Ursulines faced a hard dilemma. They opened a boys' school to help with education of families which were hard to separate. The girls' school by now was flourishing. Then, in January of 1908 fire ripped through the old Jesuit buildings. Soon only the girls' school remained, for in 1912 a gift from John D. Ryan transferred everything else to Great Falls.

The end came on the night of November 16, 1918. Fire roared through old Mount Angela, the girls' school building, leaving the nuns, with 42 Indian girls at their side, standing in the snow, watching all their hopes mount to a cold sky on the searing flames.

Today the gaunt stones still stand, and a cold spring of water runs from a pipe near old Angela. Parishioners file into the little church on Sunday morning and watch the mule deer from the hills gather around the church windows, unmindful of the agony and the glory.

The "Kid's" Wolf Pack

Blackfeet Indians called the Little Rockies the Wolf Mountains, and the toughest pack of predators that ranged these mountains was led by a mustached gunman named Harvey Logan by his mother but remembered to everyone else as "Kid Curry."

The Curry gang did pretty well for a bunch of ranch boys, but they did it with guns and horses, not a rope and a branding iron. They might have turned out fairly well if old Hank, the big brother, hadn't died of pneumonia in the 1880s. He had bogged his horse in an alkali slough, got thoroughly soaked and exposed. There were no wonder drugs in those days, and the nearest doctor was at Fort Benton, over a hundred miles away by horseback.

Hank had ridden herd on the other boys, John, Loney and the "Kid" or Harvey. They had come from Pike County, Missouri and located on a ranch on Rock Creek, just south of Landusky. From this same Missouri county came a man who was to die at the hands of the Kid and make all the Curry boys outlaws. He was Pike Landusky, a big, rough man with a rougher temper who came to the Little Rockies in 1887 to discover gold in the gulch which later spawned the town which bore his name.

The Logan or Curry boys were wild when they drank, which was no distinction in the Missouri breaks. Soon after brother Hank died they came to Landusky for a spree and made a sheepherder "dance" by shooting at his feet. The herder, who had trailed cattle in from Texas and was no greenhorn, shot Johnny Curry in the arm, and the limb had to be amputated.

The Currys were mean as teased hornets, and they soon decided it was time to run a tough old bartender, known as Jew Jake, or Jake Harris, out of town. Jake had a leg shot off in an argument with the U. S. marshal at Great Falls and used a shotgun for a crutch. The Curry boys swooped in and poured lead on Jew Jake's saloon for two days, but Jake had a washtub full of shotgun shells under the bar and wasn't exactly defenseless.

After Jake sliced a little flesh off the boys with buckshot, they took off to the hills and let him alone. The sheepherder didn't fare so well. He disappeared, which wasn't uncommon in Landusky.

Itching for action, the Curry boys decided they wanted Jim Winter's ranch and weren't about to pay for it. They told him to move along so they could move in. But Winters, who was a determined man, as befitted a neighbor of the Curry boys, didn't budge an inch. Winters had bought the ranch from Dan Tressler, whose estranged wife assertedly was interested in Johnny Curry. She asked friend John to get the ranch back, and he took a direct approach.

When John rode up to the ranch to take possession, according to his professed intention, no one knows who shot first, but Curry dropped from his horse, riddled with lead. That settled the ranch issue for the time, but Winters didn't stick around long enough to enjoy it. One morning he stood on the ranch house porch, brushing his teeth, when a bullet from ambush cut him down. No one ever saw who pulled the trigger.

Now the ranch on the south slope of the Little Rockies belonged to Abe Gill, a half-brother of Winters and land commissioner for the area. Gill sold out to the Coburn Circle C ranch and reputedly received a check at the Coburn home ranch. He was never heard of again. His clothes, in a grip checked out on the northbound stage, arrived in Harlem. He had checked in at the Landusky Hotel, but his name was neatly clipped out of the register. Another Little Rocky mystery, still unsolved.

The "Kid" and his gang frolicked frequently in Landusky. In 1894 they put on several exhibitions, including shooting up the dance hall, splintering the piano and breaking the guitars over the musicians' heads. One of them rode his horse into a saloon. The floor broke, and horse and Curry ended up in the cellar. Such antics got them in bad with the law, and late that year John Buckley, sheriff of sprawling Chouteau County, arrested the "Kid" and brother Loney. He turned the pair over to Pike Landusky, who was town constable. Pike took them home, where the Currys claim he shackled and beat them, even spit in their faces. Thoroughly angered, an easy status for the "Kid," Harvey threatened to even things up with Landusky at the first chance.

There is some question about the date of this meeting of revenge. At any rate the Currys were fined for disturbing the peace, and some days later, maybe December 27 and maybe New Year's Eve, they were back in town. With them were Jim Thornhill, a hell-raising buddy from their Wyoming days at the Hole-in-the-Wall, and Harry Longabaugh, the "Sundance Kid," apparently a name picked up in Wyoming. The assumed name Curry probably came from Wyoming, too, because Flat Nose George Curry was an outstanding outlaw in those parts.

Picked out of all the rumor and speculation are these facts. The Currys were in Jew Jake's saloon. Landusky was walking down the street when a friend told him the stage was due in shortly. He turned around and walked into the saloon after telling Bill Kellerman, an orphan boy who lived with Landusky, to go on home as he, Landusky, had some business with the stage driver.

What happened next was bloody and quick. There are many conflicting stories. The two hot-tempered men fought, with younger Curry having some advantage over the aging Landusky. Pike was beaten to his knees. Whether he was shot in this position by the enraged "Kid" or whether he pulled a derringer from his coat at the last minute and was shot in a scuffle over the arm is an unanswered question. It was the end of Landusky's namesake, and it made the "Kid" a fugitive from there out, for Landusky officially was a law man and he had died in a fight with Harvey Logan.

For all its violence, the "Kid's" career up to this point had been a matter of local concern largely. His next step was to arouse the ire of persons with far-reaching influence. True, Jim Winters was shot while brushing his teeth, but nobody ever pinned that murder on anybody. It was 1901 when the Currys were back in business in Montana. Meanwhile there were some curious happenings, such as a Union Pacific train holdup in 1897 in Wyoming and a South Dakota bank robbery, and men from the famed Pinkerton detective agency were in the Little Rockies, checking clues and Currys. In 1899 Brother Loney bought a partnership in a saloon in Harlem, but he slipped away and disappeared, owing his partner $1,000. In February of 1900 Pinkerton detectives and Kansas City police surrounded the house of Loney Curry's aunt at Dodson, Kansas. Loney broke out and took off across a cornfield, but the law's bullets cut him down.

The day before Independence Day, 1901, was hot and dry in the Milk River valley. There were men and horses in the cottonwoods along the river at a good gravel crossing near Exeter, just east of Wagner. When the westbound Great Northern train took water at Malta, it carried away a couple of unpaid passengers. Tommy Jones, the engineer, and Fireman Mickey O'Neil were told at revolver-point to stop the train at the Exeter siding. Jones complained they had to get the train off the main line, so the "Kid" consented to backing it into the west siding.

The Currys moved quickly. They had dynamite ready for the express car, and the blasted safe spewed out bank notes and a sack of gold coins, which spilled over the car floor. "Kid Curry" picked up one of the 20-dollar gold pieces and handed it to the expressman, telling him to buy himself a drink. The money was stuffed into flour sacks, loaded on the horses and soon was across the Milk River and on its way to the Little Rockies, far south. There was $40,000, all worthless, for it was unsigned and good only for starting fires. Some of it showed up with forged signatures in hi-line poker games, but most of it just disappeared.

The closest thing to an eyewitness was a tough old rancher named Cunningham, who stopped by to check on why the Great Northern train stopped at such an odd place. The answer to his curiosity was a bullet which creased his horse's neck. The bronc unloaded him and took off into the hills.

Reputedly with the "Kid" were the "Sundance Kid," Butch Cassidy and a fellow named Deaf Charlie. Nobody knows for sure. The "Kid" was picked up in Tennessee and held for identification by Engineer Jones and Fireman O'Neil.

Before the two arrived "Kid Curry" made a loop with a wire, "lassooed" his Tennessee jailer and escaped. He never was officially seen again. There is talk of his having gone to South America, of having spent his old age in the State of

Washington, talk of his being still alive, but it's all talk—talk—talk. He was even positively identified as a corpse in Colorado.

Meanwhile, with Loney Curry in his grave, his ex-partner in the Harlem Saloon still had faith in Loney's honesty. One night a hand reached in the door at the ex-partner's ranch home near Harlem and handed him $1,000 in good money. When he tore open the door there was no one there.

Great Northern, outraged over the holdup, called Pinkerton, and again the detective agency was after the Currys. Charles Siringo, top Pinkerton detective, spent much time at Landusky, but never brought the "Kid" to trial. William Pinkerton paid the "Kid" the greatest tribute: "He is the only criminal I know of who does not have one single good point." But he did. He used to help the widow Coalchak brand her calves down in Squarehead Coulee near the Little Rockies. And he didn't steal any of them, either.

In a peaceful little white enclosure in Landusky lie the bones of Pike Landusky, the headboard silvered and worn. Jim Winters and Johnny Curry are buried on the Ben Phillips ranch south of the Little Rockies. Only God knows where the souls of "Kid Curry," Harry Longabaugh, Deaf Charlie and the rest, now repose.

There is one final fillip that the "Kid" would have loved. Glasgow sent a big posse after the gang robbed the Great Northern train, sent it right to the Gill and Winters ranch. But there were no outlaws there, so the 40 possemen followed their thirst to Landusky and got uproariously drunk. One saloon threw them out, but they went to another, where the owner joined them, and they all shot up the place in good style, until Guy Manning, the local J. P., got out warrants for the whole outfit. Then they sobered up and went back to Glasgow, tickled to death they hadn't run into the "Kid."

Castle of the Silver Kings

The glint of lead and silver rather than sheen of gold drew the miners to the little mountain range where lumps of granite stand out like castles against the black firs on the slopes.

It was in 1882 when old H. H. Barnes filed the first claims, and he followed with others in 1885 to start a new mining rush in the Castle mountains south and east of White Sulphur Springs. George Robinson, who left his name on a creek, and the Hensley Brothers, Lafe, Isaac, Joseph and John, filed claims in 1886. The mining fever was on, and the prospectors were looking everywhere for the silver ore, laced heavily with lead. To the hopeful, this was another Leadville, Colorado, and they planned their town carefully, with well laid-out streets.

They picked a sloping mountain meadow on Castle Creek, just across the ridge from Hensley Creek. April 20, 1887, the town was in business, with a post office, 1,600 nearby claims and 2,000 noisy residents. For the children there was a $5,000 school. For others there was a house of ill fame, still standing on a sage-covered hillside.

An enterprising townsite company sold $100,000 in lots, and A. M. Holter of Helena fame started the Castle Water and Power Company to provide for the needs of an anticipated 50,000 residents. The earliest ore was freighted by horse and wagon to Livingston and shipped to Aurora, Illinois. The Hensleys built a smelter for their Cumberland mine, which has continued operation off and on for years, long after the old smelter fell into decay. This solved part of the transport problem, but coke still had to be hauled in from Livingston, 100 rough miles by wagon.

Still farther up the gulch was the Yellowstone mine, which has had several revivals. Just south of Castle and over a low ridge the Yellowstone's owners built another smelter, whose rock chimney or stack and some of the base still remains. As late as 1924 the slag pile from this smelter was hauled away and sold, and local residents claim yields as high as $10,000 a load came from this discarded material. Chunks of the slag still at the smelter site glow with metallic promise, as if to revive the old fever on Allebaugh Creek.

In the late 80s and early 90s prospectors swarmed all over the Castle gulches, probing into every hillside and pocket. Today's deer and elk hunters wander through the lodgepoles and firs, suddenly coming upon a log cabin with sagging roof and possibly the broken poles of an old horse corral or spring box and watering trough. Nearby will be the prospect holes, all that is left of monumental hopes and millions of man hours.

The favored few, however, did well. The Hensley smelter turned out over a half million dollars in metal in 10 months. Then in 1892 Congress abandoned silver, and the price of ore plummeted. Almost in a day the big camp closed its doors. The five-year existence of Castle was a lively one, as it was in nearby mining circles of Robinson and Smith's Camp.

The real need of the community was for a railroad. It didn't arrive until 1898, when the traffic was composed of the huge ore dumps, which gave badly needed business to the old Montana Railroad or "Jawbone" as it was affectionately called. This terminated about two miles below town, in the middle of an aspen-ringed meadow now grazed by Rancher Paul Grande's Herefords.

As mining camps go, Castle was relatively pious. Despite its seven bistros which sold both liquor and feminine affections, the tone of the town was fairly high. Calamity Jane sent her daughter to the local school with other children. Calamity was one of the town's enterprising restaurant owners. Dr. J. P. Rhoads, former mayor of Sheridan, Wyoming, came to Castle to open a store and ply his medical profession, which consisted largely of patching up injured miners and victims of saloon battles.

There was a sawmill and a slaughterhouse, the latter just across a ridge on Slaughterhouse Creek above what now is A. C. Grande's ranch. A dairy and bakery provided other everyday needs.

Castle had its laughs, too. One of the ladies of the evening found it necessary to corner an embarrassed group of males at the post office to find out who had run off with her false dentures the previous night. The local newspaper solemnly reported that a mouse in one of the houses of entertainment had caused considerable consternation during business hours one night.

Today Castle lies silent in the sun, its buildings silvered with age and surrounded by pointed firs and gray sagebrush. Its only excitement comes with fall hunters and with visitors who want to revive the silver glitter of a gone day.

To reach old Castle drive Highway 294 east from its junction with Highway 89 north of Ringling or west from Martinsdale. Turn off at Lennep and follow the signs.

The Trapper's Bride — Alfred Jacob Miller

Rising Wolf's Meadow

Hugh Monroe was the first white man ever to see the shimmering beauty of the front wall of what now is Glacier National Park, and he came, not as a tourist, but as an interpreter for the Hudson's Bay Company among the Pikuni Indians, the Blackfeet of the plains.

His was not an easy assignment, for white men were not too welcome among the Pikuni. Scarcely a decade had passed since Captain Meriwether Lewis had killed a Pikuni on the Marias River, east of the park, making Americans unwelcome in Blackfeet country for many years. However, Monroe worked for a British company, and the British were acceptable as traders among the Blackfeet.

Even Monroe, the son of a British army captain and a French noblewoman, hardly realized he would be forever lost to Glacier's allure and to the wild freedom of Pikuni life when, in the summer of 1815, he arrived from Montreal at Mountain Fort on the north fork of the Saskatchewan River. Monroe immediately was told by the fort's factor to leave with a Blackfeet party preparing to head southward to hunt and trap in Montana.

The big party, led by a head chief and including 17 wives, two lodges and huge string of horses, followed the ancient Foot-of-the-Rockies Indian trail from the Saskatchewan headwaters in Canada to the head of the Missouri River at its three forks or branches in Montana. Monroe was the first white man ever to travel this trail.

Each day's travel was leisurely, and at Sun River, or Point of Rocks River as the Pikuni called it, 100 miles south of Glacier Park, the Indians and Monroe camped for the winter to hunt and trap. In the spring they continued south, crossing the Missouri or Big River and by summer reached the Yellowstone or Elk River, where they again settled down to hunt. That summer in the Yellowstone valley Monroe fought shoulder to shoulder with the Pikuni against the Crows and earned the proud name of Rising Wolf, which stayed with him until death. By winter the Pikuni were back on the Missouri again, to camp at the mouth of the Marias. When the Indians rode back in the spring to Mountain Fort, their ponies were heavy with furs and hides for the trade.

The year was 1817, and Monroe now was as much an Indian as though he had been born in a lodge on the plains. He had married an attractive Pikuni girl, daughter of a chief. He spoke the language smoothly, and his bravery in battle had given him high prestige with the red men.

So well had he done his work that the factor at Mountain Fort ordered him to stay with the Pikuni and bring them each year to the fort to trade. He was delighted, and commented later that every day he spent roaming the plains east of the front range of the Rockies with his people was one of great enjoyment.

Monroe became a member of the Seizer band of the All Friends Society of the Pikuni, which kept order in the camp and acted as game wardens for the tribe. He rode into battle with the Pikuni, and once in the Salt Lake basin he saved the life of his friend Jim Bridger when that trapper-explorer was traveling with a band of Snake Indians. Snakes were deadly enemies of the Pikuni, and only by great persuasion did

Monroe convince the brother Blackfeet they should not shoot. They held their fire, and the two war bands even smoked together!

As his permanent camp Rising Wolf picked a beautiful meadow along Foot-of-the-Rockies trail, the flat just below Lower St. Mary Lake. Here in 1846 Father Lacombe and Monroe erected a rude cross, blessed it with prayer and named the lakes for the Saint. Here lived Monroe's wife, three sons and three daughters. He chose the valley because it swarmed with big game—bighorn sheep, goats, elk, deer and best of all—many moose. The lakes were full of Mackinaw, bulltrout and cutthroat or natives. Waterfowl blackened the lakes in the hills nearby.

Monroe's enterprising family killed wolves here by building a pyramid of logs with a hollow center. Attracted by a bait in the center, wolves would climb the outside, jump through the hole in the top and be unable to get out again. In the morning they could be easily dispatched with bow and arrow, saving costly bullet and powder for the flintlocks. A wolf pelt was worth $5 at the fort.

Wandering Assiniboine, Crow and even Yanktonais Indian war parties often attacked the camp when Monroe was gone. Once an Assiniboine war party sneaked up in early morning through the grass, but a bullet from alert daughter Lizzie Monroe's flintlock killed a warrior, and the fight was on. It was an all-day affair, but by night the entrenched Monroes had killed five Assiniboine and forced a retreat. By moonlight the attackers were back, but the Monroe aim was as good as ever and two more Assiniboine lay in the grass around the cabin before they left, this time for good. Even so, it was several days before the family ventured from the protecting walls.

This cabin was home to Rising Wolf and his family until sons and daughters had made homes of their own. The aging aristocrat lived with various members of the family until, in 1896, he followed many other Pikunis over the big divide and was buried on Two Medicine River near the buffalo bluffs where Highway 89 crosses that stream.

The Mill on the Mountain

North of Lewistown, against a blue shoulder of the Judith Range is all that is left of what no doubt is Montana's best-preserved cyanide gold mill.

The road to Maiden is a pleasant one, out of Lewistown on Highway 19's blacktop to the first wide valley to the north, then right on gravel and up Maiden Canyon between grain fields and ranches. The timbered mountains press in constantly.

Within a few miles you come to old Maiden, which roared in the lusty splendor of the 80s, then died and sank back to the earth from where it dug its wealth of gold. Today, white-faced cattle graze on the meadows and mountain slopes where men fought and drank and scrambled for nuggets.

At the forks of the road you will see all that is left of what was once a town that cast more votes than the city of Lewistown. In 1885 the town had a brewery, a small lead smelter and hundreds of soldiers from Fort Maginnis, just across the mountain, who came in every Saturday night to consume the production of the brewery.

It was 1880 when the first miners rushed into the Maiden country, which rightly is Alpine Gulch. The gulch drains into Warm Springs Creek just below the old town. Skookum Joe reputedly discovered gold in Alpine Gulch and quietly invited some friends of his from the Yellowstone to share his find. Since it was winter, all camped near the site of Fort Maginnis and waited for green grass to stake their claims.

So, the best of the old campfire stories in the Spring Creek country go, a man by the name of Maden tried to file a claim in Alpine, but nothing was left, so he went further up the creek and nailed a sign on a tree "Camp Maden, anybody welcome." Later the name acquired an additional "I."

Just above the old town of Maiden, which sits at the foot of the mountain, is the well-preserved old Maginnis mine, and the cyanide mill. Maginnis produced $1,500,000 for its owners, thanks largely to the wisdom of its engineer, Will Young.

Some of the porphyry on the mountainside above the Maginnis ran $1,100 a ton. Cyanide tanks, which still can be seen at the mill near the mine and just up the gulch from Maiden, were installed by Harry Kendall.

Kendall reputedly offered to sell the mine for half a million, then changed his mind and asked $400,000 plus a retained 10 per cent interest in the mine. This was one of the most fortunate decisions ever made. In later years the mine paid dividends of more than $6,400,000.

Today the old mill sits in dignified grandeur on the slopes of the Judiths. Still in place are the sound redwood timbers of the cyanide tanks, twisted and relaxed, but still sound. Inside the floors and stairs have rotted, but the furnaces still stand with closed doors and bricks in place. Mammoth machinery, hauled by horse team and wagon from Missouri River landings to the north, stands as it did in the 80s. The same wagons that brought in the machinery hauled out wool from the Judith Basin ranches.

There are huge laminated wood wheels, their wood silvered with age but hard and firm in the dry air of many years. Above the mill are the old offices and living quarters. A stove still stands in the corner, and a button shoe lies on the floor.

The only gold left is in the yellow of the aspens on the hills, but the air is crisp and the waters of Warm Springs Creek tinkle in the gulch as they have for centuries, surviving both men and their gold.

THE LAST OF THE BUFFALO

Last of the Buffalo

Montana's last frontier of Indian and buffalo faded in the upper Musselshell valley before a flood of rangy cattle that brought fully as much color to the Treasure State.

Grass still is king in the Musselshell country, but alfalfa and white-faced cows have replaced hump-backed brown bulls along the willow- and cottonwood-banked stream. The Musselshell trickles out through the aspens and lodgepoles in three mountain masses, the tangled Crazies on the south, the mineral-rich Castles in the middle and the blue Big Belts on the north.

Through the passes between, commerce flowed from the old Missouri River ports to the gold camps of southwestern Montana, and wagon ruts still scar the hills along the Musselshell valley.

Later, the highways and the Milwaukee railroad sought out these same passes, still hurrying the commerce across the mountains. But back to the old Musselshell, the river the Indians named for the tiny freshwater mussels in its waters, an unusual thing in an unusual land.

Camp Baker, or later, Fort Logan, in the White Sulphur Springs country brought the first cattle to the Smith River valley, and on the eastern side of the low passes lay the rich grasses of the Musselshell, only a few miles away. This was buffalo country, all across the Musselshell headwater and north into the Judith Basin.

By 1875 there were 10,000 head of cattle in the Musselshell. This was the beginning of the great cattle business in the valley, and it brought a fast change of life for the wolfers, Indian traders, trappers and wood cutters who had brawled and lusted their rowdy way into the valley since the 60s.

Ranching may have altered the economy of the valley, but changed the morals but little. Central Montana was the last stand of the buffalo and of the Indian trading post. Even Chief Joseph of the Nez Perce, on his way to defeat at Snake Creek south of Chinook, found a thriving trading post doing business with the red men just north of the Musselshell.

So, when trading, trapping and wolfing gave way to rope and saddle, the displaced residents took up horse stealing and cattle rustling to maintain their income. By the early 80s the sporadic horse thievery and rustling had turned into an organized business.

The location was perfect. Herds were large and fat, and only a day or so away to the north were the tangled badlands of the Missouri, perfect both for hiding stolen livestock and fighting a tough, rear guard action. There was grass in the badlands, and north of the river was Canada and immunity from the law if it could be reached.

There was a good return commerce, too, for stolen Canadian horses found a ready market south of the border. With a tight organization, the rustlers and thieves kept guards day and night and were bold and arrogant. The law seemed powerless to stop them.

In 1884 the cattlemen themselves stepped in and took over the enforcement job. Organizing secretly, the cowmen decided to wipe out the rustlers and with Granville Stuart of the D-S outfit as ringleader, the ranchers cornered the rustlers in the cottonwoods at the mouth of the Musselshell. Those who survived the gunfire swung from cottonwood limbs.

From there the regular enforcement officers took over. There was peace on the Musselshell. To see these historic ranges, drive Highway 12 from Roundup to White Sulphur Springs. If you wish, select Highway 294 west of Martinsdale instead, going around the south side of the Castles instead of the north.

Four years after the rustlers were wiped out, an unknown rifleman killed a wild buffalo bull between the Musselshell and Billings, probably the last wild buffalo killed in Montana and possibly in the West. The buffalo frontier was gone, and cattle had taken over the grass on the Musselshell hills.

The Captain's Wagons

His mission was to join the forts at the heads of navigation on the Missouri and Columbia rivers, thus spanning the continent for the military, and John Mullan, Captain, U. S. A., set at it with a strong will.

This bright, new graduate of West Point, seeing the mountains for the first time, saw also a monumental task of blasting, digging and clearing to get the military wagons from Fort Benton, Montana, to Fort Walla Walla, Washington. The finest monument to his genius and ability is the fact that nearly every mile of his wagon road now is occupied or paralleled by transcontinental railroad or highway.

It is easy today for the driver to follow the road which the young officer built across the prairies and through the mountains, and even a few of the old cuts and fills remain visible. Mullan explored the route from east to west, then reversed his directions in the construction, wasting no time in carrying out his assignment.

To follow Captain John more than a century later, it's best to start at riverbank in the town of Fort Benton, where the steamboats in the 1850s tied up after their long journey from St. Louis. From there climb the hills and roll across the wheatlands on highway 87 southbound to Great Falls. Mullan's wagons crossed these same hills through deep buffalo range.

From Great Falls turn westward on Highway 20. Mullan ran his road along the hills to the north of the valley, but you can cross his trail again at the town of Sun River, then known as Blackfoot Agency. To keep strictly to the Mullan road, turn south at Simms on a dirt road to St. Peter's mission, then follow the old Helena-Great Falls highway across Sullivan Hill and back to blacktop at Highway 287 just north of the Dearborn River.

Watch closely along the hills on both sides of the road and you can see tracings of the old Mullan Road, winding down into the Dearborn crossing at the present bridge for Highway 287, then along the highway to just north of the town of Wolf Creek. The highway follows the canyon of Prickley Pear Creek, but the Mullan Road stayed on top of the foothills to the west, dropping back into the valley again at Sieben. From Sieben, at the mouth of the canyon, turn off blacktop and stay with the creek, traveling a gravel road through Silver City, which lies close to the Mullan route.

From Silver City, cross the blacktop and take road heading northwest toward the mountains and Mullan Pass. Follow this dirt road until it turns sharply right at a junction on Seven-Mile Creek. Follow this road, which parallels the Northern Pacific Railway's main line, again watching for signs of the old wagon road. You will follow it all the way to the summit of the Continental Divide and down the other side. Mullan's road topped the divide at 5,800 feet, and he sighted the Columbia drainage for the first time in the waters of Dog Creek, which you follow down to Elliston and blacktop again on Highway 12, this time for good.

It was in 1853-54 that Captain Mullan first saw this country of the Little Blackfoot River at the head of the Columbia drainage. He followed the river in his exploration and in building the road five years later. Down the Little Blackfoot valley and the Clark Fork valley to Missoula the Mullan Road runs largely down the south bank, paralleling Highways 10-12 and 90 into Missoula. Across the Big Blackfoot River at Milltown, just east of Missoula, Mullan built a big timber bridge for his road.

West of Missoula Highway 10-90 follows the Mullan Road generally, but a turnoff at the west end of Missoula follows it exactly out to Frenchtown. Just south of Missoula, near Stevensville, Mullan wintered in 1853-54 and in 1854 explored south to Fort Hall in Idaho and north to Flathead Lake, seeking a good way over the Bitter Root Mountains, which hindered Lewis and Clark on their way west 50 years before.

The route he finally chose, following the St. Regis River, is the one followed today by Highway 10-90, through Superior and St. Regis, then over Lookout Pass, then called Sohon by Mullan in honor of a guide. Westward from here stay on 90 to Spokane, although it crosses Coeur d'Alene Lake instead of splitting and going north and south as did the Mullan Road.

South of the Spokane plain the branches joined and headed south over the Palouse to a crossing of the Snake, then into Fort Walla Walla.

Montana remained long in Mullan's memory. He and his party huddled in log huts the winter of 1859 near what is now DeBorgia. He had wanted to winter again in the wide valley of the Bitter Root where he knew the winters were milder, but the snows and 40-below weather caught him in the St. Regis valley. By spring much of his stock had frozen and starved, and some of his men had lost limbs to the biting cold of the mountains.

What began as a military wagon road was used far more by pioneers and settlers, who wore the ruts deep. At its completion Mullan wrote: "Thus ended my work—costing seven years of close and arduous attention, exploring and opening a road of 624 miles from the Columbia to the Missouri River at a cost of $230,000." It was a princely sum in those days, but would hardly build a good bridge a century later.

Carroll's Cutoff

Long forgotten is a town deep in the "breaks" of the Missouri River 75 miles northeast of Lewistown, a town that once was the greatest commercial port for the territory of Montana, the principal link in trade with the east.

The name of Carroll town is unfamiliar today, as unfamiliar as the Carroll road that linked the riverbank town with Helena, but at birth it was the center of attention in Montana Territory. For the first time the territory had turned north, away from the wagon road south to Corinne, Utah, and the railhead of Union Pacific.

From Helena to Corinne was 400 weary miles, but to Carroll the distance was only 200 miles by bull-train from the burgeoning mining town on Last Chance Gulch, a saving of 15 days in freight delivery. By 1874 Northern Pacific rails had reached Bismarck, N. D., and steamers could pick up passengers and freight there for the long run up the Missouri River to Carroll on the south bank of the Big Muddy 30 miles upriver from the mouth of the Musselshell.

March 16, 1874, the first wagons rolled out of Helena bound for Carroll and the new steamboat docks. The wagons belonged to the Diamond R Transportation Company, a firm headed by Colonel C. A. Broadwater, Mathew Carroll, George Steele and E. G. Maclay. The pace was 12 to 13 miles a day, with loaded wagons, and some of the wagon trains were two to three miles long.

To follow the Carroll road, cross the Helena valley by Highway 12 to Clasoil, then 284 to Canyon Ferry, where the wagon drivers saw the Missouri River for the last time until they topped the ridge south of Carroll. From Canyon Ferry the old road can be followed up White's Gulch, a passable dirt road over the Big Belt Mountains and down the eastern slope to old Fort Logan, north of White Sulphur Springs.

From here the going is, and was, better. The train turned southward up Smith River, now a good gravel road, and eastward through White Sulphur Springs onto Highway 12 and then to the Harlowton junction with Highway 19. The Carroll road swung northeastward from White Sulphur to Judith Gap along the foothills of the Belt Mountains to the northwest of the highway driver.

From Judith Gap highway and Carroll road travel much the same country by Highway 19 into Lewistown. The Carroll road again parallels Highway 19 north from Lewistown, skirting the Judith mountains, into Roy. It is only about 30 miles northeast from here to the old town, but the roads are dirt, and determined explorers should ask locally before venturing off 19's blacktop.

The remains of old Carroll are only a few "silvered" log buildings in use by local ranchers, perched on a flat below pine-covered hills, about on the Fergus-Petroleum county line. This is the flat that saw high activity in the middle 70's, when dry goods for Helena, hardware for the gold miners and soldiers for Forts Shaw and Ellis vied for space behind the teams.

A telegraph line was built in from the northeast, and stumps of the poles still can be seen in the hills. Soldiers were assigned to guard the road because it gave easy access to country where the Sioux were raiding horses and cattle. Two companies were stationed at Fort Lewis, near Lewistown.

On July 1, 1875, Captain William Ludlow, chief engineer for the department of Dakota, was ordered to survey the route from Carroll to Camp Baker, later Fort Logan. If he had time he was to make a reconnaisance in Yellowstone Park, then only three years old and under army jurisdiction.

Captain Ludlow, from his base at Carroll, took a zoologist, geologist and botanist, and made a full scale report on the Judith Basin country as well as other areas along the Carroll road. He noted bighorn sheep in the Judith mountains "so wary they are not often seen" and "great numbers of buffalo" south of Judith Gap.

Wreck of the Chippewa — O. C. Seltzer

Clagett's Landing

Ghosts of Indians and Missouri River steamboats await the traveler who follows the Judith River north to the crumbling banks of the Missouri under the ancient cottonwoods and the ruins of old Fort Clagett. Today's adventure was yesterday's vital commerce into Montana Territory and the raw vigor of a new country stretching its uncultured muscles. The road that leads to it is made of the same clay that bogged the hoofs of red warriors' horses and the wheels of freight wagons.

From Lewistown there is a good summer road to the mouth of the Judith and one of the oldest, if not the oldest, ferries in continuous operation in the state. Drive Highway 19 north out of Lewistown to Hilger, then north on Highway 236 to Winifred. From here it is only 26 miles on dirt and gravel to the fort and the ferry. Across the river the road continues to Big Sandy.

Here was one of the great commercial and military centers of Montana, even though most of the evidence has long since crumbled into the sagebrush and sand of the river banks. One great reminder is left, the old Power-Norris freight warehouse, a huge stone building, professionally mortared and still in excellent condition after nearly a century.

It stands west of the ferry landing on the south shore and serves as a barn, but the present owners are glad to let you have a look. There is an old and well-authenticated story that one of the Norris children, a boy of seven, lies buried beneath a corner of the building. He was killed when hit in the head by a singletree on one of the freight wagons loading at the docks.

Into their warehouse, with its carefully-hewn beams of cottonwood, went thousands of dollars in merchandise, unloaded from a steamer which docked at the door. The old offices at the front of the warehouse can still be visualized. The river has long since changed its main channel from directly in front of the warehouse to the other side of the island.

Just a little way up the Missouri, on a sagebrush-covered flat between the Judith and Missouri rivers, is the site of Fort Glagett, one of the least known and most interesting forts on the river. Here were stationed cavalry to guard the landings from the hostile Sioux, who resented every move to settle their country.

The Indians would wait on the hills to the north of the river for a steamboat to arrive and take advantage of the confusion and the new supply of trade goods to attack. The old fort itself was made of timbers or logs, its walls built in stockade style with blockhouses at the corners. Today only gentle rises show where these once stood, but the ground beneath is rich in treasures of the past, whiskey bottles in many shades of green, blue and brown, buttons from cavalrymen's coats, myriads of square, handmade nails and bullets of huge size—70 and 80 caliber. All around is the rusty debris of blacksmith shops that served the horses who served the cavalrymen when they rode into battle.

It was here on February 9, 1881, that White Eagle, the 60-year-old chief of the Gros Ventres died, and Bushy Head took his place as the principal chief of these friendly Indians. In the bitter winter of 1881-82 there were 600 lodges and 2,400 Indians camped at the fort—Gros Ventres, Piegan and Bloods. On June 27, 1881, the Sioux stormed into the stockade that T. C. Power and Brother had built and made off with the mules and horses. These wild horsemen who wiped out Custer's command and humiliated the United States were a constant threat at Clagett.

"Waiting for a Chinook" — C. M. Russell

The Snow-Shrinker

All along the eastern slope of the Rockies is the Chinook land, where blows a wind of mysterious birth and violent death that shrinks the snow and liberates the grass beneath.

In these foothills and prairies that front the mountains the Chinook is as much a part of Montana's winter scene as a darkened fir tree against the snow or a camouflaged jack rabbit, whose eyes alone give him away in his snow-banked hiding place. Even so, there are many who do not recognize it even when it melts the snow beneath their feet and waters their eyes in its vigorous blast.

On the streets any sunny day in winter you can hear people rejoice in the "Chinook" that is turning the ice to slush and the snow to water, but this is no Chinook, only a warm winter day. A real Chinook is a wind, a heady, portentous wind that, like Aesop's famed man in the fable, blows both hot and cold.

So there may be no more bandying of the words by winter travelers, let us, for a moment, go into the matter and identify the species. It can best be done by illustration, by a circumstance that comes only in winter and only in the northwestern United States and Canada, in the northern Alps and in southern Greenland.

The Chinook is fathered by winds from the Pacific coast, water-laden air soaring up over the Rockies and dropping its load of moisture as it moves against the cold air of the prairies. Losing this water warms the already warm air, due to heat of condensation, so this wind pushes through against the cold at

50 degrees or so. It heralds its coming with a huge band of clouds stretched overhead, dark and foreboding, known throughout Chinook country as the Chinook arch. It is a wind that comes in the night, licking at the eaves and driving out the stinging cold that has gripped the land like steel talons.

By morning the icy crystals will be mounds of mush; there will be lakes in the roads, riffled by tiny waves driven before the wind. Above the mountain crests will be the Chinook arch, and cold rain may fall when the sky darkens heavily, quickening the pace of the melting snow and the dripping eaves. Cattle and horses will drink of the new waters and seek out the wind-bared slopes with their soaked grass unlocked from marble-hard drifts.

The wind that has swooped down out of the mountains to create this miracle, to send thermometers shooting up as much as 30 to 40 degrees in an hour, is a chilling wind, cold to the touch, yet warm and caressing and certainly a scorcher to a snowdrift. It has come across the dark forests of the coast, across the sagebrush plains between the Cascades and the Rockies to work its magic on the Montana plains.

It is the salvation of the cattleman who needs the feed below the snow and a delight to the winter-weary. It is heaven, but it can end in hell.

There are memorable Chinooks all across the mountains and the plains. One I remember most clearly began at night, moaning sweetly across the hills and turning the white slopes to brown. By noon only the deepest, hardest drifts remained, and water flowed in every draw. Then the wind died, while the thermometer hovered at 40 above. In the dramatic hush, the deep quiet, the sky was leaden and nothing moved.

Then, out of the north, as suddenly as the Chinook had come in the night, came the blizzard. The mercury plummeted, the searing wind drove out of the north, the snow plunged like needles ahead of it, and everything was lost in a swirl of white bitterness, cruel in its sudden ferocity. Cattle, their bellies filled with wet grass, died in fence corners.

This was the death of a Chinook, the strange wind that named a Montana town, the county seat of Blaine. It gave its name, too, to an Indian tribe, a magnificent red-fleshed salmon and a belt of land across the northwest.

Death at the Bluff

When it is fall the time has come for the sun to shine like a bloody war shield, for the age-old ritual of the buffalo hunt must be observed.

Indians claim the buffalo came from a hole in the ground and went back into the hole when the white man came. To an Indian the shaggy brown beasts were home, food and clothing all wrapped in one hide.

The bloody war shield was an omen, for in the fall Indian enemies burned the buffalo range, and the smoke made the sun red. In the broad country west and north of Great Falls the buffalo were many when the Crows came to burn the buffalo range of the Blackfeet and the west side Indians came to fill their parfleches at the buffalo jumps or pishkun east of the divide.

This was a backdrop for war and horse stealing and the taking of women, for Sacajawea was stolen during a buffalo hunt by her people on the east side of the range. It was a grim business, and many warriors went to the Great Spirit in order that their people might eat through the long winter.

The setting is as dramatic as the hunt itself, for long ago the Indians had no horses, and they must drive the buffalo into a "V" of stone piles and force them over a cliff to be killed or wounded. The grass country just east of the front range of the Rockies is in full color when the buffalo are fat, and the sky is a blue bowl overhead. The brown grass will wave in the wind as it has always done, but the buffalo will be gone this fall day.

However, the traveler still can visit a buffalo drop or pishkun, and one of the best is just out of the town of Ulm, where any local resident will point it out. Another is just north of here, a few miles from St. Peter's mission north of Cascade.

The thousands of buffaloes mentioned by Lewis and Clark in their journals when the explorers reached Great Falls of the Missouri were the goal of Indians who worked the brown herds into position above one of these cliffs and, howling like madmen, drove their winter's meat supply over the edge to perish in a welter of dust, broken bones and squaws hacking at the dying beasts.

As the short-chested and long-winded horse of the Spaniards came north to share the grass with the buffalo, hunting changed to a chase and the kill to a deftly placed arrow, lodged neatly behind the ribs of a plunging bison.

To accomplish the kill an Indian selected for his youth and agility would strip to the waist and cover himself with a wolf skin, having first bathed in a creek to rid himself of human odor. He would perform before the herd of buffalo, dipping to the ground on all fours, then rising and all the time working toward the buffalo drop.

While the curious buffalo watched him, other Indians came quietly up behind the herd, preparing to hide themselves behind the rock piles that led to the edge of the bluff. The buffalo caller carried clutched in his hand a buffalo stone, a small limestone pebble with a remarkable resemblance to a buffalo. This had magic powers and could call buffalo by itself.

When the buffalo caller reached the very edge of the bluff he jumped up, threw away his skin and sprinted for safety. Sometimes he would jump down to a narrow ledge he had selected previously. Many times he was carried, crushed and broken, over the bluff with the buffalo he had lured to death. The risk made him a respected member of the tribe. As he threw away the skin, the Indians behind the rock piles rose up, yelling and waving their blankets to force the buffalo over the cliff.

Then it was up to the squaws. It was their job to carve the meat from the bones and cut it into strips to dry. They had the task of killing with small arrows the still struggling buffalo with broken legs or backs. They had to break the big bones with stone hammers to get at the marrow. The men feasted on warm liver, on fresh brains liberated from skulls by a blow with the hammer or on strips of intestine, wrenched from the body cavities of the buffalo.

It was a bloody but joyous occasion, and all the while lookouts kept watch for enemies, who claimed the west-side Indians left the pishkun "stinking" so that no buffalo would go near it. When the Indians went home, their parfleches heavy at the ponies' sides, there would be meat for all the red men and good medicine in the winter camps.

Blood on the Grass

Montana's greatest battle in which Indian fought Indian was over grass—the grass that the buffalo ate on the rich slopes where the plains meet the Rockies.

Where grass and buffalo were concerned, the very life of an Indian was at stake. For many years before the white man the Indians in Montana had staked out and enforced their claims to various parts of the state, and the largest territories were claimed east of the divide by Blackfeet and their allies and by the Crows of the Yellowstone valley.

The Blackfeet claimed everything east of the northern Rockies or south to about the Dearborn River, east to the Judith Basin country around Lewistown and west of Chinook. The Crows claimed all south of there on the Yellowstone, west to the Bridger Mountains and east to the Big Horn. Southwest of the Blackfeet and west of the Crows was disputed country.

It was in June of 1836 when the two great nations, the Crow or Absarokee of the south and the Blackfeet, dominated by the lordly Piegans, met on Sun or Medicine River for a great council. They met to talk the Blackfeet claims to all the lands from Belly River to the Yellowstone and the Crow claims for hunting rights in the Judith Basin and the prairies south of the Missouri River drained by the Musselshell.

It was a momentous meeting and could have had a great effect on the state's history had suspicion and tempers not flared. The days were warming, and the grass on Sun River's meadows was lush and green when more than 10,000 warriors and families of both tribes rode to the council grounds under the cottonwoods somewhere between Vaughn and Sun River, a spot not far from Highway 89.

There were cautious approaches to the problem, proposals and talks, more talks and pipe smoking, feasts on buffalo hump and fires under the greying limbs of the cottonwoods along the river. All was going well.

Then it happened. Among the Blackfeet was a medicine chief, Strong Man, whom many Crows suspected of being anything but tolerant of the Crow claims for expansion. So, under the stars of the June night several Crow warriors, without knowledge of the chiefs, caught Strong Man, dragged him into the willows by the river and tomahawked him to death.

All the old rancor between these powerful tribes rose up in a wave of rage. Two miles below the present town of Sun River, where the bluffs on both sides of the river narrow, the Blackfeet took a stand to revenge the death of Strong Man.

Flint and obsidian arrow points stilled the hearts of both Blackfeet and Crows; skulls were crushed by war hammers and ribs caved by lances. British trade rifles cracked in the summer air. Blood from Piegan, Crow, Blood Indian and Northern Blackfeet mingled as it dripped on the grass that brought about the council and the battle. In all more than 2,000 Indians died before the battle dwindled to skirmishes and ceased altogether.

Crow and Blackfeet retired to reunite their people and swear undying enmity. There was no victor and no vanquished —only hatred. No white man would have known what happened there had not Little Plume, a Blackfeet warrior who fought in the battle, put down in his own language the story of that great battle on the Medicine River.

Nepee's Secret Gold

No official record sets down the date of Montana's first Thanksgiving celebration, but one of the first was steeped in sin and greed far more than in fervent appreciation for the gifts of the Lord.

Nonetheless, a visit to this shrine of wickedness is in order. It was November, 1868, at old Fort Browning where Peoples Creek joins the sluggish Milk River. The exact location is just a few miles west of Dodson near a dirt road leading to Coburg. Highway No. 2, through Dodson, swings south of the river just west of the town, but local residents will show the road to the old fort.

Captain Buck and Major Simmons of the Fort staff dreamed up the celebration as they gazed southward at the jagged blue line of the Little Rockies and schemed ways to pry from the close-mouthed Gros Ventre Indians the secret of gold in those mountains. Two Catholic fathers who visited the Gros Ventre in 1865 had seen gold from the Little Rockies, and the priests had warned them never to tell white men their secret.

Nepee, a Gros Ventre who was a friend of Major Simmons, was the principal target of this scheme, and the plan was to ply the red man with a little fort-made whiskey and wheedle the secret out of him. The whiskey was made with a straight alcohol base, blended with Pain Killer, Hostetter's Bitters, a few bars of soap and three plugs of chewing tobacco. The last was to give it a rich color, although the makers threw in a little red ink, too, for good measure.

There was no turkey this Thanksgiving Day, but plenty of venison haunch, buffalo, antelope, "dough gods" or fried bread and a precious can of jam. The finest delicacy of all were some potatoes, tiny tubers grown at the fort for such a festive occasion.

On the great day the cottonwood buildings at the fort were filled with screaming Indian women and howling babies. The cottonwood stockade was opened wide, and the friendly Gros Ventre mixed with the dozen white men in celebration. There was to be no trading today. Tomorrow would be better, when the Indians had been mellowed with whiskey and food, and today the principal goal was to get Nepee to tell his gold mine secret.

Shortly after noon Nepee arrived and was greeted warmly by the white officers. Under the influence of a few tin cups of the wild concoction that served as cocktails, plus some persuasive conversation, Nepee showed Major Simmons a small bag of dust and nuggets. Nepee was promised all the wealth of the frontier; horses, trade goods and favors, but he clung to his secret. He would be the friend of the white man forever, but he would not divulge the location of his mine. The officers had lost their battle. There were three days of drinking, eating and fighting, but Nepee left with his lips still sealed.

Later that fall, when the snows were new on the Little Rockies, the stories of gold in the hills hadn't been forgotten. Bill Hamilton, one of the Northwest Fur Company men at the post, led a party of eight men around to the eastern side of the Little Rockies, and they dug in the rocky bed of Dry Beaver Creek about where the creek flows under the blacktop of Highway 19 south of Malta.

There was color in the pan but nothing that would pay. The Indians became unfriendly and suspicious, and snow piled higher on the foothills. The party, fearful of being snowed in or scalped, left the Little Rockies to the Gros Ventre.

There may have been a connection with the Indian mine, whose secret died with Nepee, and the Kris Kies gold strike. Kies had sent word in 1865 to his friend John Lepley in Fort Benton to come "down river" to where he had struck it rich. Lepley, three men and three Indian women started out down the Missouri but near Cow Island, just south of Harlem and near the Little Rockies, a Sioux war party killed all but one Gros Ventre woman.

The escaped Indian woman never was able to tell where the gold came from, but she said the Sioux scalped all the men in the party then slit the gold sacks and dumped the dust into the swirling Missouri. Another fortune had vanished into mystery.

BUFFALO WORSHIPERS

Sleeping Buffalo

Sun which thawed retreating glaciers in the Milk River valley at the close of the Ice Age left a scattering of boulders that became a great ritualistic symbol for the red hunters of the north.

At the crest of a hill and hard by the hot spring plunge turnoff from Highway 2 about 15 miles east of Malta is a dome-shaped boulder known to generations of Indians as the "sleeping buffalo." This stone was supposed to have amazing powers for warriors or for those whose parfleches were empty of buffalo meat.

At one time this two to three-ton rock lay a few miles north with others of its kind near the Cree crossing, an historic Milk River crossing used by Canadian Chippewa-Crees on their way south to the buffalo country of Montana, but about a quarter-century ago it was moved to the hill nearer the highway.

On its home ridge, the rock appeared to passing Indians to be the leader of a whole herd of buffalo lying on the bed ground. On the largest of these, artistic hands long stilled by death painted symbols of horns and ribs, eyes and exotic markings without meaning to modern men, red or white.

Time and again in Indian legend, the sacred sleeping buffalo of the Cree crossing raises his lordly head and commands attention, sometimes as a truly revered object and again more as a token of good fortune for hunt and battle.

Although geologically thousands of years ancient, the "sleeping buffalo" counts its symbolic history at least back to 1700, the year that the Assiniboines first saw the Milk River country and found the rock already well established and revered.

Here is the story of the venerable rock as it passed from campfire to campfire through the ages: A party of Indians looking for horses sighted a heard of buffalo lying down and crawled up to the herd only to find it turned to stone, and the largest of all the rocks was the "sleeping buffalo." This is an old Shoshone legend, but the Gros Ventres and Assiniboine both knew it well. The reference to horses dates the legend to the early 1700s, since the Shoshone first owned Spanish horses in 1717 and used them in cavalry attacks on the Blackfeet along the Milk. At that time the Snakes or Shoshone were supreme on the eastern plains of Montana.

There is another legend. An Indian youth and his wife had traveled far searching for buffalo, but he had fallen sick and taken to his bed in the lodge not far from Cree crossing. His wife had gone out each day and this day was dipping water from the creek not far from the "sleeping buffalo" when she saw a cow buffalo in the willows. She ran to get her husband, who was given strength to rise from his bed, pick up his arrows and hunt the buffalo. His wife steadied him while he shot the arrow, which killed the buffalo. Meat and soup from the animal brought him back to health, and ever after the rocks brought good fortune to other hunters.

When buffalo became scarce in Montana in the 1860s, Indians sought out the stone to ask its aid in bringing back the animal that meant life to the red man. In 1865, an old Indian tale goes, about 500 Sioux and half that many half-breeds camped near this herd of buffalo turned to stone, and Sioux Chief Medicine Bear is reported to have built his huge and colorful lodge directly over the largest rock, the "sleeping buffalo."

An Indian artist painted the buffalo's head over the entrance to the lodge, and inside the old men and women, along with the young warriors, gathered about the sacred stone. At each corner of the stone burned a fire made of the sweet grass of the Milk River hills, and in its blue smoke haze the medicine chief incanted his rituals and painted in new, bright colors the ancient symbols on the rock. For a week he neither ate nor slept, and the young men refilled and lighted his pipe for him.

When he had finished, the Indians danced and laid down their most precious belongings upon the stone, asking that the buffalo return to the prairies and make the hunting good again in their land.

The earnestness of some entreaties to the rock is amazing. The Gros Ventres were reputed to have pinched the skin of their arms, sliced off a portion and laid the bleeding offering upon the rock. The Blackfeet journeyed far to offer possessions to the rock and to receive bounty in return.

In later years Indians placed beads and bright coins or bits of cloth on the stone, usually in a hollow on the beast's back. Not until the white man came with his cattle and the buffalo were gone forever did the Indians abandon the "sleeping buffalo," to become a permanent monument to those glorious days when thousands of black hoofs shook the ground along the Milk.

To Know the Faith

Under the cottonwoods on the banks of the Teton River in 1859 Catholicism made a bid for the faith of the savage Blackfoot, a bid that shortly was to retreat to safer ground.

Three grim Jesuits, all of unswerving determination so characteristic of their calling, had planned well for their effort. In the summer of that year Father Adrian Hoecken and Brother Vincent Magri traveled with the meat-hunting Blackfeet, learning the language and the way of life of a tribe which viewed all whites with deep suspicion.

That fall Father Camillus Imoda joined the other two, who had picked a site along the Teton River which now is part of the O'Neil ranch, south of Choteau. They built three log cabins, and Father Hoecken and Brother Magri devoted the winter to studying the Blackfeet language and trying to teach the Indian children some religion.

The site they picked was hard by a spring which was open the year around, and still is, even in freezing weather. The next spring when the priests moved to a spot on the south bank of Sun River and built two cabins there, they left behind a permanent memorial, Priest Butte, directly south of the old mission and west of Freezeout Lake, not far off Highway 89.

The Sun River mission, too, was short lived. The fathers erected another mission above the mouth of Sun River and along a wide bend in the Missouri and finally a permanent mission at St. Peter near Bird Tail rock on the old Helena-Great Falls road, then the road from Helena to Fort Benton. Never again would they return to the Teton. It remained for a Protestant to take up the work of Christianizing the Blackfeet.

Four miles north of Choteau, alongside sparkling Spring Creek and just off Highway 89-287, Captain Nathaniel Pope came in 1868 to set up a trading post, which he called Old Agency. The exact spot is just east of the highway on land owned by M. J. Lyon. Still visible are the lines of the fort foundation and hollows where basement holes were dug in the valley floor.

173

Pope planted the first wheat ever grown in this area now famed for its wheat crops, and he got along with the Indians, quite a feat in itself. The Blackfeet knew the spot as "Four Persons" for the Pikuni had killed four Crows there in 1857. The graves of these Indians, plus 18 other unknowns, still can be seen just east of the old fort.

To this post on July 8, 1872, came a Methodist missionary who was to be better loved by the Indians than nearly any other man. Wesley Van Orsdal, who was "Brother Van" to all men, red or white, had walked 35 miles from Fort Shaw on Sun River following a journey from Fort Benton, where he landed from river steamer and preached his first Montana sermon in a saloon.

Major Jesse Armitage gave Brother Van a room in the rear of the store at this fort and let him use the agency schoolhouse for services. He was the first Protestant to preach to the Indians, and to begin with the savage Blackfeet was enough to test the mettle of any man.

How well he succeeded can best be judged by the comments of Indians who believed fully that after Brother Van's death the red man had a true friend in Heaven. Brother Van hunted with the Indians, riding after buffalo and seeing much of the grassy hills that were no-man's land for most whites.

At this time Old Agency was an extensive settlement, well known to the Indians and built in accord with a solemn treaty. There were offices for the agent, a store, school carpenter and blacksmith shops, quarters for a doctor and an interpreter. A 200-foot square enclosed the entire agency, and outside this square were about two dozen houses for use of Indians who wanted to live at the post.

By 1879 a log building marked the beginning of Choteau town, which was platted four years later and named after Pierre Chouteau, president of the American Fur Company. The extra "u" was dropped to distinguish the new town from Chouteau County, where Fort Benton was located and still is. Old Agency's buildings soon faded into the valley floor, their usefulness ended by the broken power of the Blackfeet and by the white man's dominance of their grassy foothills of the Rockies.

Fort on the Medicine Road

By threat more than military action the fort surrounded by green lawns and landscaped with imported shrubbery held back the last thrusts of the war-making Blackfeet and brought peace to the great grass country north of the Medicine River.

Fort Shaw, only 23 miles west of Great Falls on Highway 20, stands out in Montana frontier records for several reasons. It was named for Col. Robert G. Shaw of the 54th Massachusetts Volunteers, killed in Civil War action in 1863, leading an all-Negro fighting unit.

When established June 30, 1867, it was to be the keystone fort in the new military department of Montana, the regimental headquarters. It was to guard the rich valley of the Sun or Medicine River and police the eastern Indians in their annual journeys over the passes to the west and down Sun River to the buffalo ranges west of Great Falls. This was the famed "Great Medicine Road to the Buffalo."

Another duty of the fort was to hold back the Blackfeet to the north and west and to protect travelers and goods on the dusty Fort Benton-Helena freight road, principal commercial thoroughfare of the growing territory.

Stationed here was the 13th Infantry, whose shovels and hammers built the fort in the summer of 1867. That winter some of the men lived in tents, while the winds howled down Sun River and drifted the snow on the parade ground. When it was finished, the fort was an island of greenery and culture in the wilderness, what with its theater and dancing parties held in a special building, its post library and even an irrigation ditch from Sun River for its lawns, trees and officers' gardens.

It even had contact with civilization. In 1869 Montana's first telegraph line, built northward from Salt Lake City to Virginia City, Butte and Helena, reached Fort Shaw. Despite all this, it was an outpost on the raw frontier, facing a red enemy that even the courageous Sioux respected.

General Philip Sheridan, Little Phil of Civil War fame, in 1870 ordered Shaw's troops reinforced from Fort Ellis east of Bozeman. His action was spurred by Blackfeet raids on white residents, supposedly by bands led by Black Weasel or Mountain Chief. Major E. M. Baker of Ellis commanded, and the troops wallowed through snow and fought 40-below weather to reach the Blackfeet camp on the Marias River, not far from the present Marias Dam.

The soldiers fell on the camp in the freezing dawn of January 24, firing into the teepees and killing 175 Piegans, about 50 of them women and children. Another 150, mostly women and children, were driven out into the sub-zero weather, most of them with little or no clothing. Many were sick with smallpox. The raid was a tragic error. The camp was not Black Weasel's at all, and the Army blushingly faced heated criticism from eastern newspapers.

In 1871 Colonel John Gibbon took over command at Shaw, and in 1876 commanded the troops sent from Shaw and Ellis to help Custer on the Little Big Horn. In 1877 Gibbon again was in command when his troops fought Chief Joseph on the Big Hole, then pursued the red leader across Yellowstone Park, leaving a blue-green river and a handsome falls, both in the park, named after him.

This was the last great campaign for the men from Shaw. By 1890 the Blackfeet country was peaceful, and the fort was abandoned. In 1912 the Bureau of Reclamation took over the fort as headquarters offices for its irrigation projects on Sun River. Indian children, and whites, too, went to school in the old buildings.

For years afterward the fort served as a school. Today's traveler will find many of the old buildings still standing. Fallen are the 18-inch adobe walls, but in good repair are the wooden barracks, where on St. Patrick's Day, 1875, the Fort Shaw Dramatic Association played Robert Emmet, a stone and mud storehouse and the sutler's store. The parade ground can be as plainly seen as when the Negro troops marched across its watered grass.

Here is a grand old fortification of the twilight of the frontier, living out its days in weathered dignity.

Mail in the Saddle Bag

Hoofs of Montana's Pony Express mounts trampled the Judith and Belt foothills in 1867 on their link of the long mail route from St. Paul's metropolitan sophistication to the rowdy Last Chance Gulch gold camps at Helena.

This was a three-times-weekly Pony Express set up by Washington, D. C., planners who had drawn a line on the map from old Fort Peck to the Last Chance placer gulch. To carry out the mission on a lathered horse was another matter. To save 600 miles from the long river route was a fine idea but no one consulted the Blackfeet Indians, who expressed their irritation with bullet and knife.

The Pony Express riders had to keep a lively clip to hold the schedule which routed the mail into Montana at a point west of Fort Union on the Missouri River's north bank at the North Dakota boundary. From there the route paralleled Highway No. 2 west to a point just south of Nashua. From here the riders passed north of old Fort Peck on the river bottom, now under water, just upstream from Fort Peck Dam.

From Fort Peck the old route led southwest through black gumbo country as wild today as it was in 1867, following the north side of the Missouri River. The riders crossed the Missouri at old Fort Hawley, about 20 miles west of the UL bend at the mouth of the Musselshell River. Undoubtedly they dropped to river level off the plains to the north by following the Hawley basin down to the fort. Hawley Island, Fort Island

and the old Hawley cutoff all have been drowned in the waters of Fort Peck Lake.

Horses and riders, dripping with water of the Big Muddy, climbed the piney breaks south of the river, and, topping the rise, headed for Black Butte, the landmark at the northern tip of the Judith Mountains, 40 miles away to the southwest. Travelers on Highway 19 can sight the butte as they leave the river after crossing the Robinson bridge southbound.

The old Pony Express trail was straight, much straighter than the present road to Helena. From about the vicinity of Roy on Highway 19 the trail follows that highway around the north end of the Judiths and across the hills north of Lewistown. From Lewistown it entered and crossed the timbered draws and grassy benches of the Judith Basin itself, then up the foothills of the Big Snowy mountains and Big Belts through Judith Gap. Highway 87 west of Lewistown and Highway 19 south of Moore to Harlowton roughly follow the route.

Once on the Musselshell side, the lathered horses and their load of mail raced westward up the North Fork of the Musselshell, paralleling Highway 12 through the pass between the Belt and Castle mountains and into what now is White Sulphur Springs. Then it was only a warm spring in the hillside, but this was the main trade route from the 60s to the 80s.

From White Sulphur Springs the riders turned west toward what is Fort Logan, and the route can be followed here on gravel, then west on dirt through Watson, right on the heels of the tired ponies. These are summer roads and lead over the summit of the Belts. Take the Confederate Gulch turn at the summit to stay with the express riders down to Canyon Ferry.

From here the route led across the Helena valley north of Highway 284, which will take the soft-cushion rider into the capital city. Actually, the pony express ended at old Diamond City in Confederate Gulch, and stages picked up the mail for the last few miles into Helena.

Riders burned the mail to heat their coffee, Indians stole the strange paper with the marks on it as well as the horses and equipment. It was hardly a howling success but a rollicking part of Montana's history that ended with the stage lines and the railroads.

Love's High Price

Short lived but vivid with raw frontier color was the Reed and Bowles Trading Post or Reed's Fort on the banks of Big Spring Creek two miles north of Lewistown.

Only Major Reed's cabin still remains of the old stockade that kept horses in and Indians out, but such Reed's post authorities as Joe Montgomery point out that the cottonwood trees on the grassy flat were there a century before Reed arrived.

Reed was a pioneer dandy, who cut a fast swath with the Indian squaws and possessed a trigger-happy jealousy. At least on one occasion he gunned to death a friend who dared to make a little quick love to a Mandan squaw who was staying at the fort with Reed.

The date was around 1873, although most authorities give November, 1874, as the opening of the post, which was moved down Big Spring Creek about two and one-half miles when it was bought from Theodore Dawes. The reason for the move was to get the fort alongside the Carroll road, ill-fated freight thoroughfare from Carroll on the Missouri River to the north, into the mining camp at Helena.

It was a Spanish river boat gambler named Castro who paid love's high price. Castro had come to visit his friend Reed, who always had a few squaws hanging around his sod-roofed cabin. Castro took a liking to a Mandan Indian girl, and Reed laid a trap for the pair. Packing several horses, Reed started off up Spring Creek, ostensibly to look for a grizzly bear that had mauled "Skookum Joe" Anderson a few days before. However, when Reed got to the present site of the Fergus County courthouse he cut back to watch Castro and the squaw.

Seeing the pair come out of the stockade and walk into a clump of trees, he rode into the stockade and waited, a 50-50 buffalo gun across his knees. The returning couple looked down the barrel into Reed's jealous eyes. Reed took both about 100 yards from the stockade and, at gunpoint, forced Castro to dig his own grave. The sweating Castro and the apprehensive squaw saw Reed take drink after drink of whiskey. Finally, Reed handed Castro a drink, and as the Spaniard tipped up the cup, Reed fired the fatal shot. Castro toppled into the fresh grave. Reed sent the squaw back to the Mandan country with a pack outfit leaving the fort that night, but not before she had covered the grave of her Spanish lover.

For years the grave was a landmark along the old trail, but Spring Creek waters now have covered it with silt. The post was the only station on the Carroll road between Martinsdale and Carroll, a distance of 150 miles, and it was a great gathering spot for whites and reds alike. Although it lasted only until 1880, the two wooden-pegged log cabins and pole stockade were landmarks.

In its six years of existence its principal trade item was raw liquor, stepped up with red pepper, chewing tobacco and heaven knows what else. Since selling liquor was outlawed in Indian country, the post was a little on the shady side of the law, which bothered no one, least of all Reed. Actually, since the post was about 100 miles out of reach of organized law and order, Reed was a virtual king, backed up by his accurate gunfire.

Reed got the nickname "Major" by virtue of having served four months as Indian agent at Milk River in 1870, although he eventually was relieved of this honor. Both Reed and Bowles, his assistant, had a territory-wide reputation as handy men with a gun.

To get to the old Reed fort site, drive north of Lewistown on Highway 19. The old cabin is close by the county hospital, and a DAR tablet on the log walls tells the story.

The Lasting Wound

Two dead Indians probably forced one of the greatest shifts in American transportation and no doubt even affected the location of most of Montana's principal cities.

It was a cloudy July 26, 1806, when Captain Meriwether Lewis, co-leader of a well-known exploration, had pushed his tiny party of himself, the Fields brothers and Drouillard up the Marias River then back to a point on Two Medicine Creek not far from its junction with Birch Creek.

Lewis had wanted to make some celestial readings, but Montana's sun had stayed behind clouds. The party had reached its northernmost point on a small hill where the town of Blackfoot now stands, just west of Cut Bank. None knew that they stood within a few miles of the lowest pass in the northern Rockies, Marias Pass, not to be discovered by white men for another three-quarters of a century.

This northernmost outlook of the expedition is marked by a stone shaft just north of Highway 2, and a sign guides the turnoff into a quarter-mile dirt road.

But back to the dead Indians. Lewis and his men had found hunting so bad there was nothing to eat but grease from tainted meat mixed with a mush made from roots and cooked over a buffalo chip fire. A track of a wounded buffalo had alerted the party to Indians, and guards were posted at night.

At noon the 26th the party had reached a spot almost due north of Valier and down Birch Creek from the Highway 89 bridge. Lewis had sent Drouillard, the woodsman, hunting, while Lewis and the Fields climbed a hill above the Marias to look at the country. They saw about 30 head of horses, then a band of Indians watching Drouillard.

The air tensed, but Indian and white man advanced toward each other, equally frightened. After Lewis had presented gifts, the pipe was passed, and the Indians invited Lewis and his men to join them for the night in a shelter of skins on the creek bottom. Lewis talked to the eight Indians, who were Minnetarees and Blackfeet, and invited them to the mouth of the Marias, where Lewis expected to meet Sergeants Gass and Ordway, who were coming down the Missouri by boat.

Lewis stood guard the first half of that warm night, then woke Drouillard and fell into his blankets. At dawn he heard Drouillard yell and saw him twist his rifle from an Indian's hand. Side Hill Calf, a Blackfeet, screamed as Ruben Fields drove a knife into his ribs, and the Indian ran a dozen steps before he fell dead.

Lewis found his own rifle gone and saw the Indians escaping with the party's horses. After running about 300 yards, the winded Lewis gave up and shouted to the Indians he would shoot if they didn't give up the horses. One Indian turned to face him and Lewis fired, bringing the Indian to his knees but not before he fired at Lewis, the bullet grazing the captain's face.

It was over in minutes, and the party, with newly acquired Indian horses, rode their mounts into the sunrise, rode them 140 miles in 24 hours to a miraculous meeting with the boats at the mouth of the Marias. Lewis heard the firing of army rifles, and identified them by the heavy sound, as distinguished from the light firing of Indian rifles. He mounted the bluffs, saw Ordway's boats on the river. Gass and Willard, who had gone overland, met the party at the Marias mouth, just below the town of Loma on Highway 87.

Meanwhile, the Indians, as told years later by the Piegan Wolf Calf to George Bird Grinnell, rode off as fast in the other direction. But the white man's knife and bullet had enraged the Blackfeet. He held them away from his country, bent the westward flow of commerce southward through Mullan Pass into the Bitter Roots and down the gorges of the Clark's Fork of the Columbia.

In 1807 David Thompson recorded in his writings that the Blackfeet were still keeping an eye on the Missouri River, hoping to avenge the deaths of their brothers at the hands of the white men.

Possibly it was a coincidence, but no part of Montana was as forbidding to the whitemen, as dangerous to any who entered it, as was the Blackfeet country. Not until 1889 did white men open Marias Pass to commerce so strong was the medicine of the Blackfeet and so long their memory.

Old Engraving of Fort Benton

Paddle Wheel Port

For nearly 40 years the queen port of the upper Missouri was Fort Benton, and its main thoroughfare still faces the coffee-colored waters which made it rich, powerful and famed on the frontier. To many Montanans, Fort Benton still is "the" pioneer city of the state, and its basic history the commercial story of the old territory.

Benton was born in 1846 when its log houses were moved from old Fort Lewis, which was across the river and upstream a few miles. Its mover was Alexander Culbertson, one of the really great fur traders, whose Piegan wife, Natawista Iksana, a true Indian princess in every way, brought him friendship of the Blackfeet, who were friends to few men, white or red.

Not until Christmas eve, 1850, however, was the baby christened. That year Major Culbertson had put up the first adobe building, and as the fiddlers sawed out the dance tunes that Yuletide, Culbertson called for a toast to Senator Thomas Hart Benton of Missouri. It was a sincere toast, for Senator

Benton had saved the American Fur Company's license following a brush with authorities over liquor smuggling.

Fort Benton thus had a name, but it had yet to mature. For years it would be a brawling, river-front town, then a town of warehouses and clerks, before it reached its majority.

It was the coming of the first steamboat that put red blood into Benton's commercial arteries. That boat was the Chippewa, which made the big try in 1859, only to fall short on June 17 at Brule bottom, six miles up the Missouri from the mouth of the Marias and the site of old Fort McKenzie. It was the burning of the fort that gave the flat its name of "brule" or "burned." Lack of dry fuel put off the Chippewa's arrival at Fort Benton until the summer of 1860.

Missouri River navigation had arrived by stages. In 1831 the Yellowstone, oldest of the Missouri River steamers, reached Fort Pierre, South Dakota, from St. Louis. In 1832 the Yellowstone was at Fort Union on the Montana-North Dakota line. Then it was the Assiniboine to the mouth of Poplar River at the town of Poplar, followed by the El Paso to the mouth of Milk River south of Nashua. Charles Chouteau of the American Fur Company was responsible for the Chippewa's voyage to Brule bottom and then Fort Benton, and John LaBarge was the captain. Missouri River navigation to its head was a reality.

The first trip allegedly was sponsored by the Chouteaus, but some claim it was government-sponsored, which is more in accord with present-day river transportation.

The Chippewa, for all its distinction, went out in a blaze of glory, and liquor was its downfall. On May 15, 1861, the Chippewa was plowing up the Missouri just below the mouth of Poplar River at Disaster Rapids when some deckhands bored a hole in a barrel of trade alcohol to wet their whistles. As they drank this raw material from which trade whiskey was made, they knocked over a candle, and in moments the whole boat was afire.

Passengers scrambled up the banks, the boat flamed out at water's edge, then burst into violence again as heat touched off the powder kegs in the hold. A party of Crow Indians nearby, attracted by the flames, picked the Chippewa's soggy bones of calico, blankets, tobacco and trade goods. To add one more dash of drama, the Crows stood off an attack by a party of Sioux who tried to horn in on the spoils.

Hundreds of boats followed the Chippewa. Gold discoveries and the completion of the Mullan Road from Fort Benton to Fort Walla Walla, Washington, spurred the traffic. In 1879, the peak year, 49 boats docked at Benton, some of them carrying 600 tons of freight. The end was near, however, for by 1883 the Northern Pacific Railway had punched through to the coast and on September 29, 1887, Mrs. James J. Hill drove a silver spike at the Fort Benton depot of the Manitoba Railroad, forerunner of Great Northern.

By 1890 it was virtually all over, although the last steamboat docked at Benton as late as 1922.

To visit Benton drive Highway 87 to the Benton turnoff 40 miles north of Great Falls. Descend the hill down which Indians came to Culbertson's trading post and up which hundreds of freight wagons, loaded with steamboated supplies for the mines, struggled, creaking behind ox teams and headed for Helena.

Once in town, drive to the cottonwood-shaded river front, park and walk up and down the street in the footsteps of Indians, fur traders and scalawags, and look across the waters which closed over the head of Thomas Meagher in 1867 to end the sparkling career of Montana's acting territorial governor.

See the old adobe fort walls and the cannon with their muzzles pointed outward as if to protect the old fort town from enemies by land or by sea.

Lewis and Clark Discovering Black Eagle Falls — C. M. Russell

Sublimely Grand Waters

All the bulk of America's longest river pours over the cliffs in a spectacle that amazed Meriwether Lewis, defied his pen and left him numbed with an impression that the Great Falls of the Missouri River were "sublimely grand."

The falls themselves have yielded prominence to their namesake city, just upriver, but when the waters are not rerouted through turbines they are no less grand than when Lewis first saw them at high noon June 13, 1805. His were the first white men's eyes to see the "spray arise above the plain like a column of smoke" and the first white ears to hear "the agreeable sound of a fall of water."

Almost boyishly, Lewis "hurryed down the hill which was about 200 feet high and difficult of access to gaze on this sublimely grand spectacle." For the moment he forgot that Sacajawea was alarmingly ill a few miles downriver in her tent, that the country was filled with grizzly bears and rattlesnakes. He was preoccupied with the "sparkling foam" rising from the river, a tiny island with Indian lodges below the falls and skeletons of buffalo lying below the falls "which I presume have been swept down by the current and precipitated over this tremendous fall." He wished for artistic talents to describe the fall, noted the rainbow which later gave rainbow falls its name and finally decided to rest at the base of a cottonwood on the river's edge.

That night he feasted on native trout, caught at the base of the falls and described in detail in the journal, along with buffalo hump, tongue and marrowbones. Lewis was delighted with his discovery, for there had been some question at the mouth of the Marias River as to which branch was the main stream. Now, Lewis was prepared to notify Clark and the rest of the party and "settle in their minds all further doubts as to the Missouri."

The party's work had just started. For the first time since they left St. Charles, the expedition must leave the river and go overland. "One of the grandest views in nature," as Clark put it, presented a barrier that meant moving all the possessions of the party across 18 miles of broken country to the place where the Medicine River joined the Missouri above the falls.

The party cut a huge cottonwood tree into rough wheels and built carts, then struggled over rocks and cactus to the riverbank above the cataracts. It was hard work, and Clark wrote: "many limp from the soreness of their feet and some become faint, but no man complains, all go cheerfully on."

Perils were added to frustration and fatigue. Captain Lewis was attacked by a grizzly bear while dressing out a buffalo, and he beat off the bear from a position waist-deep in the Missouri. On his way back to camp a mountain lion crossed Lewis' trail, and three buffalo bulls challenged his way. At camp he lay down under the stars to find a rattlesnake sharing his bed.

Thirty-two days later all the expedition's goods were safe ashore on White Bear Island above the mouth of Sun or Medicine River, and the captains broke out their supply of spirits for a drink in celebration of victory over the falls.

Today, a river road on the north bank of the Missouri leads out through Black Eagle and follows the bluffs, eventually leading back to blacktop on Highway 87.

Fort of the Daring

Its cottonwood logs have long since sunk into the soil of the Missouri River banks from which they grew, but Fort McKenzie is green in memory as the fur fort that most defied the Indians.

The Blackfeet myth that clothed these Indians with the most warlike reputation in the Northwest, most of it deserved, had, since Lewis and Clark discovered the mouth of the Marias River, kept the fur traders at a respectful distance.

Not until 1832 did the lure of the rich, soft furs of the shining-mountain-land of the Blackfeet overcome the terror. Outright fear was replaced by extreme caution, even though the Blackfeet, Piegans, Bloods and Gros Ventres, as Alexander Culbertson put it, were "so hostile and bloodthirsty as to make the trading, or the erecting of a fort among them too dangerous to be attempted."

Nevertheless, it was Culbertson who completed Fort McKenzie on the north bank of the Missouri, six miles above the mouth of the Marias, which is just below the town of Loma. The site was in the very heart of these tribes, and the American Fur Company prudently erected a temporary fort at this point to protect the handful of men under first David D. Mitchell and then Culbertson, who were building the permanent fort. Both were then American Fur clerks, but Culbertson later became a partner, and Mitchell U. S. Superintendent of Indian Affairs.

Since Culbertson noted 2,000 Blackfeet lodges nearby, this precaution couldn't be questioned. The fort slowly rose into place on the upper end of a meadow, 225 feet from the river, facing southward and 15 feet above high water. The site, Culbertson noted, was formerly covered by timber but by that time was bare. Directly across the river was a black bluff, from the summit of which an Indian could see everything going on in the fort. Although this seemed a disadvantage, Builder Culbertson pointed out the fort site was the only one in the area and besides, the Blackfeet guns wouldn't shoot that far.

The architect and builder of this outpost describes it as

built of 18-foot cottonwood pickets, planted three feet below ground and forming a rectangle 200 feet on a side.

Cottonwood bastions were on the northeast and southwest corners, ball-proof, 20 feet square and two storied. In these were cannon, plus plentiful supplies of powder, ball and rifle. Apartments on the rear wall, inside, housed the "bougeois" and clerks, and the principal living room even included a library with books on science, history, poetry and fiction to "drive dull care away" or so Culbertson asserted. With 2,000 Blackfeet lodges readily available, dull care shouldn't have been a problem.

The walls also enclosed a room for interpreters, a council room and a reception room for chiefs, who were the only Indians allowed inside the fort. The "Bourgeois" room even boasted pine doors made from planks sawed in the Rocky Mountains, a real luxury on the lumber-hungry plains.

Functional rooms in the fort included a kitchen, a special room for salting buffalo tongues, a frontier delicacy; tailor and blacksmith shops and an ice house which held forty loads of ice and kept meat "several days in summer."

Stables completed the service buildings, with room for the 30 to 40 horses, a dozen cattle and a few hogs that belonged to the fort. Principal boast of the livestock department was a Durham bull which Culbertson called "one of the most splendid in the United States or Territories. It must have been the model for the one on the old "roll your own" tobacco sack.

To Culbertson, the most magnificent aspect of the fort was its American flag, flying from a 50-foot staff in a square in front of the stockade. "From this," wrote Culbertson, "wave the glorious folds of the starry banner of our native land, made more beautiful by its situation in the dreary wilderness around it. The wanderer, as he sees the bright folds from afar, hails them with gladness, as it means for him a place of safety. No sight is more welcome to the voyageur, the hunter or the trapper. That flag cheers all who claim it as theirs, and it protects all, white men or red. Here in the wilderness all fly to it for refuge and depend on it for security."

Sounds better today than it did 130 years ago.

Father of the People

His Cree name was We-Shask-Ka-Chask and his lodge was on the little flat place at the very top of Middle Butte in the Sweet Grass hills north of Chester.

We-Shask-Ka-Chask was an Indian giant with long, white hair and a snowy beard, but he was thin and wiry and, though aging, had bright, piercing eyes. He had set up his lodge on top of the butte the Indians called the Middle One because he had become very old and he could see all over the prairies where the buffalo ate the short grass and grew fat.

For this legendary Cree had been here before the buffalo. So strong was his medicine that he drank from the morning dew, and the great spirit supplied him with food. His name meant he was indomitable or invincible, and he so believed, for he thought himself the father of all the people on the earth.

This was Blackfeet country, too, and the Blackfeet believed the Great Spirit had created the Sweet Grass hills as a place to look for buffalo and used them just for that. But this was before there were Blackfeet, in the long-gone centuries when We-Shask-Ka-Chask walked the earth, from ocean to ocean, crossed the mountains and the plains and returned to the three Buttes on the prairie.

He knew that he was father of all the people, but he knew another person, called Round Man, who was as short and fat and weak of legs as We-Shask-Ka-Chask was tall and straight and thin and strong of limb. Round Man thought he was father of the people, too, and this angered We-Shask-Ka-Chask, who sought for Round Man to contest the title, but Round Man was not to be found.

Round Man, who lived somewhere to the south, finally came to see We-Shask-Ka-Chask, and with the help of many of his people, Round Man climbed to the top of the Butte where the Cree leader lived. We-Shask-Ka-Chask sneered at Round Man and reviled him for trying to claim to be father of all the Indian people.

Round Man took his scolding in silence, then said he had come to prove to We-Shask-Ka-Chask that he, Round Man, had come to this land before the wild animals, before the buffalo, that he had known huge animals on the plains, some of them many times the height of a man.

This infuriated We-Shask-Ka-Chask, and he retorted that he had been on these plains when fogs and mists covered the earth and big reptiles wandered over the earth. They argued and argued, and finally Round Man tired of the argument.

Then We-Shask-Ka-Chask suggested each would lie on his couch until death came to one of those who claimed to be the father of all people. This suited Round Man, who was sure his fat body would outlast that of the thin, emaciated We-Shask-Ka-Chask.

So the two lay on their couches atop the Middle Butte overlooking the buffalo plains. After 50 years Round Man raised himself on his elbow and peeked at We-Shask-Ka-Chask, but the old Cree still breathed strongly, so Round Man lay down again upon his couch.

Another 50 years passed, and the summers and winters came and went, and the buffalo grew fat and were killed at the pishkun, and Round Man again raised himself from the couch and prepared to leave the lodge. But We-Shask-Ka-Chask called in a small, thin voice to come back, for he was still alive.

Sorrow and disappointment crossed the face of Round Man, then his fat body collapsed into a pile of grey dust on the floor of the lodge. We-Shask-Ka-Chask had proved himself to be the father of all the people.

To see these hills as did the great We-Shask-Ka-Chask or as did the Stevens expedition in 1853, guided by Hugh Monroe or Rising Wolf of the Blackfeet, drive Highway 2 east from Shelby or west from Havre. Just west of Chester a good gravel road heads north to the hills at Whitlash. North from Galata another road will take you to the same town. Explore from there. The great spirit will guide you to the legendary hills.

Ghost of the Judith

Some called this lone killer "Snowdrift" and others the "Ghost Wolf" of the Judith Basin, but all who knew him admired the cunning and skill that for 15 years gave him the power to slash down hundreds of steers and arrogantly avoid the rage of their owners.

When at last he fell, it was old age that brought his end as fully as did the rifle in the hands of a sworn enemy. When this end came he had left a legend of terror and destruction that still is a conversation piece around the fireplaces of ranch houses in the "Basin."

Snowdrift was white, a great disadvantage except in winter, so he hunted by night or in the grey of dawn or dusk. In daylight he hid where he could pick up the scent of anyone approaching from his blind side and where he could watch miles of country below him. For this purpose he selected a pocket in a high rock ledge of the Highwood, Belt or Bear Paw mountains, or a sagebrush hilltop from which he could slip away unnoticed at the approach of man.

For Snowdrift feared only man. He was master of all else and could pull down a four-year-old steer and tear out its warm flesh in huge chunks as fuel for the wolf's constant roving. He moved always at a high, flowing lope, a tireless, mile-devouring gait that accounted in no small part for his long life against tough odds.

It was 1915 when ranchers first noticed the big white wolf and his kills. He would take a calf or steer on Dry Wolf Creek and the next night would be in the Highwoods or even the Bear's Paw Mountains, far to the north across the Missouri River. He killed and moved on, fast, for he knew man would be after him. His range was from the Belts to the Bear Paws, curving into the Highwoods on the west and to the hills east of Stanford. He knew it intimately. He marked every change, then avoided it. Once some ranchers tore down an old sheep fence which he had crossed many times. He never went that way again, for men had been there and changed it, and that was bad.

He was known to travel as much as 125 miles in 24 hours and to kill 50 miles from a kill of the previous day. To roam his range from end to end he had to cross two railroad rights-of-way fenced with wolf-proof fence. He slipped through culverts or under bridges, but never the same ones twice in succession.

Always alone, the big white wolf scorned other wolves, except for a quick dalliance with a lady of his choice. He would check out a wolf caught in a trap, circle widely and be on his way. He never ate from any carcass except that he had freshly killed himself. He left it to the magpies once he had gorged himself.

At the height of his infamy, there were two other light-colored wolves in Snowdrift's area, both living in the Highwoods. Neither could match the old killer in cunning, for one was taken in 1922 and the other in 1923. No one knows how many cattle the white wolf killed, but it has been estimated at thousands. One rancher alone claimed he lost 40 head over the years to Snowdrift's appetite.

All the while he roamed and killed, hunters were hot after him. Earl Neill hit him in the left hind leg on a long shot, but otherwise he was charmed. Hunters used captive female wolves to lure him, employed the best scents and secret lures and the most carefully prepared trap settings. Snowdrift scorned them all. He was chased by car, spotted by a Great Northern train crew near Stanford, hunted by imported Russian wolf hounds and trained coyote dogs. He was pursued with gun and rope.

Once the Skelton brothers of Geyser hunted him for a week in the mountains and had given up, their packs and rifles loaded in the wagon box. Snowdrift leeringly crossed the trail in front of them, flashing a taunting farewell with his long, white tail.

The end came on a May morning in 1930, when Earl Neill, the only man ever to mar Snowdrift's magic in all those years, sighted the white wolf near the Al Close ranch. Close and Neill moved in with two dogs and cornered the anicent killer in heavy timber.

Snowdrift broke out, only 40 yards from Close and Neill

and stood, like snowy marble, defiant and discarding all the old caution. He was aging, suffering from Neill's bullet wound, and Close's shot caught him just under the left eye.

All Stanford came to see in the flesh the terror of the range. The body was six feet long and weighed 83 pounds, and the legs were long as a greyhound's, the most unusual part of an unusual animal. The men who had cursed and hunted him had his skin mounted, and visitors today can see under glass in the Judith Basin County courthouse at Stanford the most famed of all wolves in Montana's range history.

Karl Bodmer's Famous Picture of Fort Union. The Noted European Artist Came to the Fort with Prince Maximilian in 1833.

Stockade at the Forks

Just above where the muddy Yellowstone's waters mingle with the equally turbid Missouri there is a meeting place that brought many of the world's great to its sun-seared and blizzard-blasted prairie.

The remains of Fort Union are meager, but the memories of civilization in this remote spot are many. The actual confluence of these two great rivers, marked by Lewis and Clark as a suitable place for a trading post, is a buffalo-bone's throw across the line into North Dakota, but the actual fort site is six miles above the junction and well inside Montana.

In 1822 Fort Henry was built at the junction, but Indians soon destroyed the old fort. Henry was one of the famed company of traders which included William Ashley, Jim Bridger, Hugh Glass and William Sublette.

It was the fall of 1829 when Kenneth McKenzie, the efficient but not-too-popular executive of the American Fur Company's Missouri "outfit," began building Fort Floyd, whose name was soon changed to Fort Union. Not until four years later was the big fort, a virtual palace in the wilderness, completed. By that time it had competition from Fort William, just downstream, a post built by Sublette.

Probably more Indians came to Union than to any other post—Crees from Canada, Assiniboines, Chippewa from Dakota's Turtle Mountains and Red River valley, Crows down the Yellowstone valley, Hidatsa, Mandans and Arikara up the Missouri. Even Sacajawea's Shoshone occasionally came to the fort, as did the historic lady herself.

Edwin T. Denig, business manager at the fort, described Union as "the principal and handsomest trading post on the Missouri River" and described the site as "beautiful" and "well chosen." He says it is six and a half miles up the Missouri from the mouth of the Yellowstone and about 25 steps from the north bank of the river.

The fort was laid out nearly due north and south, with a 220-foot frontage facing the river and 240 feet depth. Palisades 20 feet high, made of cottonwood logs on end, and laid on stone foundations, surrounded the entire fort. Around the inside of this stockade was a walkway or balcony five feet below the top, and from this vantage point wolves were shot at sunset.

On the southwest and northeast corners were stone bastions 24 feet square and 30 feet high, with three-foot walls. Two flagstaffs flew flags from the roof, each with an American eagle. Two weathercocks, one an eagle and the other a buffalo bull, decorated the shingle roof. A three-pound iron cannon and a brass swivel were mounted in the bastions, and both usually were loaded.

For a frontier post in these raw days, Fort Union had much luxury. Alexander Culbertson, a partner in the company, and Mrs. Culbertson occupied a suite. Others had apartments. There was a large ice house, a meat house, a stable for buffalo calves, another for horses, a dairy and a milk house. Offices, a storehouse for trade goods, a gunsmith's shop and other buildings completed the fort. A parade ground filled the interior. The large outside gates were 12 feet wide and 14 feet high, one each in the middle of front and rear. Over the top of the front gate was a painting of a treaty of peace between the whites and the Indians.

In the center of the parade ground was a 63-foot flagstaff, surmounted by Old Glory, and around the base of the staff grew a practical garden of radishes, lettuce and water cress.

Life at the fort was good. Besides the nightly wolf hunt from the palisades, Culbertson and his Indian princess wife, Natawista Iksana, would saddle their horses and gallop out to shoot any buffalo that ventured near. Mrs. Culbertson, an expert swimmer, would dive into the Missouri River and come up under swimming ducks with a captured mallard in each hand, a feat that delighted John James Audubon in 1843.

From Fort Union were mounted the expeditions into the Blackfeet country to the west. As a feeler, a Chippewa half-breed named Jake Bergier was dispatched up the river to the Great Falls country to contact the Piegans. He brought them to Fort Union with the promise that the Indians could kill him if he had not told the truth about the Fort's location. McKenzie wooed them with medals and gifts, then arranged to have James Kipp, a man skilled in Indian ways, a genius of frontier relations, to set up a fort in 1831 at the mouth of the Marias River. It helped considerably that Kipp's wife was a Mandan princess.

Kipp succeeded, and a golden flow of furs came from the Blackfeet country. Although his fort, named Piegan, perished at the hands of the Assiniboine in 1832, Kipp was on his way downriver with more than 6,400 beaver skins worth $46,000, a fortune in those days.

Fort McKenzie, built just six miles above the Piegan site and on the banks of the Missouri, and Fort Benton, brought further riches to American Fur, but Fort Union was still head of navigation on the Missouri as far as commerce was concerned.

The same year Kipp brought in his fabulous haul of furs, George Catlin, the artist and writer, visited Fort Union, and in 1833 Prince Maximilian of Wied came to the fort to study the great American West. In 1843 John James Audubon brought his keen naturalist's eye and accurate artist's brush to the junction of the rivers. With Maximilian was Karl Bodmer, recording for European amazement the life of the upper Missouri.

Audubon was a popular and respected guest at the fort, and the fact he was nearly 70 years old at the time did not stop him from participating in buffalo hunts or from roaming the hills in search of specimens. Audubon was no admirer of Catlin, calling that writer's descriptions of the plains Indians and their lives "trashy stuff."

Audubon was fascinated with Fort Union and praised Mrs. Culbertson's culinary art and her grace as a hostess. He drew countless detailed pictures of birds and animals and found time to write: "The prong-horned antelope often dies on the open prairies during severe winter weather, and the remains of shockingly poor, starved, miserable individuals of this species, in a state of utmost emaciation, are now and then found dead in the winter, even near Fort Union and other trading posts." What he wrote is true even today.

Through Fort Union came Father Pierre DeSmet to bring faith to the Flathead Indians, far to the west, and on his return visits to St. Louis he and his Iroquois companion passed through Fort Union.

In 1866 the army built Fort Buford, a few miles on the Dakota side, to stem the growing menace of the Sioux, who pressed to its very gates and even held it in siege. This was the end of the trading forts at the forks of the river. It is ironic that Sitting Bull, who often led forays against Buford, was to surrender here in 1881. Brilliant Joseph, chief of the Nez Perces, was a prisoner of war at Buford.

To visit Fort Union's site today turn off Highway 2 at Bainville, drive to Snowden, then four miles east to the fort. From the south turn off Highway 16 just east of Fairview and drive north to Snowden.

Paxson's "Early Arrivals"

Fight No More

It was a cold, rainy October day when the Indian wars ended in the United States, and the exact spot was a grassy slope above the valley of Snake Creek south of Chinook.

For five days Chief Joseph of the Nez Perces, called Thunder-Traveling-Over-the-Mountains by his people, had stood with his warriors and his women and children to fight Colonel Nelson A. Miles, the fourth army officer who had been sent to stop his flight into Canada. A dozen times he had tangled with the bluecoats since he left the Wallowa country and crossed the Snake River into Idaho in June of 1877, and this was the only battle he lost.

His defeat ended not only the nearly 2,000-mile flight of the Nez Perces into Canada and safety. It ended the Indian wars, for this was the last battle in which an organized Indian force met the United States army. Four times in Montana Joseph had outsmarted, bested or fought a drawn battle with the troops.

The Nez Perce had slipped around Fort Fizzle in the Lolo, leaving an embarrassed General Howard and a number of citizens entrenched and with no one to fight. It was a standoff at the Big Hole, where the soldiers under General Gibbon fired into the lodges at dawn. General Sturgis was whipped and outmaneuvered by Joseph at Canyon Creek near Laurel. Now the time had come. General Howard and Colonel Miles were both at the Indians' flanks.

Joseph had crossed the Missouri River a day ahead of Miles, who had to be ferried across by a Missouri River steamboat below Cow Island. Only a few more miles and Joseph would have been safe in Canada, where he intended to go to Sitting Bull's camp in Saskatchewan. From there he intended to bargain with the U. S. government over Nez Perce lands in Oregon.

It was September 30, 1877, when fate decreed the Nez Perce and the U. S. Army would meet on Snake Creek. Miles, who had force-marched his men from Fort Keogh, just west of Miles City, had more than 600 soldiers and Indians with him. Joseph had around 400 Indians, most of them women and children.

Miles charged into the Indian camp, cutting it in two and capturing nearly all the 100 horses of the Nez Perce. Joseph handed his little daughter a horse and told her to escape, which she did. The leader's clothes were cut by army bullets and his horse wounded, but he got his gun and jumped into the close-in fighting among the lodges. When night fell 18 Indian warriors and three women were dead. Miles had lost 26 soldiers, with 40 wounded. He sent for Joseph, and the leader sent Yellow Bull to talk to the colonel.

The next four days were of fighting and talking, with messengers, including Cheyenne Indian scouts, going back and forth across the lines between the rifle pits on the grassy hills. At 11 o'clock October 5 communication was established, and Joseph came over to the military camp to meet Howard and Miles. At 2 that afternoon Joseph offered his rifle to Howard, then gave it to Miles, surrendering on conditions set up by Miles: "If you will come out and give up your arms, I will spare your lives and send you back to the reservation."

Miles kept his word but the U. S. government didn't. Some, including Joseph, eventually got back to Oregon, but most of the Nez Perce sweltered to death in Kansas, drinking dirty river water.

On his surrender Joseph told Miles: "I am tired of fighting . . . the little children are freezing to death. My heart is sick and sad. From where the sun now stands, I will fight no more with the white man."

Joseph surrendered 89 men, 184 women, 147 children and had lost an estimated 100 Indians on his retreat. During the fighting on Snake Creek 104 Nez Perce slipped away and into Canada, including Chief White Bird.

General Howard's aide-de-camp and adjutant said many years later of Joseph: "(I) . . . can bear testimony to Joseph's fine character—conduct of the war on the lines of 'civilized' warfare—our unjust treatment which brought on the war and the repudiation of what were the clearly understood terms of surrender."

The Snake Creek battlefield is just south of Chinook; turn off Highway 2 in the town and drive about 13 miles due south.

The Battle at Snake Creek — C. M. Russell

The New Land of Shining Mountains

Southeast — Land of the Indian Wars

Custer's defeat in 1876 was the most famous, but southeastern Montana was one of the major Indian battlegrounds of the West, and eventually the Indians took second money.

Of all the forts in Montana built to protect the constantly increasing population from the Indians, Fort Keogh was no doubt the busiest. General Nelson Miles had an efficiency in battle and a fairness in conquest that made him a genuine leader, and it's too bad his wisdom wasn't shared in Washington.

History began early in the Yellowstone country, and most of this southeast is drained by the river Rochejohne as the Indians called it. Only a little more than a year after Lewis and Clark returned home, or in November of 1807, John Colter and Manuel Lisa, St. Louis fur trader, arrived at the mouth of the Big Horn and built Montana's first permanent dwelling.

Even before that Francois Antoine Larocque, an educated Frenchman and clerk for the Northwest Company, had visited Pryor Creek south of Billings, probably about September 6, 1805, although his journal leaves some doubt.

An interim visitor was Captain William Clark in the summer of 1806, on his way to a rendezvous with Meriwether Lewis at the fork of the Missouri and Yellowstone.

These were peaceful visitors, but their followers invoked the wrath of the Sioux and Cheyenne. The Crow, who ruled the upper Yellowstone, were peaceful as far as whites were concerned, although they did steal all Clark's horses and forced him to float the river below Park City. Stealing horses was no sign of hostility. It was a legitimate way to acquire property.

Among the distinguished persons who felt the ferocity of the Indians were Custer, Benteen, Reno, Miles, Forsyth and dozens of lesser citizens, both military and civilian. There is always the question of just how much of this boiling animosity was stirred by Sir George Gore, the Irish nobleman who hauled his luxurious wagons through the Powder River country in 1856, slaughtering thousands of buffalo and antelope with his custom-made rifles and leaving their stinking carcasses on the plains. He may well have left much behind him besides the name of Glendive on the creek which reminded him of the vales of Erin.

Whatever the cause, there was blood on the moon in the country of the Powder and the Yellowstone, and this was the only spot on the nation's map where the U. S. Army ever came to defeat at the hands of red men defending their homeland.

How They Got Their Names — Towns and Cities

Absarokee—This is the country of the Absarokee or Absaroka Indians, best known as the Mountain Crows. Up-sa-rah-qu is the name the Crows were given by other Indians, meaning "sharp people."

Baker—Renamed from Lorraine for an engineer with the Milwaukee railroad, A. G. Baker.

Big Timber—After Big Timber Creek, which flows into the Yellowstone River here. The creek had huge cottonwood trees on its banks.

Billings—Frederick Billings, president of the Northern Pacific Railway, furnished a name for this town in the early 80s when the city was growing up between the Yellowstone River and the NP tracks.

Bridger—This one-street town in pioneer coal-mining days was called Stringtown, the easiest name to come by. However, "Daddy" Town, the village's father, wanted it named after his buddy "Jim Bridger." Calamity Jane took in washing at her tent home in Bridger and operated a freight line.

Broadus—By a "red tape" error in Washington, D. C., one "d" was dropped from the family name of Broaddus when this county seat was named. Broaddus cattle ranged over much of southeastern Montana.

Clyde Park—Take your choice on this one. Some claim its namesake was Clyde DuRand, an early rancher. Others say the Clydesdale horses raised around the valley in its beginning as a ranch country were to blame.

Colstrip—Coal mined from deep beds by the strip process both created the town and gave it a name.

Columbus—Either Columbus, Minnesota, or the discoverer of America is responsible.

Comanche—The sole survivor of the Custer battle was Captain Myles W. Keogh's buckskin horse, Comanche. Found wandering on the battlefield he was taken to Fort Riley, Kansas, where he died when he was 29 years old. His mounted form is at the University of Kansas, displaying a typical cavalry horse of that period.

Cooke City—In 1880 Jay Cooke, Jr., had 10 feet of snow shoveled off the ore veins around Cooke City so he could decide whether to buy the Republic claims. He did, and Cooke City was off to a boom. Later Major Eaton tried to change the name to Eidelweiss, a German flower that blooms through the snow, but the miners stuck by old Jay.

Crow Agency—For the Crow Indians their agency is at this town in the Big Horn valley.

Custer—This Yellowstone valley town is named for General George Armstrong Custer, leader of the Seventh Cavalry, who died with his command in the most famous Indian battle of the West.

Ekalaka—David H. Russell, frontier hunter and the first settler in this area, married the daughter of a Sioux Indian chief name Ijkalaka, and Russell named the town after her. He was coming to Montana with a load of trade whiskey and his wagon stuck in the mud. He said, "Hell, any place in Montana is a good place for a saloon," and stayed.

Fallon—A contraction of the name O'Fallon, a nephew of Captain William Clark and prominent St. Louis fur trader.

Forsyth—The first army officer to land here from a Yellowstone River steamboat was General James W. Forsyth. For a long time the place was known as Forsyth's landing.

Gardiner—Took its name from the Gardiner River, which flows into the Yellowstone River near town.

Garryowen—Memories of the Custer campaign live in this name of the Seventh Cavalry marching song.

Glendive—Sir George Gore, while hunting in southwestern Montana, saw in the small creek entering the Yellowstone River here a resemblance to Glendive Creek in his native Ireland. This was in 1856 but the name stuck to both creek and town.

Hardin—Probably for S. H. Hardin, Texas cowman and friend of the man who platted the town.

Harlowton—The town was the eastern terminus of the Montana Railway Company's line across central Montana, and Richard Harlow was president of the railroad. The railroad was called the "Jawbone" because Harlow's fluent persuasion substituted for cash in getting labor and materials.

Hysham—Charles Hysham was an early cattleman in this area on the Yellowstone.

Ismay—Two girls, Isabelle and Mary Peck, combined their names to give this town a moniker. They were daughters of George W. Peck, oldtime Milwaukee Railroad officer.

Lame Deer—Chief Lame Deer of the Minneconyoux, a Sioux tribe, gave his name to this Cheyenne Reservation town. Lame Deer swore he would never surrender to the white man but General Nelson Miles changed his mind May 7, 1877.

Laurel—Apparently from the laurel growing on the river bottom here. This site, at the mouth of the Clark's Fork of the Yellowstone, was discussed by Lewis and Clark as a good site for a trading post. The town was known for a time as Canyon Creek, and the Indians called this point "The Lodge Where All Dance."

Livingston—Named for Johnson Livingston, a director of the Northern Pacific Railway. Since the 80s this city has been identified strongly with the railroad and with Yellowstone National Park to the south.

Lodge Grass—A mistake named this town. Crow Indians called the surrounding country "greasy grass," because the grass left a stain on their moccasins. The Crow names for "greasy" and "lodge" were so similar that pioneers hung the wrong name on the town. Nearby Greasy Grass Creek is correctly named.

Miles City—General Nelson A. Miles, who commanded the forces at Fort Keogh, just west of Miles City, gave his name to one of the greatest cow towns in the West. From Fort Keogh General Miles went out to bring the Indians to terms following Custer's smashing defeat on the Little Big Horn. Miles City once was the greatest horse market in the world and still is a leading livestock center.

Mill Iron—Named for the old Mill Iron ranch, whose brand was the same shape as the irons used in the pioneer lumber mills.

Nye—After Jack Nye, one of the early prospectors in the Stillwater country and founder of the Stillwater Mining Company in 1884.

Park City—This town had a hard time making up its mind. It was here that Captain William Clark first found trees large enough to make canoes for his descent of the Yellowstone River. Its first name was Clark City for a real estate promoter, not the explorer. Northern Pacific Railway officials wanted to save the name Park City for the present Livingston, gateway to Yellowstone Park by rail at that time. However, the residents decided they wanted Park City, and the name stuck.

Plevna—After Plevna, Bulgaria.

Pompey's Pillar—Nearby, on the banks of the Yellowstone River, is a stone formation noted by Captain William Clark in 1806 and named for "Little Pomp," Sacajawea's baby.

Powderville—Only town in Montana with only one official inhabitant. Named for Powder River.

Pryor—From the nearby Pryor Mountains.

Rapelje—After J. M. Rapelje, Northern Pacific Railway official.

Red Lodge—The Crow Indians at one time had a council tepee or lodge here, painted red with ocher.

Rosebud—For the many wild roses found along the river bank.

St. Xavier—After the St. Xavier school and Roman Catholic mission established here in 1887.

Sanders—After Wilbur Fisk Sanders, U. S. Senator from Montana, member of the Vigilantes, who first established law and order in the territory.

Sidney—Named for Sidney Walters, member of a pioneer family in the lower Yellowstone valley.

Sioux Pass—A natural pass in the bluffs here was used for years by the Sioux Indians.

Terry—After General Alfred H. Terry, Custer's commander in the Little Big Horn campaign.

Twodot—Just south of here lived "Two Dot" Wilson, nicknamed from his brand of two dots on the side of a cow.

Wibaux—After Pierre Wibaux, pioneer cattleman and Frenchman of excellent background who operated in southeastern Montana and southwestern North Dakota.

Wilsall—Combination of Will and Sally, son and daughter-in-law of Walter B. Jordan, who laid out the townsite.

How They Got Their Names — Lakes and Streams

Yellowstone River—Called Rochejohne by the Indians, the reference is to the large yellow boulders in the bed of the river at some points. Rising in Yellowstone Park and flowing through Yellowstone Lake, both of which took their name from the river, it flows north, then eastward, draining all of southern Montana, and joins the Missouri at old Fort Union, just east of the Montana border in North Dakota. This valley was the way west for not only thousands of Indians but wagon trains by the dozens into southwestern Montana.

Glendive Creek—Named by Sir George Gore, Irish nobleman in Montana in a big game hunt, because the little badlands creek reminded him of a creek by that name in Ireland. Flows into the Yellowstone at Glendive, and rises in the rough country just west of the Dakota border. Crow Indians came into the valley by way of Glendive Creek.

O'Fallon Creek—Runs into the Yellowstone River from the south at Fallon. Captain Clark named it Coal Creek or Oaktar-pon-er, but it later was renamed after Clark's nephew, a prominent St. Louis fur trader.

Powder River—Rises in northern Wyoming, west of the Black Hills and flows almost due north to join the Yellowstone west of Terry. One of the best known western rivers, it has been called "too thick to drink, too thin to plow, a mile wide and an inch deep." During World War I the 91st Division made it famous with their battle cry "Powder River, Let 'er Buck." Francois Antoine Larocque in 1805 ascended the Powder and said: "The current of the river is very strong and the water so muddy that it is scarcely drinkable. The savages say that it is always thus and that it is for this reason that they call the river Powder, for the wind rises and carries from the slope a fine sand which obscures and dirties the water." It was a coincidence that when Captain Clark named the river Red Stone when he reached its mouth July 30, 1806, he found the Indians called it Wa ha Sah, meaning the same thing. Clark commented on the "great quantities of red stone thrown out of this river" at its mouth. He didn't like the water here, either, and again crossed the Yellowstone to spend the night. Between here and Miles City are Buffalo Rapids, named by Clark because a buffalo carcass floated in them, and Bear Rapids, after a grizzly standing on a rock there.

Tongue River—Rises along the Wyoming border and flows northeasterly through the Cheyenne Reservation to join the Yellowstone at Miles City. Indians called the river Lazeka or Tongue. Clark camped at an island across the Yellowstone from the mouth of the Tongue July 29, 1806. He didn't like the taste of Tongue River water any better than Powder River.

Rosebud River—Flows northward out of the Rosebud Mountains on the western edge of the Cheyenne Indian Reservation and into the Yellowstone just west of Rosebud. Named for wild rosebuds along the river bank. Indians called this the Little Big Horn River. Records have vanished on a long ago trading fort at the mouth of the Rosebud.

Great Porcupine Creek—Flows from the north into the Yellowstone at Forsyth. Captain Clark passed here July 28, 1806, and commented that the stream was called Little Wolf by the Indians and "containing little water." It still doesn't have much water.

Sarpy Creek—Flows northward out of the Sarpy hills between Hysham and Forsyth, and into the Yellowstone. Captain Clark named it Labiech's River, after a party member, but it was renamed after John B. Sarpy, St. Louis fur merchant with interests in the area.

Big Horn and Little Big Horn Rivers—The Big Horn flows in from Wyoming and enters the Yellowstone about 15 miles west of Hysham. The Little Big Horn flows into the Big Horn at Hardin. Both were named for bighorn sheep along the banks. On the latter stream General Custer was defeated in his famed battle of June 25, 1876. At the mouth of the Big Horn Manuel Lisa erected Montana's first permanent habitation in 1807.

This fort was abandoned in 1811 and succeeded by forts Benton (1822-23) and Cass (1832-35). Don't confuse with Fort Benton on the Missouri.

Pryor's River—Flows northward out of the Pryor Mountains into the Yellowstone River just above Billings. Named for Sergeant Pryor, who accompanied Captain Clark on his Yellowstone exploration. The party camped just below the mouth of this river July 24, 1806.

Canyon Creek—A small but historic creek flows out of rimrocks to the north and into the Yellowstone near Laurel. Here, in September, 1877, the U. S. Army under General Sturgis and Nez Perce warriors under Chief Joseph fought a battle in the canyon. The Indians won, hands down.

Clark's Fork of the Yellowstone—One of two streams in the state to honor the co-leader of the Lewis and Clark expedition. Rises in Yellowstone Park, flows eastward through Wyoming, then northward to join the Yellowstone at Laurel. Crow Indians called the junction "The Lodge where all dance." This valley from earliest times has been a road for Indians, pioneers and soldiers. Chief Joseph led his Nez Perce down the valley in 1877, followed by General Gibbon. John Colter used this trail in the winter of 1806-07, after leaving the returning Lewis and Clark expedition to come back to Montana and trade for furs. Some of Montana's first coal mines are in this valley.

Stillwater River—Drains the northern slope of the Absaroka plateau, flowing northward into the Yellowstone at Columbus. Indian legend has it that a young Crow lover jumped into the river during a violent storm to join his sweetheart, whose body had been washed into the flood by the storm. As the storm quieted and the waters stilled, the Indians called the place the sacred "still water," and the whole river took this name. America's only chrome mines are at the head of this river.

Sweet Grass Creek—Flows southward into the Yellowstone at Greycliff, draining the eastern slope of the Crazy mountains and Cayuse hills. Pays a practical tribute to the fine grazing on the slopes of these mountains.

Boulder River—Huge boulders in the river bed and on the

banks gave it this name. Flows out of the Absaroka Mountains northward into the Yellowstone at Big Timber.

Big Timber Creek—Flows out of the Crazy Mountains to the north and into the Yellowstone at the town of the same name. Big cottonwood trees growing along the creek gave it that name, but none was big enough to make canoes for Captain Clark. He had to wait till he got to Park City.

Shields River—Named for John Shields, who accompanied Captain Clark on his exploration of the Yellowstone and arrived at the point where the Shields River flows into the Yellowstone below Livingston July 15, 1806. The river drains the valley between the Bridger and Crazy Mountains.

How They Got Their Names — Mountains

Absaroka Range—Montana's highest mountain range contains 12,799-foot Granite Peak, the loftiest point in the state. This range borders Wyoming at the northern boundary of Yellowstone Park and lies between the upper Yellowstone valley and the Boulder River valley south of Big Timber. Highest highway pass in Montana carries the Red Lodge-Cooke City road across the Beartooth plateau at 10,940 feet from the Yellowstone valley to Yellowstone Park. In these mountains is Grasshopper Glacier, with its millions of frozen prehistoric grasshoppers. From the ancient name of the Crow Indians—Absaroka.

Bull Mountains—South of Roundup. Rolling hills timbered with yellow pine. Name came either from buffalo or elk bulls found in the area.

Cayuse Hills—East of Melville. Cayuse is the old frontier name for a range horse.

Chalk Buttes—Southwest of Ekalaka. Named for the distinctive white walls of the "breaks" of the Powder River.

Crazy Mountains—East of Wilsall. This high, rugged range, populated with Rocky Mountain goats, was named because a woman member of a pioneer wagon train moving westward along the old Bozeman trail became insane at the foot of these mountains. First called the "Crazy Woman Mountains," this was later shortened. Crazy Peak at 11,214 feet west of Melville is the highest.

Makoshika—Badlands south of Glendive, named for the old Indian term for such broken country. The most scenic portion is a state park.

Pryor Mountains—South of Laurel. Named for Sergeant Pryor of the Lewis and Clark expedition, who accompanied Clark on his Yellowstone exploration in 1806. It was Pryor who, after the Crow Indians had stolen all the Clark party's horses, managed to build two bowl-shaped "bull boats" of buffalo hides and navigated the cranky craft to the mouth of the Yellowstone. The Pryor Mountains contain a number of ice caves.

The New Land

Dawn of white man's history in Montana could have come on a bleak New Year's Day more than 200 years ago, but no one can say for certain except two Frenchmen long since in their graves. The red bluffs of southeastern Montana and the silent waters of the Little Missouri do not talk.

In the early 1700s the ambitious French yearned to step boldly into the path of the southward-expanding Hudson's Bay Company, and Sieur de La Verendrye, the French agent at Lake Nipigon, north of Lake Superior, in 1728, had the support of French-governed Canada in setting up western trading posts to accomplish this cutoff of the British.

Although he visited the Mandans in North Dakota in 1738, he later fell ill, and when a major expedition was mounted in 1742 he had to send his sons, Francois and Louis Joseph. These leaders were at the Mandan village in Dakota from May to July of 1742, since these Indians were supposed to know the way to the Pacific. They didn't, but the Verendryes waited here, as did Lewis and Clark a half century later, for Indians who knew the way to salt water.

First the Crows, then the Bow Indians, were the Verendryes' traveling companions. The latter urged them to help in a planned fight with the Snake Indians, which surely would result in their reaching the ocean. On this trek southwestward there is evidence the party crossed Montana's southeastern corner, sighting on January 1, 1743, a range of mountains shining in the winter sun off to the southwest.

Some believe this range was the Big Horns in Wyoming, others the Black Hills of South Dakota, but the vantage point could easily have been along the Little Missouri river in the Albion or Alzada country, not far from Highway 212. The French and the Bow Indians found an abandoned Snake camp somewhere west of Sheridan, Wyoming, and retreated eastward, fearing encirclement by the enemy.

Eventually the Verendryes returned to Manitoba, where the elder Verendrye had a post, but whether they really reached Montana is one of the great mysteries of the West. However, any adventurer can follow Highway 212 southeast from Miles City and mentally roll back two centuries on the hills and breaks of the Little Missouri.

While Lewis and Clark were waiting out the winter of 1804-05 at the Mandan camp on the Missouri in North Dakota, they refused Francois Antone Larcoque, a North West Company clerk, permission to join their expedition. Next June he joined a party of Gros Ventre headed west, followed the Heart River, then the Little Missouri and crossed the bluffs and cinder buttes of southeastern Montana to the Powder River.

Here Larcoque learned that the Indians called this river the Powder because "the wind rises and carries from the slope a fine sand which obscures and dirties the water." Even in those days it was a mile wide, an inch deep, too thick to drink and too thin to plow.

July 3 the party saw the Big Horn Mountains, reached their foot, then swung northwestward until, on September 6, 1805, it reached Pryor Creek south of Billings. Although he bought 122 beaver skins, four bear and two otter, he never followed up his contacts with the Indians. Even his original journal was lost. Only a copy at Laval University tells of his journeys to Montana.

To reach his trail across Montana, again take Highway 212, which must roughly parallel his way between the Little Missouri and the Powder. To follow him after he left Sheridan, travel Highway 90 south of Billings, then turn off on blacktop east and south of Billings and drive straight to the town of Pryor, where the Plenty Coups museum recalls the achievements of a later day.

Whatever these explorers found, they probably knew nothing of all Montana that lay to the west and north. Only rumor came from the Indian bands they traveled with. Soon afterward the star of France declined and faded in the western world, and Napoleon sold Montana east of the divide to a young nation which succeeded in finding its way to the salt water.

The Battle Custer Won

Summer haze hung softly over the lower Yellowstone valley August 4, 1873, the day General George Armstrong Custer whipped the Sioux among the tall cottonwoods near the mouth of Tongue River.

Custer's defeat and death three years later at the hands of this same tribe are part of every school boy's historical lore, but the Custer campaign preceding that fateful date in 1876 on the Little Big Horn is virtually unknown. Barely known, too, is that the general's prime duty in the West was to guard survey crews driving a line westward for the new Northern Pacific Railway from Lake Superior to Puget Sound, a railroad that was to join the northern coasts and bring troops to the outposts of a young country.

The year 1873 was a bad one for the surveyor escort. The

Sioux didn't want anyone in their buffalo country and said so with arrow and rifle. To protect the transit-and-chain men the army brought a regiment of cavalry from the south and set up a supply depot at the mouth of Glendive Creek, about where the city of Glendive now stands. Major General D. S. Stanley commanded 1,700 men from Fort Rice on the Missouri River in Dakota Territory.

At 5 o'clock the morning of August 4 General Custer left camp along the Yellowstone leading 91 cavalrymen. At his side was Bloody Knife, Custer's Arickaree scout, who died with the general at the Little Big Horn. Bloody Knife quickly picked out Indian sign along the bluffs, which was not surprising. There had been skirmishes almost every day. At 10 o'clock the column topped the rimrocks along the river and Custer stopped his command to let the sweating men and horses rest. It was a fine day, and the general decided to drop off into the river bottom, which looked so attractive from the bluffs, and to spend a little while under the shade of the heavy-limbed cottonwoods.

His horses drank heavily from the "clear, crystal water of the Yellowstone," a far cry from today's roiled river, and Custer picked a "most inviting spot for my noonday nap" near his picketed horse, his rifle within easy reach.

Captain Tom Custer, the general's brother, snoozed nearby. Then all hell broke loose under the warm summer sky. Pickets' rifles cracked, and a half-dozen plumed Sioux closed in at a fast run across the grassy river bottom which bordered the cottonwoods. Stopped by trooper fire, the Sioux galloped back across the meadow, giving Custer time to mount his Kentucky thoroughbred and his men time to saddle up. The Sioux tried to lure the cavalry into a trap by the river. For two miles blue-coated riders chased red-skinned horsemen, then the cavalry stopped just short of heavy timber at the river's edge.

From ambush nearly 400 Sioux warriors, stripped and painted for battle, screaming defiance, raced their steel-muscled ponies against the army. They moved in perfect formation against the cavalry, now 400 yards away, and Captain Custer ordered his men to dismount so they could fire from steadier positions. One man in four held the bridles of his buddies' mounts.

The first ripping volley cut down so many Indians that the line wavered, and live warriors scooped up wounded and dying on a dead run. Moylan and his troops were moving up fast from the rear, guidons and manes flying in the wind. The 15 cavalrymen on the ground loaded and reloaded, and soon the Sioux turned back to the protecting timber. The officers quickly decided to make a defensive stand on foot, depending on carbine firepower to overcome the rush of the mounted Indians. The soldiers still were outnumbered 10 to one.

Fighting from a tight circle the soldiers dropped back to the grove where they had rested earlier. The ground between was covered with dead Indians and horses. A single Indian, galloping back and forth across the line of defense, tempted Bloody Knife and General Custer. Bloody Knife's Henry rifle cut down the Sioux, and Custer's rifle killed his pony. His comrades snatched up the body almost as soon as it touched the ground.

The hot afternoon wore on. The Sioux tried crawling through the grass on their stomachs, then they set fire to the grass in front of the dug-in troopers. The grass was still green and failed to burn. Indians sneaked around the end of the defense line and tried to move up under cover of the river bank to steal Custer's horses. All attempts were fought off.

Both sides gathered to firm up their positions, warily watching the other. Custer noticed the Indians moving quickly into a tighter formation on the left. The Sioux had seen, even before the cavalry, a cloud of dust on the bluffs above the river. Four squadrons of cavalry were moving up fast, vieing as to which would be the first to relieve Custer's command. Custer called it a "grand and welcome sight."

Even before the reinforcements arrived, Custer's men were in the saddle and hot after the scrambling Sioux, even though the odds were still five-to-one in favor of the Indians. The pursuers picked up a few Indian ponies but soon gave up the chase and returned to camp opposite the mouth of Tongue River. Custer estimated Indian dead and wounded at "that of half our entire force engaged." The troopers lost two men— the post veterinarian and the sutler. It was a clear cut day of victory for the general, but the Sioux were to have their day, and it was not long coming.

Little Big Horn – Bloody Mystery

For all its fame as the symbol of Indian battles, Custer's defeat on the green hills of June above the Little Big Horn remains one of the greatest mysteries of the West.

Conflicting stories of what happened when Yellow Hair's troops ripped into battle against the Sioux and Cheyenne began the day the battle ended, and they still are rampant. This very mystery makes the battleground even more intriguing to today's amateur strategists and casual visitors to this shrine of the romantic frontier.

No one who reaches Hardin on Highway 90 or its smaller neighbors Crow Agency or Garryowen, just south, can miss the Custer Battlefield National Monument or the nearby Reno-Benteen Battlefield memorial. Even the excellent markings on the fields and the well-informed attendants can't penetrate the welter of conflict that obliterates what really happened that bright June 25, 1876.

These things are well known. George Armstrong Custer had capably earned the bitter hatred of the Sioux and Cheyenne. He had led the butchering troops into Black Kettle's camp on the Washita in the Texas panhandle, driving half-naked Cheyennes into the foot-deep snow and searing cold. Custer had earned his general's stars well, for he had fought in the major campaigns of the Civil War ever since he left West Point, where he graduated at the foot of his class.

On a bitter, raw May 17, 1876, Custer, together with Reno, Benteen and the command of Seventh Cavalarymen rode west from Fort Abraham Lincoln on the Missouri River. A mirage in the sun breaking through foreboding clouds made the column appear to be riding into the sky. It was a portentous symbol, for 39 days later many of them were dead, and a nation was humiliated to the quick.

So, the Cheyennes who were brutally mauled at Washita and the Sioux who had seen the U. S. government callously break its treaty to keep gold miners out of the Black Hills of South Dakota, were in the proper mood to receive the Seventh on the morning of June 25. An added stinger was that General George Crook, moving from the south toward the Little Big

Horn, attacked a Cheyenne camp, thinking it to be a Sioux encampment, and later Crook tangled again with Crazy Horse's Sioux, this time on June 17, 1876.

The stage was being beautifully set for maddened battle. General Alfred H. Terry, in overall command, was correctly confident that the Indians would be found on the Little Big Horn. General Terry had persuaded General Grant to restore Custer's command for this Indian duty, and Custer was eager to re-establish himself.

The strategy was for Custer to move up the Rosebud River on June 22, and two days later he camped at what now is Busby, about 15 miles east of the battlefield and in the open pine hills at the head of the Rosebud. Crook's Indian troubles kept him from making contact from the south. From the north Colonel John Gibbon was bringing troops down the Yellowstone from forts Shaw and Ellis.

While Custer was watching the Tongue and Powder valleys for possible encirclement, scouts returning to camp told of large Indian encampment on the Little Big Horn. On the morning of the 25th Sioux or Cheyenne scouts were checking out Custer's command, and no one will ever know whether Custer really was fully informed on the size of the Indian camp on the Little Big Horn.

Meanwhile, General Terry had talked with Colonel Gibbon at the mouth of Powder River. All was going fairly well, except that Major Reno had irritated General Terry by not following orders.

About 2 o'clock the hot afternoon of June 25 a band of about 40 Indians was seen going down the river. Captain Fred Benteen already had been sent out to scout east and south, and all units were marching. Major Reno was sent after the small Indian party, and either unknown or unheeded was the fact that he was heading straight into what undoubtedly was the largest Indian battle force ever assembled. There were from 12 to 15,000 Sioux and Cheyenne in the camp, and their horse herds, peacefully grazing above the river bottom, could have numbered well over 30,000. Never before on the North American continent had so many savages and their horses gathered at one time.

Reno, with only 112 men, galloped through the cottonwood

trees on the river bottom, splashed into the waters of the Little Big Horn and met the withering onslaught of the Sioux-Cheyenne under Sitting Bull's top command. The battle was under way. This was about 2:30, and Reno met more Indians than he thought were in the whole camp. By 4 o'clock he was in full retreat, having to cross the river in a new place and expose his men by climbing a six-foot bank with frightened horses.

Custer met the Indians on the hogback above. There were no white survivors of the massacre itself. Thousands of Indians fought Custer and lived. Thousands more watched the fight. Even here there is disagreement. Some claim that Custer tried to cross the river to help Reno, and that advancing Indians drove him back to the hills. Many Indians supported this view. Others claimed Custer advanced down the Little Big Horn, hoping for ammunition packs he had requested from Benteen, who was a mile south. Some Indians claim he held this position well until a premature advance by two companies of soldiers under Reno caused him to overextend his defense.

Benteen and Reno brought their commands together. Heavy fighting was heard on the hills above, but everyone on the river bottom was too busy with hordes of red warriors to find out what happened to Custer. Night ended the firing, and in the dark Benteen and Reno's commands brought water from the river, tended to the wounded and prepared for more fighting at dawn.

Soon after noon the 26th, scouts were seen going to the big camp upriver, and soon the travois were under way. The Indians were moving up the Little Big Horn. Gibbon's Montana column and General Terry soon found what had happened to Custer and his men. All 225 lay dead on the ridge. In all, including Reno's losses, 262 soldiers died in the battle. The world found out what happened to Custer through Curley, Custer's scout, who crawled from the brush at the mouth of the Little Big Horn to tell Captain Grant Marsh of the steamer Far West about the disaster. The wounded from Reno's command were bedded down on grass beds on the deck of the Far West to return to Fort Abraham Lincoln, by way of the Yellowstone and Missouri rivers.

Black Kettle had his revenge. So did Rain-in-the-Face,

who threatened to cut out Captain Tom Custer's heart after the captain had jailed him at Fort Abraham Lincoln. When Tom Custer's body was found, his midsection had been ripped open with a lance. Immediately the rumors started. No one can say finally even today whether Custer was scalped and mutilated. No one knows who killed the yellow-haired general. No one knows whether Wooden Leg, the old Cheyenne, told the truth when he said Indians killed not more than 20 or 30 of Custer's men, and the rest committed suicide. There is no proof of the Indian claim that a can of whiskey hung at the pommel of each soldier's saddle. Ugly rumors as to Custer's and Reno's bravery have persisted over the years.

As clear as the air on a June day along the Little Big Horn is that the Custer defeat electrified a lethargic nation. It demand revenge and got it. Within a year all organized Indian resistance on the North American continent was stilled forever.

Little Pomp's Tower

Morning rain showered the rimrocks of the Yellowstone valley and the first white visitor to climb Pompey's Pillar and watch the shimmering blue of southern Montana's mountains.

The day was July 25, 1806, and Captain William Clark was on his way to a rendezvous at the mouth of the Yellowstone River with Meriwether Lewis. During breakfast the party had killed two "fat buffalow" and two equally fat deer, Clark's journal records.

By noon the rain had ended, although the expedition had to sit some it out under a cottonwood log and deerskin shelter along the river and dry itself by a "large fire."

Clark described the discovery of the pillar itself: "I proceeded on after the rain lay a little and at 4 p.m. arrived at a remarkable rock situated in an extensive bottom on the starboard (south) side of the river and 250 paces from it. This rock I ascended and from its top had a most extensive view in every direction. This rock which I shall call Pompy's Tower is 200 feet high and 400 paces in circumference and only accessible on one side, which is from the N. E., the other parts of it being a perpendicular cliff of lightish coloured gritty rock."

Clark carefully noted in his journal that the tower top was covered with five or six feet of soil and supported a crop of short grass. He also observed that the Indians have made two piles of stone on the top and engraved on the face of the rock some figures of animals.

Near this Indian handwork Clark carved his own name and the date, as have so many tourists after him in so many places. The Clark autograph, however, eventually was protected by a screen erected by the Northern Pacific Railway and so preserved for generations to see.

Clark carefully looked over the country from the top of the rock. At his feet on the north was the Yellowstone River, called Rochejhone by the explorers, and the craggy rimrocks, a gray and brown pattern of sandstone. Clark recorded that the "hills are ruged and some pine" and that the "plains are open and extensive."

Looking farther off, beyond the Yellowstone valley, Clark saw two mountain ranges, the Big Horns to the southwest, which he called "Rocky mountains covered with snow" and to the southeast the Rosebud Range or "what the Indians call the Little Wolf mountains."

The latter were generally then called the Wolf or Cheetish Mountains and not until later became known as the Rosebuds. Opposite the pillar Clark noted a "stream running muddy water" and named it Baptiests' Creek after Baptiste Lepage, one of the expedition members. The expedition was a little careless with its spelling. The creek now is Pompey's Pillar Creek.

Although Clark named the rock "Pompy's Tower," later journal corrections showed the name Pompey's Pillar, after Sacajawea's baby, or "Little Pomp," as Lewis called him, and the name stuck, much better than most of the expedition's names. Clark named another stream from the north Shannon's Creek, but it now is Bull Mountain Creek.

Clark noted "emence herds of Buffalow, elk and wolves," then killed two bighorn sheep out of a herd of 40, but could recover neither of them. Landing the canoes, he went ashore and killed a ewe and a small ram and recovered both, but wished he had killed a bigger ram, like so many hunters after him.

Clark then pried part of a fossilized fish off the rimrock and the party swept off down the river, ending the day in another shower amid the rutting grunts of the buffalo bulls "a very loud and disagreeable sound." Minus the bighorn sheep, the pillar is very much an attraction today, between Billings and Hysham, just off Highway 94.

Red Farmers

Sugar beets and alfalfa grow in the valley where Montana's first farmers lived and grew their stunted, many-colored corn, the Lower Yellowstone.

Corncrib and power machinery are reminders that here the earth was turned for the first time in Montana so a seed could grow a crop. That the farming tools soon were dropped by hands which preferred to drive an arrow into a plunging buffalo's rib case is of little matter—here was the birthplace of Montana agriculture.

It was the Crow Indians, the Absaroka who ruled southern Montana and disputed even the warlike Blackfeet, who came as farmers to the level river bottom beneath the bluffs, about where Glendive now stands. Natives of the now great cornlands of Iowa, the Crow and Hidatsa, were a single tribe before history, and they moved first to the Devil's Lake country of North Dakota, then to the Missouri valley near the mouth of Heart River, which enters the Missouri at Mandan, North Dakota.

Here they learned to build earth lodges; then the Crows split away from their Hidatsa brothers to follow the sun westward along the Heart River and across the badlands into the winding valley of the Yellowstone, at the mouth of Glendive Creek.

While they planted their corn and molded heavy pottery vessels to contain their harvest, they built a ceremonial center, one of the last they would ever build. This was in the mid 1700s, half a century at least before Captain William Clark passed this way.

Already the Crows were becoming hunters, forsaking the soil for the buffalo chase, and in 25 years they were wanderers, following the herds and growing nothing but their ceremonial tobacco. Long before horses came to the plains, the Crows were hunting for a living, and even the Hidatsas came to Montana for an occasional hunt or raid.

Soon these farmers possessed most of the Yellowstone ranging to the mountains and up and down the great rivers that flow into the valley from the south, the Big Horn, Clark Fork, Stillwater, Rosebud and Tongue, although they had long since forgotten how to till. The Absaroka loved their country, loved it so much their great Chief Black Otter was carried miles with an enemy spearhead in his hip so he could die and be buried on the rimrocks above the Yellowstone.

The Crow Chief Arapooish, who must have been a one-man Indian Chamber of Commerce, described the Crow country: "It has snowy mountains and sunny plains; all kinds of climates and good things for every season. When the summer heat scorches the prairies, you can draw up under the mountains, where the air is cool and sweet, the grass fresh and bright streams come tumbling out of the snow banks.

"There you can hunt the elk, the deer and the antelope when their skins are fit for dressing; there you will find plenty of white bears and mountain sheep. In the autumn, when your horses are fat and strong from the mountain pastures, you can go down into the plains and hunt the buffalo or trap beaver on the stream. And when winter comes on, you can take shelter in the woody bottoms along the rivers; there you will find buffalo meat for yourselves and cottonwood bark for your horses, or you may winter in the Wind river valley (in Wyoming), where there is salt weed in abundance.

"The Crow country is exactly the right place. Everything good is to be found there. There is no country like the Crow country."

Go follow the good counsel of Arapooish. Highway 94 from Glendive to Billings winds through the valley of the Crows, from the badlands of Maco Sica to the cool shadows of the Absaroka Range. Go soon, for the medicine is strong.

The Waters of Little Moon

It was here on the banks of the Stillwater River, where it clatters over the rocks on its downward plunge from the snow-filled Absarokas, that the Indian girl gave the river its name, many snows ago when the Crows were young.

The Stillwater River, right down to where it empties its trout-filled waters into the Yellowstone at Columbus, just across the river from Highway 90, is a fascinating stream. Cross the bridge onto Highway 307, and from Absarokee a road follows the river to its head at the Mouat Mines, only chrome mines in North America.

To call this rushing river the Stillwater seems to be a contradiction, but there is a story beyond the talking waters, a story as old as the Crow Indians, who hunted the plains for their buffalo along the rimrocked Yellowstone and lived the winter in the foothills of the Absaroka where the grass was sweet for the horses.

Some say these Indians were older even than the Crows, but they were peaceful people until Weeluna, the Little Moon, was born. Little Moon had refined features and a pleasing voice even as a child, and she grew to lithe womanhood, the object of attention of every young man in the tribe. Her voice was as the murmur of the waters and her heart was filled with friendliness.

To have such a beauty in this Indian camp along the Stillwater was to cause jealousy among the young braves for her hand, and soon they fell to bickering over her attentions. The old men feared for the consequences of this rivalry, but had to await the decision of Weeluna and her father.

Weeluna selected a particularly handsome brave of powerful physique and exceptional skill in the woods and as a huntsman. His name was Nemidji, the finest hunter in the tribe, and though this was fall and the aspen leaves were as gold on the mountains, Weeluna wanted to wait until spring to be married, wait until the earth was born again.

Black were the hearts of the rejected lovers, who planned to rob the camp at the first snowfall and teach the tribe a lesson for its rejection. The night this storm came the young braves stole the warm buffalo robes and broke the arrows and spears, stole the horses and took with them all the food.

Weeluna tried to rally the girls of the camp to go out and hunt, but finally she and her lover, Nemidji, started off alone through the snow. They came to a herd of elk, exhausted and bogged down in the heavy snow, and killed easily enough to feed all the old men, women and children of the camp.

But Weeluna had sickened herself with this great effort, and though the snow melted and Indian summer returned, although the winter was mild and there was plenty to eat, Little Moon worsened. When the first flowers of spring came to the Absaroka she died with a smile on her lips for her people and for her love, Nemidji.

The sorrowing camp wrapped her body in a blanket and buried it in a gnarled fir tree by the Stillwater's banks, as was their custom. As grief ruled the Indians, lightning brightened the sky and thunder brought down the rain in great sheets, driving the river from its banks. A huge boulder rolled down the mountainside, tearing the burial tree from its roots and throwing it into the flash flood that carried it to the river. The moving mass of rock and trees blocked the river, damming it into a pool.

The body of Little Moon floated in the suddenly stilled waters, and the moon, breaking through the storm clouds, painted her face with the softest of light. When Nemidji saw her smile in death he plunged crazily into the pool to rescue her. As he swam back to shore, the dam gave way and swirled the pair of lovers downstream.

When the flood waters dropped away and quiet returned to the river, it left a smooth, still backwater which the Indians called a holy place and gave its name of stilled waters to all the river. With Little Moon's death came peace to the tribe, and each autumn saw the parfleches filled with buffalo, and the warm sunshine danced on the riffles in the Stillwater.

John Colter – Salesman

First winter explorer—and first salesman—in Montana was the fabled John Colter, and to follow his tracks in the snow, even today, is a rare adventure.

Colter was with Lewis and Clark, but before he reached civilization he turned back to the mountains with a pair of Illinois hunters he met at the Mandan villages in Dakota.

With these two fur-hungry men, Colter ascended the Yellowstone River, then the Clark's Fork, and camped in the winter of 1806-07 at the mouth of the Clark's Fork Canyon, in the Bridger country. To visit this campsite drive Highway 310 south out of Laurel.

You will have been on Colter's trail all the way, for he is reported to have camped at the edge of the Absaroka plateau. By spring Colter had his fill and started back down the Yellowstone and Missouri, but not before he took a quick swing through sunlight basin, just over the Wyoming boundary from his winter camp.

When he reached the mouth of the Platte River he ran into Manuel Lisa, a shrewd fur trader, who persuaded Colter to go back upriver with him. Along with the party went George Drouillard or Drewyer, Lewis and Clark expedition hunter, who later was to die at the hands of Blackfeet near the Three Forks of the Missouri.

Again Colter ascended the Yellowstone, and on a cottonwood covered flat at the mouth of the Big Horn River the walls of the first permanent building in Montana rose into the fall air. By late November of 1807 the post was finished. Its site is four miles west of Big Horn on Highway 94, at the junction of the Big Horn and Yellowstone rivers. It was named Manuel's Fort, or Lisa's Fort.

Bitter cold and heavy snows kept the Indians away from the fort, so Lisa sent Colter out to bring them in to trade, thus making Colter the first traveling salesman in Montana. He started out up the Big Horn River, a route that can be traveled on Highway 47 from Custer to Hardin, then by Highway 313 to St. Xavier. No road follows across country to Pryor Creek, which he ascended to Pryor Gap and then to the Clark's Fork somewhere south of the town of Belfry on Highway 397. From here he followed the Clark's Fork south on about the route of Highway 120.

Colter left the Clark's Fork where Dead Indian and Sunlight creeks enter the river, then crossed the foothills to the Shoshone River somewhere east of Yellowstone Park's Sylvan Pass. He may have entered Sunlight basin, which he knew from his previous trip. He did go to the head of Wind River and warmed himself at the boiling spring on Warm Spring Mountain.

In any event he turned back north to the head of the Yellowstone, followed around the west side of Yellowstone Lake and unwittingly discovered the world's most famed park. He may have gone farther south, for in 1931 a stone was found near Jackson Hole with Colter's name and the date 1808. The stone is in the museum at Grand Teton National Park.

Colter saw the hot springs and geysers of the park, thus becoming the park's first winter visitor, a rather commonplace event today.

From the roof of the Yellowstone plateau, Colter dropped back to the Clark's Fork again and retraced his steps to the fort. So good were his reports that when Lisa returned to St. Louis he formed a new company which included such partners as William Clark and the Chouteau brothers. When it left St. Louis in 1809 for the Big Horn the company party contained 300 men.

The effort, though, was doomed to fail. Eight men, including Drouillard, were killed by Blackfeet at Three Forks in the spring of 1810, and Colter was lucky to get away. Partner Andrew Henry went to the Snake River country to open a post, first American fur post west of the Rockies, and Pierre Menard, one of the original partners, returned to the Big Horn. In 1810-11 fire destroyed from $15,000 to $20,000 in furs and buffalo robes, and when Henry returned from the Snake he found Menard gone and the post abandoned. The Indians once more were in full command in Montana.

Thomas Moran's "Yellowstone Wilderness"

Wilderness White House

For two April weeks in 1883 the United States was governed from a Montana town long since sunk into the sagebrush and by-passed every year by thousands of whizzing automobiles.

Cinnabar, which was three miles north of Gardiner, historic entrance to Yellowstone National Park, was itself the park entrance at that time. The town was doomed from birth, even its name resulting from a mistake. Cinnabar, a mercuric sulphide ore, is bright red, and the eternal optimists of that time thought the red streaks in nearby Devil's Slide were pure cinnabar that would make them rich. When they turned out to be only colored stone, the name of the new town on the sagebrush hillside was too firm to be changed.

Northern Pacific was the first railroad ever to reach a park entrance, and Yankee Jim, a white-haired patriarch who ruled the only canyon route to the north entrance of Yellowstone, made NP pay well for the privilege of passage. He had carved out a road around the rocks above the frothing, green Yellowstone river, and he wasn't about to let anyone use his right-of-way for nothing, especially a railroad.

While the old wagon road and the rails ran west of the river, Highway 89, the road from Livingston to the park, uses the east side of the river most of the way.

This was in 1883, and August 31 of that year NP rails reached the town. Although hopes of mining mercury had vanished, there were good coal deposits west of the river from Cinnabar in what still is called Cinnabar basin. In the middle 80s, when Cinnabar was at the height of its rugged splendor, coke ovens were built near the mines, and coal was shipped to Helena to make gas and coking coal. A ferry carried the coal. across the Yellowstone to the rail cars.

By 1885-6 Northern Pacific trains were letting off tourists on the platform at Cinnabar, where they were picked up by stagecoach for a visit to America's greatest wonderland, a status which hasn't changed.

There were runaway teams, scared tourists and smashed outfits, all of which fitted into the flamboyant atmosphere that Cinnabar loved so well. Its reputation was as red as the streaks in Devil's slide that named the town.

Betting always was lively in Cinnabar, on anything from the standard Sunday horse races to game of stud poker. There were three saloons, plenty of fights and an occasional fatality of some drunk during a horse race. When this happened, the races were held up for the funeral, after which all bets were on again.

With all this, Cinnabar's great day was April 8, 1883, when President Theodore Roosevelt arrived in town by private railroad train, complete with staff, to dedicate the new stone arch at the entrance to Yellowstone. A great naturalist, Teddy couldn't wait to see the park, and he had with him as guide and companion the famed John Burroughs. The previous year rails had been extended to the site of Gardiner, but the Roosevelt train and the capital of the United States remained at Cinnabar, three miles north.

Trail Above the Eagles

Across the crown of the loftiest of all Montana mountain ranges—the Beartooth plateau—is laced the Trail Above the Eagles, happily paved for the benefit of travelers.

Even midsummer storms have the sting of a blizzard at the peak of this range, even though grass grows on its rolling summit and sheep graze as placidly as on an eastern Montana meadow. This is a land of contrasts, for warming sunshine is alternated with quick blizzards and plunging canyons with open slopes. Slide rock can end quickly in a mountain lake.

To approach this plateau from below is to be impressed, as an ant aspiring to maximum achievement. The approach from Red Lodge or from Columbus, by highways 312 or 307 respectively is lordly and revealing. It recalls the world's great vistas of valleys beneath towering mountains, such as the snowline behind the vale of Kashmir, the Himalaya from the Indian plain and the crest of the Olympics from Puget Sound. The summits appear to float in air and be supported by cloud rather than dense granite.

Highway 312 is the cold, official designation of the Red Lodge-Cooke City highway, which winds rapidly from valley floor to the ice corridors at 10,940 feet which carry the road over Beartooth Pass and into Wyoming for a quick loop before it reenters Montana and Yellowstone Park. There is water everywhere, flowing over the boulders and under the highway, and alpine lakes are bordered by wind-whipped pines.

The summit is a beautifully eerie world, as apart from the Yellowstone valley far below as the surface of the moon. Pilot and Index peaks guide the way, as they did the Indians who named this Trail Above the Eagles and the pioneers who followed this way to the mines at Cooke City.

Although the Red Lodge-Cooke City road runs among the peaks, they are more impressive from below. On highway 37 to Nye the plateau goes up and up on the south side of the valley, reaching to 2,000 feet and over. Left of the road out of Dean is Mount Wood at 12,660 feet, only 119 feet below the summit of Granite Peak at 12,799, highest piece of real estate in Montana.

Dominating all this valley country is the Beartooth summit, high and white and overhanging. Its snows are perpetual and a constant reminder of the Beartooth Glacier that blanketed these peaks 8,000-odd years ago and pushed its tentacles into the valleys. The boulder-covered river banks recall, too, that this was not long ago and could happen again, in maybe 8,000 years, give or take a century or so.

Hayfield Victory

Breech-loading rifles under a broiling sun stilled the fanatical heart of Crazy Mule, the Cheyenne chief, because he underestimated the fiber of the men in the hayfield.

The day was August 1, 1867, and most of the savagery of the Sioux-Cheyenne war machine was concentrated on the Rosebud River 25 miles east of Fort C. F. Smith on the banks of the Big Horn River at the site of Yellowtail Dam.

A detachment of 19 men had been sent out from the fort to cut about 350 tons of hay to winter the fort's horses and mules. As the sun set on July 29 at the hayfield about three miles east of the fort, Iron Bull, a Crow chief, rode up with a few warriors to warn that Crazy Mule would attack the hayfield. The soldiers shrugged him off, as did General Bradley later at Fort Smith. The truth was too hard to believe.

Sweet-smelling timothy scented the peaceful air that morning of August 1, and the soldiers ate their breakfast under a tarpaulin, looking out at a brilliant summer sky. The teamsters moved their wagons out to the hayfield, while soldiers wrote letters home or played cards. In all there were 19 troopers and hay cutters at the little log corral when the Cheyenne tornado struck.

Gunshots to the north warned the teamsters, who raced their lathering mules to the corral ahead of the solid front of war-bonneted braves, stripped for battle and riding prime mounts with gay plumes in their manes. At the edge of the field the painted warriors swung their war clubs and galloped in for the kill.

First to die was Lieutenant Sternberg, whose Prussian training and Civil war experience taught him to stand up and fight. As he stood on the log corral, shouting defiance, a Cheyenne bullet tore away his right eye socket. The soldiers' breech-loading rifles, first to be used in the West, kept up a steady hail of lead and soon forced the Indians back out of range.

The Cheyenne counseled briefly, then countered by setting fire to the hayfield, and the wind drove the flames directly toward the little corral. As if by magic the fire blew itself out just short of the corral, and the soldiers peered through the smoke, waiting for the next charge, watching the Indians huddled on the Big Horn cliffs just out of range.

Another sheet of lead from the breechloaders drove back the second charge, but Private Nevins was dead and Sergeant Norton and Teamster Hollister wounded. Norton refused to give up, though, rising from his bed under the tarpaulin every time the Cheyenne charged and firing into them with his good pistol hand.

The Indians withdrew but after noon roared in with renewed frenzy, even sniping at the corral from the willows along Warrior Creek. Crazy Mule led this attack himself, splashing through Warrior Creek right into the barrels of the breechloaders. Every soldier had vowed to use his last cartridge on himself in preference to being captured by Crazy Mule.

The chief fell under the searing blast, and his men attacked again and again to recover Crazy Mule's body. Each time they left more Indians beside it. Captain D. A. Colvin probably killed more Indians that day than any other man before or since, an estimated 300 with his 16-shot rifle. All the stock in the corral, except two, had been killed by Indian bullets or arrows. The corral was a bloody shambles, but a victorious one.

With the Indians gone and the sun slanting down to the west, Private Bradley strapped on two service revolvers and offered to go to Fort Smith for help. It arrived in the form of Captain Thomas Burrowes and a command. The returning, victorious soldiers scalped a Cheyenne lying just outside the corral, hoisted his severed head on a pole and marched off to Fort Smith, in some ways as savage as their attackers.

Teamster Hollister died next day in Fort Smith's sick bay, and he and his two military companions in death were buried south of the fort, subsequently to be moved to Custer Battlefield.

To re-fight the hayfield battle, drive Highway 90 east of Billings to Hardin, then south on Highway 313 through St. Xavier to the old Fort Smith site at Yellowtail Dam. The timothy field that was watered that summer day with Indian and soldier blood lies three miles east.

Ice Age Trophy

Big game trophies of 10,000 years ago lie buried beneath gumbo and gravel of eastern Montana's hills and, like gold, are where you find them.

If the way to one of these ancient treasures were well marked, there would be no adventure in the hunting. Of the millions of these massive grass-eaters, the bison of the ice age, that once roamed Montana's plains country, very few have been traced to their last resting place.

Most recent find was that which turned up on the shovel of a pipeline trench digger south of Miles City in the Tongue River country, a huge skull that belonged to Bison Occidentalis, oversize granddaddy of the famed western buffalo. Buried under a layer of gumbo, the skull rested in a gravel bed and looked as though it were blackened by charcoal, possibly from a campfire of the very first Yellowstone valley residents.

This would have been a good place for a camp, down on the valley floor and near the Tongue River. Grass in the Miles City country has fed range animals for years and still does—Occidentalis probably was one of the first. Very likely he was not the only one to be roasted and eaten on this camp site along the ancient Tongue, and his 2,200-pound body must have provided plenty of eating for whatever or whoever devoured him.

Although no bones of the earliest Montanans have been found with bison remains, many human bones, weapons and tools have been found in other parts of the West in company with Ice Age bison bones. This is what makes the search more intriguing. Since it is strictly an off-highway pursuit, it's best to look over the general country as to the possibilities—Anywhere that offers protective clay, old river bottoms and steep cut banks to reveal any skulls that might be left around in a happy hunting ground.

Take any good road that leads into the hills or badlands, but first check the weather and ask a local expert where this road will take you.

Badlands are good possibilities, for here the cuts into the ancient sands and clays are deep. There are thousands of these draws and canyons to be explored, and watch out for places where you can get bogged down with your car. Most of these eastern Montana badlands have roads of a sort into them, from fair to good traveling in spring or summer. Nearby ranchers usually will be able to tell you where the roads lead and how good they are.

Typical badlands are those south of Glendive, between Glendive and Wibaux, and all along the Missouri River east of the UL bend or clear to the toe of Fort Peck Lake. There are others, such as those north of Havre, but they are smaller. This doesn't diminish the possibility of finding the remains of Occidentalis.

In the Chamber of Commerce office in Lewistown you can see an excellent Occidentalis skull, with its sweeping horns, wide skull and arched nose bones. Thousands of years back this huge, shaggy animal died, by accident, illness or by the hand of an equally uncultured man. His skull sank into the side of a Missouri River badlands hill and stayed there for centuries, until dug up and brought to Lewistown. This will give you an idea of what you are looking for.

You will know that somewhere in a tangle of gumbo and pine trees an ancient bison went down to death, probably as he came to a waterhole to drink, and met a shower of spears from black-maned, naked men. Possibly these same men later met death in these hills in a one-sided fight with a cave bear, the short-faced ancestor of the grizzly bear that Lewis and Clark met here on their way west.

Anyway, happy hunting. If you find an Occidentalis skull, you will have an incomparable conversation piece for your basement room. Even if you don't you will have found for yourself a whole new face of Montana, tangled and weird and lost to itself under the blue sky.

Bear Coat's Fort

From Fort Keogh on the Yellowstone the gauntleted hand of the United States Army reached out to crush the last Indian resistance in the nation. Miles City sprang up near the fort to preserve the memory of the general who led the final Indian campaigns.

The year was 1877 and the Army still smarted from the whipping it had taken on the little Big Horn from Crazy Horse and his Sioux-Cheyenne cavalry. The previous fall, soon after the Custer defeat, the Tongue River Cantonment had been set up by General Nelson A. Miles and his Fifth Infantry. Congress soon decided to build a permanent fort on this site at the junction of the Tongue and Yellowstone rivers, and Fort Keogh's log walls began to rise February 19, 1877.

The fort was named for Captain Myles W. Keogh of the Seventh Cavalry who, with others, died beside Custer at the Big Horn battle. Fort Keogh, then, was a fort with a mission. It had the duty of avenging those who died on the Little Big Horn and bring peace to the frontier. In a sense, Fort Keogh was General Nelson Miles and vice versa.

Where others had failed, the heroic and capable Miles took over. A congressional medal of honor holder, General Miles had served all through the Civil War with the Army of the Potomac, was wounded four times. He came to Keogh with a thorough knowledge of Indian fighting, having campaigned against the Cheyenne, Comanche, Kiowa, Sioux, Nez Perces, Bannocks and Apaches.

Miles had captured the wily Geronimo in the southwestern desert mountains after bushy-bearded General George Crook had given up the chase in the cactus country. General O. O. Howard had worn out his wagons and men in a 1,300-mile pursuit of Chief Joseph and his Nez Perce all through Idaho and Montana only to see General Miles force-march his men from Keogh to the Bear Paws and receive Joseph's dramatic surrender, forever ending the Indian wars.

The Indians called Miles "Bear Coat" because he wore heavy winter clothing and a round fur cap, but they respected his military genius and his fairness in battle.

It was Miles who pursued the victorious Sitting Bull north from the Little Big Horn, cut off his support and pushed him into Canada, where he stayed until he surrendered in 1881. In January of 1877 Miles and his troops marched up the Tongue to Crazy Horse's headquarters to start a campaign of weakening the remaining forces who defeated Custer. By that spring all Indians but Lame Deer and his Minneconyoux, a tribe of the Sioux, had been rounded up and placed on their reservations. Miles attacked Lame Deer's camp on May 7, 1877, destroying it and killing the chief. Custer had been avenged and his attackers either subdued or driven out of the country.

The last real campaign from Keogh, in fact the last real Indian campaign anywhere, was the march to cut off Joseph in his retreat to Canada. The military suspected Joseph would head from Idaho for the Yellowstone country, for the Nez Perce for years had hunted buffalo with their friends, the Crows.

Joseph crossed Yellowstone Park, and Colonel S. D. Sturgis was sent to intercept him on the Shoshone. However, the Nez Perce scouting was better than the Army's and Joseph came down the Clark's Fork of the Yellowstone two days ahead of Sturgis. The red man won a brisk contact at Canyon Creek north of Laurel and hurried north. Miles and his troops scrambled out of Fort Keogh, were ferried across the Missouri east of Cow Island and, marching day and night, brought Joseph under their rifles on Snake Creek that wet October morning in the Bear Paws.

Fort Keogh by 1878 had telegraphic contact with the war department through Fort Buford in North Dakota. It had come of age but its reason for existence was nearly over. A little mop-up in the Yellowstone valley and the Fifth Infantry had done its work. A short drive from Miles City west across the Tongue River on Highway 94 will show the visitor where Miles commanded under the cottonwoods.

Torch to the Wagon

Wagon train burnings and scalped pioneers are dished up as standard fare in TV and movie versions of the old West, but only two authenticated wagon burnings are documented in Montana history—the most spectacular one only yards off blacktop in the Yellowstone valley.

The year was 1866, the day August 24, and wagons were moving along the old Bozeman trail, a hated "knife" driven by the white man directly into Indian territory. This was Crow country, and Crows were generally friendly to the whites, but Sioux were everywhere, and they knew the whites were coming in increasing numbers to the Gallatin valley and the southwestern Montana gold mines.

With most of the wagons were blue-coated soldiers, able and experienced Indian fighters with plenty of guns, and this held the Sioux back. Only when they could see a quick opportunity to punish these white invaders did the red horsemen of the plains move in for a kill.

William K. Thomas, his eight-year-old son Charles, and Joseph Schultz, a young Canadian, left St. Clair County, Illinois, on May 15, 1866, to join George Thomas, William's brother, in the Gallatin valley of Montana Territory. The trio traveled by steamboat up the Missouri River to Atchison, Kansas, where they bought a new prairie "schooner" plus a team of mules and joined the Waller and Langworthy wagon train for the Bozeman trail. They picked up other westering wagons on the way, including two government trains of 40 and 100 wagons respectively, the latter led by Jim Bridger, and headed for Fort C. F. Smith on the Big Horn River.

Thomas kept a journal of the trip, noting hardships in Wyoming and skirmishes with the angry Sioux, who hesitated to make a direct attack on a military train bristling with arms. Thomas noted worriedly that the Indians would attempt to cut off any wagons that lagged behind.

At Fort Smith, where the Big Horn River breaks out of its canyon, the military wagons and soldiers stopped. Thomas had been sobered by an attack on ox train wagons in Wyoming and by the sight of a fresh grave of five men killed by the Indians only days before. Wolves had opened the new grave.

However, at Fort Smith, Jim Bridger told the civilians they were now in Crow country and that the Crows probably wouldn't let the Sioux enter their territory. After three days at Fort Smith the wagons ferried the Big Horn river and headed west for the Gallatin.

Taking comfort from old Jim's words, Thomas and his wagon moved ahead of the rest of the wagons on August 17. This was the last time the other pioneers saw the Thomas party alive. On the afternoon of August 24 the trailing wagon party, with Jim Bridger guiding, saw smoke reddening the sun and came cautiously upon the blazing Thomas wagon beneath the sandstone bluffs nine miles west of what now is Reed Point and just off Highway 90.

Blood was still fresh on the bodies of the two men and the little boy. Bridger cursed his misjudged advice. The bodies had been scalped, the mules and everything of value were gone and arrows stuck out of the flesh of the newly dead. Nearby were 21 peeled willow sticks with cloth tied on the tips and the other ends pushed into the ground. Bridger read this Indian message as a party of 21 Sioux, leaving their brand on their bloody work.

Hastily, Captain Waller buried the bodies in a common grave and left three rough headboards nearby with the names of each. Waller took Thomas' notebook and the fatal arrows to the man's brother George in the Gallatin. The arrows and willow sticks now belong to the State Historical Museum in Helena, mute witnesses to the wagon burning.

INDEX

Absaroka Mountains	213
Absarokee	206, 228
Adobetown	24
Ajax Mountains	8
Alberton	58
Alder	10, 24
Alder Gulch	23
Alexander, Chief	83, 107
Altitude, lowest, highest	2
American Fork	111
American Fur Co.	15, 189, 197
Amsterdam	10
Anaconda	58
Anaconda Range	56
Antelope	129
Arlee	58, 108
Armstead	7
Ashley, Cong. James	35
Ashley, William	197
Aspen, tree	16
Assiniboine Indians	170
Audubon, John J.	198
Augusta	129
Avalanche Gulch	40
Avon	98
Baker	206
Baker, Camp	45
Bannack	5, 7, 24, 33, 36
Bannock Indians	8
Basin	10
Bear Paw Mtns.	127, 193
Beartooth Pass	234
Beaverhead Mtns.	6, 8
Beaverhead River	6, 7, 27
Beaver's Head Rock	6
Beaver Tail Hill	95
Belgrade	10
Belly River	127
Belt	9
Belt Mountains	9, 127
Benteen, Capt. Fred	220, 221, 222
Benton, Fort	14, 44, 131, 135, 155, 183
Benton, Thomas Hart	183
Big Hole	5, 6, 7
Big Horn Mtns.	216, 225
Big Horn Rivers	211, 217, 220
Big Muddy Creek	124
Big Timber	206
Big Timber Creek	212
Billings	206
Bitter Root Mtns.	6, 56
Bitter Root River	53, 54, 117
Bitter Root Valley	73
Bison Creek	17
Bison, extinct	238
Bison Range	104
Blackfeet Indians	14, 113, 135, 147, 164, 166, 167, 177, 181, 226
Blackfoot City	98
Blackfoot Rivers	54, 55, 78
Blacktail Creek	7
Bloody Knife	218
Bonner	58, 79
Boulder	10
Boulder River	8, 212
Bovey, Chas. and Mrs.	24
Bow Indians	215
Bowdoin Res.	127
Box Elder	129
Bozeman	10
Bozeman, John	47
Bozeman Pass	21, 47
Bozeman Trail	21, 242
Brackett Creek	21
Brenner	8
Bridger	206
Bridger, Jim	9, 21, 193, 242
Bridger Mtns.	9, 21
Bridger Trail	21
Broadus	206
Broadwater, Col. C. A.	158
Browning	129
Browning, Fort	168
Buffalo	129
Buford, Fort	200
Bull Mtn.	9, 213
Butte	30, 52, 58, 175
Cabinet Mtns.	56
Camas Prairie	58

Cameahwait, Chief	28
Canyon Creek	30, 212
Canyon Ferry	10, 39
Cardwell	8
Carroll	21, 158
Carroll, Mathew	158
Cascade	129
Castle	21, 144
Castle Mtns.	127, 144, 153
Cat Creek	129
Cattle	18
Cayuse Hills	213
Chalk Buttes	213
Charlo	59
Charbonneau	27
Chester	129
Chestnut	48
Cheyenne Indians	220, 236
Chinook	129, 162
Chippewa, boat	183
Choteau	129, 173
Chouteau, Pierre	174
Cinnabar	232
Circle	130
Clagett, Fort	160
Clark's Fork, Columbia	53
Clark's Fork, Yellowstone	212
Clark, William	13, 47, 224, 231
Clarke, Malcolm	45
Clearwater River	55
Cleveland, Jack	33
Clyde Park	21, 206
Coeur d'Alene Mtns.	56
Colorado Gulch	120
Colstrip	206
Colter, John	13, 47, 205, 230
Columbia Falls	59
Columbia Mtns.	57
Columbia River	28
Columbus	206, 234
Colville, Fort	74
Comanche	207
Confederate Gulch	40
Connah, Fort	89
Conrad	130
Cooke City	207, 234
Copperopolis	21
Cordilleran Glacier	85
Council Grove	83
Cowen, John	43
Cow Island	201
Cover, Thomas W.	23
Crab, John	11, 43
Crazy Horse	221
Crazy Mtns.	153, 213
Crazy Mule	236
Cree Indians	170, 191
Crook, Gen. George	220
Crow Agency	207
Crow Indians	164, 166, 167, 215, 226
Cruse, Tommy	197
Culbertson	130
Culbertson, Alexander	183, 189, 198
Curry, "Kid"	139, 140
Custer	207
Custer, battlefield	220
Custer, George A.	46, 217, 220
Custer, Tom	218, 220
Cut Bank	130
Cut Bank Creek	127
Daley, Pete	33
Dearborn River	80, 126
DeBorgia	59, 157
Deer Lodge	59
Deer Lodge Pass	19
Deer Lodge Valley	19, 102
DeSmet, Father Pierre	20, 73, 81, 199
Devon	130
Diamond City	40
Diamond R Transportation Co.	158
Dillon	6, 11
Dixon	59
Dodson	130, 168
Drewyer or Drouillard, George	27, 181, 230
Drummond	59
Duck Lake	126
Dunquerque	130
Dupuyer	130
Edgar, Henry	23
Edgerton, Judge Sidney	34

Ekalaka	207
Elkhorn	9
Elkhorn Mtn.	9
Elk Park Pass	17
Ellis, Fort	48
Elliston	156
Eureka	59
Fairfield	130
Fairview	131
Fairweather, Bill	23
Fallon	207
Fields, Ruben	182
Finlay, Francois	51, 90
Finley Point	77
Firehole River	8
Fisher River	52, 92
Fizzle, Fort	201
Forest Service	117
Forsyth	207
Flathead Indians	107, 113, 115, 199
Flathead Pass	22
Flathead Lake	53, 76
Flathead Mtns.	58
Flathead River	53, 54
Flint Creek	56
Flint Mtns.	57
Floyd, Fort	197
Frances, Lake	127
Frazer	131
Frenchtown	59, 157
Fresno	131
Fresno reservoir	127
Galata	131
Galen	59
Gallatin City	14
Gallatin Gateway	11
Gallatin Mtns.	9
Gallatin River	8, 47
Gardiner	207, 233
Garfield, James A.	84
Garnet Mtns.	57
Garrison	59
Garryowen	207
Gates of Mountains	43
Gass, Sgt. Patrick	181
Georgians, Four	43
Geraldine	131
Gibbon, John	201, 221
Gibbon River	8
Gibson reservoir	127
Glacier Park	123
Names, Geographical features	63 - 72
Glasgow	131
Glass, Hugh	197
Glendale	30
Glendive	207
Glendive Creek	210
Gold Creek	59, 111
Gore, Sir George	205, 207
Grant, John	18, 103
Grant, Richard	18
Granite Peak	2, 213
Grasshopper Creek	7, 36
Grass Range	131
Grass Valley	83
Gravelly Mtns.	9
Great Falls	131, 187
Great Northern Ry.	82, 97, 142, 185
Great Porcupine Creek	211
Grotevant, Jerry	30
Gros Ventre Indians	168
Hamilton	60
Hangman's Gulch	37
Hardin	208
Harlem	132, 140
Harvard University	24
Hauser, Samuel P.	34
Havre	132
Harlowton	208
Hawley, Fort	177
Heart Butte	132
Hecla	30
Helena	5, 11, 158, 175
Hell Gate	40
Hell Gate Treaty	84
Henry, Andrew	231
Henry, Fort	197
Highland	24
Highland Mtns.	9
Highwood	137

Highwood Mtns.	128, 193
Hingham	132
Hinsdale	132
Hobson	132
Hoeken, Father Adrian	107
Holter, A. M.	144
Homestead	132
Horse Prairie Creek	6, 7, 27
Horse Shoe Hills	10
Hot Springs	60
Howard, Gen. O. O.	201
Hudson's Bay Co.	89, 99, 147, 212
Hungry Horse	60
Hysham	208
Idaho Territory	33, 34
Immel, Michael	14
Inverness	132
Ismay	208
Ives, George	33
Jeffers	9
Jefferson City	11
Jefferson River	6
Jefferson, Thomas	5, 6
Jocko River	53
Jordan	132
Joseph, Chief	5, 19, 38, 44, 200, 201, 241
Jones, Robert	14
Judith Basin	21
Judith Gap	21, 132, 159
Judith River	125
Kalispell	60
Keogh, Fort	201, 205, 240
Kevin	132
Kicking Horse reservoir	54
Kies, Kris	169
Kipp, James	198
Knippenberg, Henry	31
Kohrs, Conrad	18, 103
Kootenai Falls	81
Kootenai River	52, 91
Kremlin	132
Lame Deer	208, 241
Landusky	132
Landusky, Pike	139
Langford, Nathaniel P.	34
Larb Hills	128
Larocque, Francois Antoine	205, 216
Last Chance Gulch	43, 177
Laurel	208
LaVerendrye, Sieur, Louis, Francois	215
Lemhi Pass	8, 28
Lewis & Clark	5, 6, 13, 27, 36, 44, 78, 115, 164, 197, 205, 216, 224
Lewis, Fort	183
Lewis, Meriwether	27, 181, 187
Lewis Range	57
Lewistown	160
Lima	10
Lindbergh, Chas. A.	87
Lion Creek, City	30
Lisa, Manuel, Fort	14, 205, 230
Little Moon	228
Livingston	208
Lodge Grass	208
Logan	11, 13
Logan, Capt. William	46
Lolo	60
Lolo Creek	115
Lott, Mortimer	35
Lyons, Jack	33
MacDonald, Angus and Duncan	90
MacDonald Pass	119
Maginnis, Cong. Martin	45
Maginnis, Fort	151
Madison Mtns.	9
Madison River	6, 8
Magpie Gulch	41
Makoshika	214
Maiden	150
Mandan, Fort	27
Mandan village	215
Manhattan	11
Marias River	43, 125, 175, 181, 182, 187
Marias Pass	181
Marysville	97
Martinsdale	145
Masonic Lodge	35

Maximilian, Prince 199
McDonald, Finan 91
McKenzie, Fort 185, 189
McKenzie, Kenneth 197
Meagher, Thomas 185
Melrose 97, 30
Melstone 132
Menard, Pierre 231
Mengarini, Father 75
Miles City 208, 238, 240
Miles, Nelson A. 201, 205, 240
Milk River 105, 124, 168, 170
Miller, D. J. 43
Mill Iron 209
Milltown 60
Milwaukee Railroad 153
Minnetares Indians .. 27, 79, 181
Mission Mtns. 57, 88
Missoula 60
Missoula Lake 85
Missouri Rivers 5, 6, 124, 215
Mitchell, David D. 189
Moccasin 133
Moccasin Mtns. 128
Moiese 60
Monida 11, 18
Monroe, Hugh 147, 192
Montana Auto Ass'n VI
Montana Post 24
Montana Railroad 145
Moore, Bill 33
Mullan, Capt. John
.... 3, 108, 119, 155
Mullan Pass 121, 182
Mullan Road 44, 84
Musselshell 133
Musselshell River 125, 153

Nelson Reservoir 127
Nevada City 24
Nevada Creek 55
Nez Perce Indians ....
.... 5, 78, 109, 115, 201
Neihart 133
Nine-Mile Divide 57
Nine Pipes Reservoir 54
Northern Pacific Railway ....
        21, 97, 121, 156, 217, 224, 232

Northwest Fur Co. ....
.... 92, 100, 169, 205
Nye 209

O'Fallon Creek 20
Ogden, Peter Skene 15
Oilmont 133
Old Agency 173
Oregon Trail 21
Ordway, Sgt. John 181
Outlook 133
Owen, Fort 20
Owen, John 75
Oxalatl 9

Pablo, Michel 105
Pablo Reservoir 54
Pablo Town 60
Paradise 6
Park City 209
Parker, Rev. Samuel 109
Pease, Fort 49
Peck, Fort 131
Peck, Fort, Lake 125
Pfouts, Paris 35
Philanthropy River 7
Philipsburg 60
Philosophy River 13
Pilcher, John 14
Pine Grove 24
Piney Buttes 128
Pioneer Mtns. 6, 9, 30
Pishkun 164
Plains 61
Plentywood 133
Plevna 209
Plummer, Henry 33, 37
Point of Rocks 6, 23, 27
Pompey's Pillar 209, 224
Pend Oreille Indians 102
Pony Express 177
Poplar River 124, 183
Portage 133
Powder River 210, 221
Powderville 209
Power, T. C. 161
Prickly Pear Valley 43
Priest's Pass 119

Pryor Creek	205, 212
Pryor Mtns.	214
Purcell Mtns.	57
Quake Lake	8
Railroad, first in Montana	5
Ram's Horn Tree	93
Rattlesnake Cliff	6
Rattlesnake Creek	54, 79
Ray, Ned	34, 37
Ravalli	61
Ravalli, Father Antony	71, 136
Red Lodge	209, 234
Red Rock Creek	7, 27
Reed and Bowles Fort	179
Reno, Major Marcus	220, 221, 222
Riel, Louis	137
Ringling	11
Robber's Roost	33
Rochejohne River	210
Rock Creek	55
Rocky Mountain Fur Co.	15
Rodgers, Harry	23
Rosebud	209
Rosebud River	211, 221
Ross, Alexander	15, 89, 93
Roosevelt, Theodore	233
Ronan	61
Roundup	133
Ryegate	133
Ruby	24
Ruby Mtns.	9
Ruby River	6, 23
Sacajawea	6, 27, 197
Saco	133
St. Ignatius	18, 61, 107
St. Mary's Lake	149
St. Mary's Mission	8, 73
St. Peter's Mission	135, 164
St. Regis	54, 61, 157
St. Xavier	209
Saleesh House	113
Salish Tribes	83
Saltese	61
Sapphire Mtns.	57
Sand Coulee	133
Sanders	209
Sanders, Wilbur Fisk	35
Sarpy Creek	211
Scobey	133
Seeley Lake	61
Shaw, Fort	45, 131, 135, 175
Shawmut	133
Sheep	18
Sheep Mtns.	128
Shelby	134
Sheridan	11, 32
Shields River	21, 212
Shoshone Indians	6, 7, 27, 171
Sidney	209
Sieben	156
Silver Bow	11, 61
Silver Bow Creek	52
Silver mines	30
Sioux Indians	217, 220, 242
Sioux Pass	209
Sitting Bull	200, 222
Skalkaho Creek	54
Snake Creek	201
Snake River	201
Snowcrest Mtns.	10
Snowdrift (wolf)	193
Snowy Mtns.	128
Smith, Fort C. F.	21, 236, 242
Smith, Jedediah	15
Smith River	126
Somers	61
Spanish Peaks, Creek	9
Springdale	21
Squaw Peaks	58
Stevens, Gov. Isaac I.	79, 83
Stanley, Reginald	43
Stanford	193
Stevensville	61
Stillwater River	53, 212, 228
Stinson, Buck	37
Story, Nelson	49
Stuart, James, Granville	18, 111, 154
Sturgis, Gen. S. D.	201
Sublette, William	197
Sula	19
Summit	24
Sunburst	134
Sun River	126, 135, 148, 156, 167, 173, 175, 188

Superior	61
Swan River	54, 87
Swan Mtns.	58
Sweet Grass	134
Sweet Grass Creek	211
Sweet Grass Hills	128, 191
Targhee Pass	9
Tendoy Mtns.	10
Terry	209
Terry, Gen. Alfred H.	251
Teton River	126, 173
Teton-Sawtooth Mtns.	128
Thompson, David	81, 91, 99, 113, 182
Thompson Falls	61
Thompson Pass	100
Thompson River	53, 113
Three Forks	5, 6, 12, 13
Tiber Reservoir	127
Tobacco River	52
Tobacco Root Mtns.	10
Tongue River	211, 238, 240
Two Dot	210
Townsend	12, 39
Trapper Creek and City	30
Traveler's Rest	78, 115
Trident	12
Tullock, Samuel	15
Twin Bridges	6, 7, 12
Ulm	164
Union, Fort	177, 197
Utah Northern Railroad	5, 31
Valier	134
Vandenburgh, Wm. H.	15
Van Orsdal, Wesley	174
Varina	12, 24
Vaughn	133, 167
Victor	61, 83
Vigilantes	32, 37
Virginia City	5, 12, 23, 33, 175
Wagner	142
Wagner, Dutch John	37
Walking Coyote	105
Walla Walla, Fort	155
Wells Fargo	44
Westby	134
West Glacier	61
West Yellowstone	12
Whitefish River	53
Whitefish Mtns.	58
White's Gulch	40
White, John	36
White Sulphur Springs	12, 45, 153
Whitman, Marcus	109
Whitetail	134
Wibaux	210
Willard, Alexander	7, 36, 182
William, Fort	197
Williams, James	35
Wilsall	22, 210
Winnett	134
Wisdom	2
Wisdom River	6
Wise River	7
Wolf Creek	12
Wolf Point	134
Wyoming	6
Yaak	52
Yankee Flat	37
Yellowstone Park	5, 231, 232
Yellowstone River	210
Yellowstone Valley	6, 148
Yellowtail Dam	237
Zortman	134
Zurich	134